MEN

OF

STEEL

MEN
OF
STEEL

The Lives and Times of Boxing's
Middleweight Champions

PETER WALSH

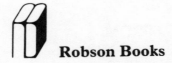
Robson Books

To Jayne, with Love

First published in Great Britain in 1993 by
Robson Books Ltd, Bolsover House, 5-6
Clipstone Street, London W1P 7EB

Copyright © 1993 Peter Walsh
The right of Peter Walsh to be identified as
author of this work has been asserted by him
in accordance with the Copyright, Designs
and Patents Act 1988

British Library Cataloguing in Publication Data
A catalogue record for this title is available
from the British Library

ISBN 0 86051 847 7

Typeset in Plantin by EMS Photosetters,
Thorpe Bay, Essex.
Printed in Great Britain by St. Edmundsbury
Press, Bury St. Edmunds, Suffolk.

Contents

Acknowledgments

I am particularly grateful to boxing collectors Bob Hartley, of Wembley, and Ron Wells, of Birmingham, for allowing me to visit their homes and drink their tea while ploughing through old books and magazines. Thanks to the staff of the National Newspaper Library and the British Museum. The staff of *Boxing News* were kind enough to allow me to look through their files and Daniel Herbert helped to find information.

Introduction

MEN of Steel tries to chronicle the history of the world middleweight boxing championship. It's a big subject. My dilemma in writing this book was not what to include but what to leave out. Perhaps this is why the 160-pounders have been neglected by writers. Yes, there are biographies about many of them. Even a few films. But no one has written a history of all the champions, their fights, their lives.

The heavyweights, by dint of sheer bulk, have always held the public attention. 'As the heavyweights go, so goes boxing' is one of those ring aphorisms that fight fans love to throw at each other. Yet it is the middleweights that truly represent the best, and worst, of the sport: its skill, drama, thunder and cruelty.

This introduction sets out a brief outline of the inception of the middleweight title under Queensberry rules. It then touches on some of the changes which altered boxing over the years that followed. A deeper understanding of this development can be found in two excellent recent books, Elliott J. Gorn's *The Manly Art* and Jeffrey T. Sammons's *Beyond the Ring*. I have simply examined a few topics which are relevant to the middleweights in particular.

This is not an exhaustive study; that would take volumes. Nor does it claim conclusive accuracy: accounts of many early boxing matches differ from source to source. It is an attempt to deal fairly and, I hope, clearly, with the 70-odd men who have claimed the middleweight title, in one form or another, since the last century.

The middleweight class appears to have been established in Britain when Richard Humphries beat Sam Martin in a bareknuckle fight in 1776. There was great interest in the contest and about £100,000 is said to have changed hands on the result. Other bruisers associated with the division over the following decades included Bob Watson, Hooper the Tinman, Jack 'Nonpareil' Randall, Harry Harmer, Arthur Mathewson, Pat Halton, John Callaghan, Tass Parker, Nat Langham, Posh Price and Jack Baldock. All fought under London Prize Ring rules.

A 'world' title fight at that time would have had to involve a fighter from Britain against one from America, with each weighing in the region of 154lb. However, in the US the middleweights were not recognized as a separate class until much later. Any man worth his salt fought in the heavyweight, or open, class, no matter what his weight. So it is doubtful if there were any world champions except in the open class during the bareknuckle days.

In the mid-1860s an Englishman called John Graham Chambers penned a set of rules for boxing with gloves. His friend the Marquis of Queensberry lent his name to the new code. Rounds were to last no more than three minutes, with a minute's rest in between, and contestants were given 10 seconds to rise if knocked down. The rules had their critics — some diehards thought gloves were for sissies — but they were more acceptable to the authorities than bareknuckle fighting. Gloves or 'mufflers', as they were called, ultimately saved the sport from extinction.

In 1872 the Bow Cups began. These were competitions under Queensberry rules to determine British champions in different weight categories. The first middleweight (11 stone) champion was Bill Brooks of Mile End, east London, in April 1872. In a foretaste of the tragedy that was to haunt the division, he fell ill and died later that year. His successor, Charley Davis, was himself forced to retire through illness. The title passed to an Irishman, Denny Harrington, who has the distinction of being the first middleweight champion of the world under Queensberry rules. Harrington was born in Cork on 13 December 1849. Emigrating to England, he entered a few gloved tournaments and befriended Charley Davis. When Davis retired, Harrington claimed his title. By September 1876 he was established as champion in England, there being nobody willing to challenge him.

To be world champion, however, he had to beat the best from the

United States. There the popularity of knuckle fighting had received a fillip from the Civil War, which introduced men to the sport in army camps and barracks. Waves of Irish immigrants bearing a tradition of fisticuffs also helped. A contest in April 1867 between Tom Chandler and Dooney Harris, an Englishman living in America, is often seen as the genesis of the US middleweight title. They fought for $5,000 at Port Isabel, California. The London-born Harris was favourite, but it was written of Chandler: 'No finer specimen of a man has ever featured in the prize ring on the Pacific Coast. His appearance and expression are eminently pleasing and gentlemanly.' Chandler won. He weighed 9st 10lb, too light to count as a middleweight today.

A year later, Chandler's claim was disputed by George Rooke, a Dundalk Irishman who had served a gunsmith's apprenticeship in England before emigrating to Boston in 1862 at the age of 23. There he made rifles during the Civil War. He was a well-proportioned and athletic man with an alert gaze and huge moustache. He lost a severe fight with Rocky Moore for the American middleweight title; Moore refused a return bout and retired. Over the next few years, Rooke established himself as American champion by beating several tough opponents.

In 1876 he sailed to England and made a match with Harrington at 11 stone in what was the first-ever world title fight under Queensberry rules. It was clearly advertised as such in the British *Sporting Life* of 17 November 1877: 'George Rooke (The American Champion) made challenge to the world at 10st 12lb for the Middleweight Championship and a £50 or £100 cup under Marquis of Queensberry Rules', and again on 9 March 1878: 'March 13th, on which occasion George Rooke and Denny Harrington (Middleweight Champions of the World) will appear.' Harrington was four inches shorter but slightly heavier at 10st 13½lb. In a wild fight, during which the Englishman was bitten on the wrist by one of Rooke's supporters and the referee and timekeeper were manhandled, Harrington laid Rooke out with a right to the cheek after six rounds, lasting 22 minutes and 40 seconds.

Harrington defended his title 14 months later against Florrie Barnet under a gaslit railway arch in Bermondsey Street, in London's East End. The hard-punching champion won in two rounds. In November 1879 he met Birmingham's Alf Greenfield in a fight advertised for the title. Harrington had trained only for five days and weighed 12st. Greenfield outboxed him for 70 minutes until, in the 18th round, he knocked the champion through the ropes, then hit him twice while he was helpless. The referee disqualified Greenfield, who had been on the verge of victory.

In December 1880 Harrington met 33-year-old William Sheriff of Leicester for £50-a-side. Both were well inside the stipulated limit of 11st 3lb. Sheriff gradually wore his man down and floored him repeatedly before police stopped the fight in the 11th round. At a meeting that night, the referee insisted the fight be renewed, but the backers of Harrington demurred and Sheriff became champion. Harrington retired and later worked as a stevedore. He died in January 1911, aged 61.

Sheriff, known as 'the Prussian', was born on 1 August 1847. Details of his early bouts are sketchy, but they included wins over three members of the same family, the Haughtons. Chunky and game, he never defended the crown he took from Harrington, but put on weight and later went to the States to fight as a heavyweight. He drew with Charlie Mitchell in 1883 and fought an incredible five-hour draw with John Welch: 76 three-minute rounds with gloves. Not surprisingly, he was never much good after that. He died on 4 June 1893.

The Americans had different ideas about the world title. They never acknowledged the significance of Rooke's loss to Harrington. Instead, his claim was seen to have fizzled out, and in 1872, according to *Boxing News*, he 'was apparently supplanted by Jimmy Murray, a natural 154-pounder who obtained recognition partly because his friends presented him with a belt inscribed "Champion".' In 1873 Murray was challenged by Mike Donovan, who generally weighed about 154lb but happily tackled heavyweights. They met on a cold May morning at Port Erie, outside Philadelphia. No ring was pitched for fear of interference; the spectators linked arms to make a human arena. The men fought with bare fists under London Prize Ring rules. After 44 rounds the bout broke up on the approach of police and was declared a draw. Donovan and Murray were arrested and shared a jail cell for four days. Murray subsequently retired.

Donovan, who was born in Chicago in 1847, was never world champion, but became an important figure in popularizing gloved boxing in the US. A wiry, balding young man, bursting with energy and rude health, he joined the Union side in the Civil War as an adventurous teenager and marched with General Sherman through Georgia. He engaged in his first fist fights in the Army.

The title lay dormant after Murray's retirement. Bareknuckle fighting was going through a bad time, with regular police interference, rowdy gangs and corruption. In 1877 a husky youth called William McClellan claimed the crown and challenged all comers. He fought a number of minor bouts, then met Donovan in April 1878 for the vacant title. They fought in a room over a New York saloon, wearing two-ounce gloves but under prize ring rules. After 14 rounds, Donovan was disqualified. They were matched again in May under special rules, when Donovan won decisively in seven rounds to receive some acknowledgement as American champion.

In 1880 a contest between Donovan and Rooke in Canada was called off when a sheriff arrived with a posse and a boatload of British soldiers who, according to Alexander Johnston, 'probably would much rather have watched a fight than stop it'. Rooke still claimed the title, but his claim had no basis. He was beaten in three rounds by John L. Sullivan in June 1880 and in two by Donovan in 1881. Donovan did practically no more fighting as a middleweight and retired in 1883 to devote himself to teaching. He gained fame as the boxing instructor of New York Athletic Club and as a good friend of future president Theodore Roosevelt, with whom he sparred regularly. 'Professor' Donovan taught the noble art to 'gentlemen eminent in science, literature, art, social and commercial life'. The new-found public taste for amateur sparring helped redeem professional ring fighting, which enjoyed a resurgence, aided by the popularity of heavyweight John L. Sullivan. Donovan, who trained 'Gentleman' Jim Corbett to beat Sullivan, died in New York in 1918.

George Fulljames was apparently the next claimant, but he was beaten in July 1884 by Jack Dempsey, a New York Irishman (see next chapter). England's Charlie Mitchell, who usually weighed about 150lb, was probably the best in world, but was interested only in the heavyweight title. It was Dempsey who emerged to earn recognition and who brought the division into the modern era. Boxing as we know it today was taking shape.

★ ★ ★

The sport was still to see many important changes. In the late 19th century it was still illegal, or quasi-legal, in many parts of the world. Its three centres were Britain, Australia, and certain states in the USA. In Britain the National Sporting Club in London emerged as the authoritative voice of the sport. In Australia, the game developed under the tutelage of Larry Foley, who taught many internationally acclaimed boxers. His influence was continued by two promoters, Hugh McIntosh and Snowy Baker, who for a spell made Sydney one of the world's premier fight cities.

It was America, however, which held most influence and which has dominated the middleweight title to the present day. In the 1890s the boxing clubs of New Orleans helped to systematize US boxing, recognizing six distinct weight classifications. Referees were allowed to stop contests and to award decisions. In New York the sport was run under the Horton Law between 1896 and 1900. Fights were permitted without any limit. In 1900 the Lewis Law took over, permitting boxing only in recognized, members-only clubs. The system was widely abused. According to writer Alva Johnston, 'Every new arrival was scrutinized by sentinels; anybody who looked like a reformer or stool pigeon was barred. There was no public sale of tickets. Only duly elected club members were admitted. The payment of two dollars at any saloon near the arena made any man a duly elected club member and provided him with a card calling for a good seat; one dollar made him a junior member, with a card entitling him to a bad seat . . . every card was issued in the name of John Smith, in order to simplify the clerical work.'

In 1911 the Frawley Law legalized boxing in New York State and permitted ten-round fights but not decisions. Corruption became endemic. Nat Fleischer, who worked the New York beat as a young sports reporter, wrote: 'The fight game was a racket then and truly could be referred to as the sport of rogues. Although there were some honest promoters in New York . . . boxing as a whole was ruled by ruffians, gangsters and politicians. The many fixed fights that soured the public on the sport were engineered by politicians with headquarters in Tammany Hall, which . . . had tremendous influence over the game. They told the police what to do and how to do it. They made the odds, brought about the fixes, and collected their bets.'

The no-decision clause was open to abuse in other ways. Managers and backers would influence the reporters who rendered the important 'newspaper' decisions on which bets were settled, or would rush to the telegraph wires first to send biased reports to the city papers.

The repeal of the Frawley Law in 1917 removed boxing's legal sanction in New York state for three years, until the Walker Law of 1920, which set up a model commission. This didn't stop the gang lords, now strengthened by their control of booze during Prohibition. Fleischer wrote: 'They not only muscled in on boxers . . . but on the prosperous clubs as well. It was a case of take it or leave it with them. There was no middle channel. They often stole fighters outright, and it was not worth one's life to defy them. Practically every big city's fight clubs had bootleggers' dough financing the operation. The Dutch Schulz and Owney Madden mobs held sway in New York, the Boo Boo Hoff mobsters in Pennsylvania and the Al Capone gunmen in Illinois.'

Hoff was a regular promoter and manager in Philadelphia. It is hard to assess the true extent of the gangsters' power, which was by its very nature unseen. Certainly some cities, such as Chicago, were very shady; one prominent referee, Dave Miller, was part of a leading Jewish gang family and another, Dave Barry, was a close pal of mobsters such as Spike O'Donnell. Another contemporary sportswriter, Paul Gallico, wrote: 'Whether or not they really influenced the referees and officials, they no doubt *said* they did and it behooved a pugilist to receive them politely and meet them socially.'

Around 1911 the International Boxing Union was formed in Europe in an attempt to co-ordinate various worldwide authorities and to standardize weight categories. It had some success, establishing the middleweight limit at 160lb. In 1920 another organization, the National Boxing Association, was formed after a meeting at New York's Flatiron Building by a group representing American states that wished to work together. Sadly, the most influential state, New York, refused to join — something which was to cause a split in the middleweight title during the 1930s.

In the 1940s and 1950s, a period which saw the boxing commissions cease their feuding, more sinister forces were at work. Mobsters led by a powerful New York gangster called Frankie Carbo gained control of some of the game's top promoters and managers., They effectively decided who boxed for the title, and who didn't. They set the terms. Carbo's grip was broken only when he was jailed in the early 1960s.

A brief period of sanity followed, but in the 1970s the game was split by two warring sanctioning bodies, the World Boxing Council and the World Boxing Association (formerly the NBA). These have now been joined by a pack of imitators, reducing boxing to its present-day state, something almost akin to professional wrestling. Only the boxers, much maligned and often abused, have kept their dignity.

1

From Skin to Gloves

IT WAS a good trade for a poor young immigrant. John Kelly was lucky to find work at Palmer's cooperage, a large, grimy building in the Williamsburg section of Brooklyn, one of the five boroughs of New York. Like Kelly, most of its workers were Irish-born, driven overseas in the wake of the Great Famine. They sweated at the benches to make barrels to be taken by horse-drawn wagon all over the bustling city. Some of them had dreams, however.

Kelly wanted to be a fighter. Two of his pals, who also worked at Palmer's in their time, shared the same idea and together they put the old cooper's shop on the sporting map. Each went on to fight for a world title. There was Jack McAuliffe, who retired as undefeated lightweight champion; Jack Skelly, who boxed for the featherweight crown in his professional debut; and there was John Kelly who, under the name Jack Dempsey, became the first widely accepted middleweight champion of the world. Sportswriters called them the 'Three Jacks'.

Dempsey bridged the gap between the old and new styles of 'milling', between bare fists and padded boxing gloves. His movements would look comical today but in his time he was an innovator. Dark-haired, with a Barrymore profile, he was agile and graceful, a student of footwork and feinting in an era of plodding bruisers. His fans thought he was unbeatable; they called him 'the Nonpareil' (the peerless, the incomparable).

He was born near Clane, in County Kildare, Ireland, on 15 December 1862. His family joined the exodus to the New World and settled in Williamsburg. There he met McAuliffe and Skelly and they became firm friends. In his teens, Kelly wanted to be a champion wrestler and won a string of bouts at the sport. He turned to fist fighting at 20, using the name Jack Dempsey to avoid offending his parents. He trained with McAuliffe, a fellow Irishman, in an improvised gym in the rough Fourteenth Ward. They used flat irons for dumbbells and punched an old sack filled with sand and sawdust.

Backed by bar owner Jack Shanley, Dempsey made his debut against Ed McDonald in a wooden hall on Long Island in April 1883. His fitness from wrestling stood him in good stead; the bout was in its 21st round when McDonald was ruled out for a low blow. Dempsey, who weighed 9st 2lb, collected a purse of $100. He fought 13 more times without loss in the next 12 months, all in the New York area. Sometimes the police arrived and the boxers had to flee. Dempsey took the risk; he loved to fight. Wins over the likes of Billy Dacey soon marked him as one of the best lightweights in America.

On 30 July 1884 Dempsey met George Fulljames for a stake of $1,000 each at Great Kills, Staten Island. This contest is often cited as the first for the middleweight title, which Fulljames, from Toronto, Canada, is said to have claimed some time in 1884 (see previous chapter). In fact, it was almost certainly for the *light*weight title. Neither of the men exceeded 10st. They fought with heavy driving gloves under London Prize Ring rules and Dempsey won by knockout in 22 rounds.

Dempsey gradually abandoned the lightweight division to make way for his pal McAuliffe, now a rising boxer in his own right. The mantle of middleweight champion seemed to settle on Dempsey imperceptibly (though he usually weighed about 140lb, then the welterweight limit, there was little interest in that division at the time). Charlie Mitchell, the best middleweight in the world, was competing at heavyweight and so in the absence of any foreign challengers, the Nonpareil won acceptance first in the US, and then abroad, as the leading 154-pounder. His claim was backed by a string of wins in gloved bouts over the next 18 months, including a successful tour of the West Coast.

His next title bout, against Jack Fogarty in February 1886 in New York, typified the age of illicit fighting. The pugilists, along with about 300 fans, met at a pre-ordained spot in Manhattan, then took the New Jersey ferry across the Hudson river. The New York police watched the ferry leave and returned to their normal duties, satisfied there would be no trouble on their patch. According to Patrick Myler in his book *The Fighting Irish*, 'This was what the fight crowd had been waiting for. The ferry took them back again to New York, where the contest was staged at the Clarendon Hall on 13th Street with not a lawman in sight. Dempsey gave Fogarty a savage hiding and won in the 27th round. He picked up $1,500 in prize money and a world championship belt donated, ironically, by the *Police Gazette*.' Fogarty came round to see the spectators holding a collection for him. 'Tell them to stop it,' he said. 'I lost and I don't deserve any money.'

A month later Dempsey defended his crown against George La Blanche, real name Blais, a fierce former US Marine and lumberjack with a bristling handlebar moustache. Dempsey won in 13 rounds. He cashed in on his fame with a coast-to-coast tour, boxing with the new padded gloves and winning about a score of gloved matches. Outside the ring he was a confident, flamboyant figure, never slow to employ his fists in a bar or street brawl. On one occasion he met his match and was thrown through a restaurant window by a belligerent waiter.

The Nonpareil's next serious challenge came in December 1887 against a hard-hitting New Yorker named Johnny Reagan. Twice postponed after police interference, the contest finally began on an isolated Long Island beach. By the fourth round, the tide was rising and the boxers were ankle-deep in water. They carried on until the referee called a halt with the waves lapping their shins. A tugboat was summoned and took contestants and spectators to higher ground, a grassy knoll 20 miles away. As they then resumed, a snowstorm suddenly descended. The men fought on through the freezing blizzard and Dempsey knocked out his foe in the 45th round with a right to the jaw. The bout lasted four hours from start to finish.

After several more contests, including a draw with the veteran Mike Donovan, Dempsey again risked his title against LaBlanche at the California Athletic Club, San Francisco, on 27 August 1889. The Quebecois, now 32, had improved considerably since their previous meeting and had recruited a clever English lightweight, Jimmy Carroll, as his trainer. Again he was outclassed, but he gamely persevered. In round 32, LaBlanche missed with a wild left hook. Pivoting on his foot, he swung back his left arm with great force. Some reports say he caught the champion with his elbow, others with the back of his glove. Dempsey fell flat on his face, breaking his nose, and was counted out. His manager, Dan Costigan, and backers protested that the punch had been a foul, but the referee gave the fight to LaBlanche. The so-called 'pivot' blow was afterwards declared illegal by the fight fraternity; though the result stood as a win for LaBlanche, Dempsey retained recognition as champion. Incidentally, LaBlanche had weighed 161lb, well over the limit.

Dempsey restored his credibility against Billy McCarthy, a former Australian middleweight champion who had fought in the US for several years. They met on 18 February 1890 at the California AC. There was a delay before the start while the gloves were changed; gamblers had tampered with them. Dempsey was the lighter man but carried the day in 28 rounds to win international recognition as champion. McCarthy showed his courage years later, saving 17 lives in a Texas flood.

Though he was only 28, Dempsey's health now began to fail. He was plagued with a hacking cough and sometimes choked up blood; in fact, he was in the early stages of tuberculosis. Despite this, he was made chief instructor at the California AC, a move which indirectly hastened his demise. A month after beating McCarthy, Dempsey prepared to second his old friend McAuliffe at the club in a match against Jimmy Carroll, LaBlanche's former trainer. However, Major Frank McLoughlin, the club's managing director, intended betting heavily on Carroll and forbade Dempsey from helping McAuliffe. Dempsey resigned as instructor and was in McAuliffe's corner to see him knock out Carroll in 47 rounds. McLoughlin was furious and vowed to find an opponent to take Dempsey's title.

A lanky blacksmith called Bob Fitzsimmons, English-born and newly arrived in the States, seemed to fit the bill. After watching him box, Carroll and McLoughlin courted his friendship and set about luring Dempsey into the ring. Knowing the champion would no longer risk his title at the Major's club, they hoped to tempt him to New Orleans, another city which permitted gloved contests. To whet appetites, they arranged a bout for Fitzsimmons there in June; he knocked out Arthur Upham in five rounds.

McLoughlin next told the matchmaker of the New Orleans Olympic Club that he would guarantee any purse offered for a title match with Fitzsimmons. This enabled the club to telegraph Dempsey at his home in Portland, Oregon, and offer a purse of $12,000, with $11,000 for the winner. The champion couldn't resist what was, for that time, an enormous sum. It was a coup for the

Olympic, an impressively ornate building with electric lights, Turkish baths, a bowling alley and a rifle range. Extra seats were installed and all 4,000 were filled on the evening of 14 January 1891, when the two boxers climbed into the ring. The resultant publicity made the Olympic for a spell the most important prizefight venue in the world.

Dempsey was favourite to win but McLoughlin made the biggest wager ever known in New Orleans, accepting $50,000 to $30,000 on Fitzsimmons. It was billed as a fight to the finish, which meant 45 rounds, at a stipulated weight of 154lb. They weighed-in in the ring, which was laid with flattened sand; Dempsey was 147½lb, Fitzsimmons 150½. 'May the best man win,' said the challenger, offering his hand. 'He will,' retorted Dempsey. The local police captain, evidently a man of the old school, was unimpressed by their five-ounce gloves. 'If they can hurt themselves with these pillows, then I'm mistaken,' he said.

Dempsey should never have been in the ring. Weak with illness, he was facing an opponent who was bigger, stronger, fitter, and hit harder. To the crowd's astonishment, he was floored as early as the second round. Dempsey fought back but went down twice more in the seventh and was saved by the bell. In the tenth, he was felled three times. Blood came from his brows, nose and mouth. McAuliffe, who was in his corner, later recalled, 'As the one-sided scrap went on, with Dempsey taking the punishment like the hero that he was, there were cries from all over the building, imploring me to throw up the sponge and end it. The referee would have halted that fight today, but those were stern times. Men fought until they dropped, as a general rule, and the sight of blood didn't faze either spectator or the third man in the ring.'

Dempsey refused to quit. He had bet $1,000, equal to the loser's purse, on himself and so would get nothing if he lost. But his cause was hopeless. He fell six times more in the 11th and 12th. In the 13th, after flooring him yet again, Fitzsimmons said, 'You've had enough, I don't want to hurt you any more.' Dempsey replied, 'I'm good enough to beat you yet.' Fitzsimmons cracked over another wicked right cross to the jaw, Dempsey went down again, and McAuliffe threw his sponge in the ring to signify defeat.

In his dressing room, the badly mauled ex-champion lamented, 'It wouldn't hurt so much if I lost my title to an Irishman or an

American, but to an Englishman; that's what kills me.' McAuliffe cushioned the blow a little; he had bet his expected $1,400 training fee against $1,000 that Fitzsimmons couldn't stop Dempsey in ten rounds. His friend's brave defiance had won the bet and McAuliffe gave Dempsey his winnings.

Nonpareil no longer, Dempsey fought just three times in the next four years. He beat Mike Keogh, drew with Billy McCarthy, then lost in three rounds to Tommy Ryan, the world welterweight champion. Against Ryan he was a spare, gaunt figure, weighing 135lb. After three rather gentle rounds, Dempsey was so exhausted he fell over from a push. The referee awarded the contest to Ryan to save Dempsey the indignity of being counted out. His last ring appearance was an exhibition with John L. Sullivan at Madison Square Garden. It was a benefit for Dempsey, who had squandered his ring money and was now terminally ill. He died of TB five months later, on 2 November 1895, in Portland, Oregon. He was only 33. He had made friends with Fitzsimmons and on his death bed told his wife to bet on his old foe whenever he fought, advice which would have made her a rich widow. His own name would live on; it was adopted by a young heavyweight called William Harrison Dempsey, who went on to become one of the most famous boxers of all.

Opponents were known to laugh when they saw Bob Fitzsimmons. It was a foolish thing to do. Despite his spindly legs, impossibly pale skin, bald head with its fringe of red hair, and his freckles, Fitzsimmons was an iron man, his power latent in an upper frame developed through countless hours at a blacksmith's forge. According to a contemporary, his 'arms and shoulders were heavily-made, his chest was plated with muscle; his back so strongly developed that his shoulders stooped. His waist was as slender as a girl's, his hips were a minus quality and his legs mere gangling shanks. Above the belt-line he was a heavyweight, below a spindly lightweight.' He won lasting fame as the first Englishman to win the world heavyweight title (Lennox Lewis recently became the second) and the first man to win world titles at three different weights.

Fitzsimmons was born in the tiny village of Helston, Cornwall, on 26 May 1862, the last of 12 children to an Irish father and a 47-year-old Cornish mother. James, the father, was a trained blacksmith and the borough police constable, while his mother was the local midwife. Robert was an energetic child and the bane of his school friends, who suffered from his penchant for rough-and-tumble boxing practice. Around 1872, his parents emigrated to New Zealand with their five youngest offspring. Their journey was probably a search for work, as the tin industry vital to Cornwall's economy was in terminal decline.

They settled among an expatriate Cornish community at Timaru, in Canterbury Bight. James set up a smithy and taught his son to make horseshoes, iron farm equipment and wagon tyres. He shaped his freakish physique at the anvil. Fitzsimmons's accounts of his teenage years varied according to which reporter he was telling. In one version he learned to box to avenge himself on a bully. In another, he began after belting a boy who beat him in a Bible-reciting contest. In his first bareknuckle fight, at the age of 15, he caused a local sensation by beating Tom Baines, a huge blacksmith known as the 'Timaru Terror'.

In 1880 and 1881, 'Fitz' won two amateur tournaments promoted by Jem Mace, the last of the great English prize ring men, who was scouring New Zealand for talent. In the second of these shows Fitzsimmons beat five opponents in one night, then challenged Mace's protégé, a 200lb Maori called Herbert Slade. A big crowd gathered to watch their hero give Slade such a thrashing that Mace stopped the contest in the second round. Fitzsimmons, angry at being denied a knockout, challenged the old warrior himself. Mace was ready to fight when the crowd prevailed on him to spare the younger man. The two shook hands and Mace advised Fitzsimmons to go to Larry Foley's boxing academy in Sydney, Australia, to learn the game properly.

It was two years before he took that advice, but he never regretted it. Foley played a key role in developing all the famous Australian fighters of the era, men like Peter Jackson, Frank Slavin, and Young Griffo. Watching and competing at his ramshackle arena known as the 'Iron Pot' transformed Fitzsimmons from a rough-and-ready scrapper to a first-class ringman. He was to stay in Sydney for the next seven years. His fight record is patchy; there was very little reporting of boxing, and only a couple of dozen fights can be traced, but he must have had many more. He won most of them and in February 1890 challenged the Australian middleweight champion, Jim Hall.

Hall had been contacted by the California AC, keen to match him with Dempsey for the world title. It was explained that a win before he left Australia would boost his stock in America and create greater interest in the bout. Foley arranged for Hall to fight Fitzsimmons. It was a 'schlenter', an Australian word for a fake. Hall gave Fitzsimmons £55 to 'lie down' in the fourth round. A report in the local *Evening News* said Hall was 'manifestly out of condition' and the two fighters 'were pushing one another about the ring without strength enough to do harm of the mildest description'. In the fourth, 'Fitzsimmons advanced and Hall accommodated him with a right somewhere in the vicinity of the jaw.' Fitzsimmons was counted out.

Hall, who always denied the fight was fixed, never got his reward. He was stabbed in the hand in a drunken brawl soon after and had to postpone his trip to America. It was to change the course of boxing history. Fitzsimmons was invited in his place and sailed in April 1890 with his wife Alice and baby son. One fellow passenger recorded, 'He is like a big kid and always playing jokes. On the way over he took delight in tripping over a sailor in order to get him mad enough to try and hit him. Bob would just laugh and duck and dodge, brushing off every intended punch, until the other man had to stop in admiration of Fitzsimmons's defensive skills.'

They arrived in San Francisco 24 days later. At the California AC, Fitzsimmons was told he would have to prove his worth before stepping in the ring with the champion. He was matched with Frank Allen, a local middleweight; Fitzsimmons punched him around the ring before flattening him in the first round. Allen broke his wrist in the fall, while the blows had shattered a gold bridge on his jaw. Another test was arranged, against Billy McCarthy. The two had once sparred in Sydney and McCarthy expected little trouble. He called his opponent a 'bald-headed kangaroo' and there was laughter at Fitzsimmons's appearance as he removed his dressing gown. The laughter stopped when McCarthy hit the deck almost as soon as the bout started. He was dropped several more times in the next few rounds and in the sixth swung low in desperation. Fitzsimmons went down in great distress, but persuaded the referee it had been an accident. The bout continued and McCarthy's punishment grew even more severe. He collapsed in round nine.

Fitzsimmons's emphatic title over Dempsey came as a great surprise to the fistic fraternity. They would have been astonished had they known he would box for 23 years more and win titles at three weights. Fitzsimmons would defend his first title only once, before abandoning it to pursue the heavyweight championship. Yet he was undoubtedly the dominant middleweight of his day and still the best in the world at the turn of the century.

After beating Dempsey he set off on the usual variety tour, giving exhibitions of ball-punching and sparring and offering $100 to anyone who could stay four rounds with him. He enjoyed theatrical life and was always something of a showman. He also kept the boxing writers employed thinking up nicknames: 'Freckled Bob', 'Ruby Robert' and 'the Fighting Blacksmith'. He beat Irish heavyweight Peter Maher in New Orleans in his next serious appearance and whipped a number of men on another stage tour. In September 1892 he was back in the Crescent City to watch 'Gentleman' Jim Corbett end John L. Sullivan's reign as heavyweight champion. The new king was not much bigger than Fitzsimmons, who challenged him. Corbett said, 'Tell him to stick to his own class.'

First, Fitzsimmons settled matters with Jim Hall, who had reached America and was bad-mouthing his old adversary. Their rivalry fuelled enormous interest and a bidding contest between the new Crescent City AC in New Orleans and the Coney Island AC in New York resulted in an unheard-of purse offer of $40,000 from New Orleans. New York actually topped this bid, but Fitzsimmons's new manager, Martin Julian, preferred the Louisiana offer. Julian was an acrobat the champion had met on his theatrical outings. He had fallen for one of Julian's sisters, Rose. Julian, in turn, took a fancy to the boxer's wife. This cosy arrangement allowed Julian to worm his way in as manager, which did little for Fitzsimmons's finances.

Eight thousand attended the bout in March 1893. It was recognized at the time as being for the title, but both men were well over even the modern middleweight limit of 160lb. In the fourth round, Hall pulled back from a Fitzsimmons feint. Wrote Gilbert Odd: 'Like lightning, Fitz darted forward and whipped a hard left to the jaw, followed by a tremendous right hand swing that landed full on the point of the Australian's chin. Down he went in an untidy heap and did not move a muscle while the full count was called.' Hall's English backer, the eccentric 'Squire' George Abingdon Baird, lost heavily on his man. The wealthy Baird, Hall and their party then set out on a monumental spree in the city's bars and bordellos to drown

their sorrows. After several nights of debauchery Baird collapsed of a
heart attack 'while dancing a mad fandango with a dazzling Creole'.
He died 10 days later.

Fitzsimmons applied for US citizenship, which he believed would
help him secure a fight with Corbett. He also divorced Alice to marry
Rose Julian; Alice in turn married Martin Julian. Rose, a short,
muscular trapeze artist with a wistfully pretty face and thick ringlets
of hair, became one of the first women to attend boxing matches
regularly, breaching social barriers to support her man and creating
much pious indignation among newspaper editors. Fitzsimmons
returned to the stage to star in the boxing play *A Man's A Man* and
fought several heavyweight contests before defending his title against
Dan Creedon, another pupil of Larry Foley.

Creedon came from New Zealand. He had been unbeaten in
Sydney, and claimed the Australian middleweight title after beating
Tut Ryan. He was 5ft 8½in tall, with a short, thick neck and big
shoulders. Reaching the US at the end of 1892, he was an instant
success, winning his first five contests by knockout. The Olympic
matched them as the last bout of a three-day title carnival in
September 1894. On the first day Billy Plimmer and Johnny Murton
drew for the 'world' bantam title. On the second Stanton Abbott and
Jack Everhardt drew for the lightweight title. For the middleweight
bout, Fitz raised the weight limit to 158lb, where it stuck for about 20
years. Creedon did most of the attacking in the first round. But in the
second, Fitz dropped him with a right. Up at 'eight', the challenger
was swamped and was flattened with another perfect right. He was
unconscious for several minutes.

Though Fitzsimmons did not formally relinquish the middleweight
title, he never defended it again. His whole career almost ended soon
after when he was charged with manslaughter following the death of
an opponent, Con Riordan. At the subsequent nine-day trial it was
established that Riordan entered the ring drunk, fell from a light blow
and probably died from apoplexy. Fitzsimmons was acquitted.

Meanwhile, Corbett retired and named Peter Maher as his
successor. Fitzsimmons promptly knocked him out in a bout held
over the Mexican border to avoid a posse of Texas Rangers. Then
there was an equally bizarre fight against Tom Sharkey. The referee
was Wyatt Earp, the famous Western marshall, who was friendly with
Sharkey. In round eight Fitzsimmons knocked out his opponent.

Earp disqualified him for an alleged low blow. Fitzsimmons and the crowd protested but were silenced when Earp strapped on his gunbelt and stood ready to draw.

Finally, on 17 March 1897, he challenged Corbett at Carson City, Nevada, for the heavyweight title he craved. After being outboxed and outsmarted, he switched his attack to the body and in the 14th round caught the champion with a pile-driving left to the solar plexus. Corbett fell to his knees with the breath driven out of him and was unable to rise before the count reached 'ten'. Fitzsimmons was champion at 34.

He lost the heavyweight title two years later when he conceded 64lb to the daunting Jim Jeffries and was kayoed in the 11th round. He gave away even more weight a year later when beating the 300lb-plus Ed Dunkhorst, known as the 'Human Freight Car', and secured a rematch with Jeffries in 1902. Fitzsimmons was later said to have encased his fists in plaster of Paris; if so, the plan backfired. He broke both his hands on Jeffries's jaw and lost in the eighth. The *San Francisco Examiner*, which received an anonymous letter beforehand predicting the result, said the bout was a fake.

It was not the end of Fitzsimmons's career. In November 1903, at the age of 41, he won his third world title, at light-heavyweight, by outboxing George Gardner over 15 rounds. He held it for two years until he was pulverized by 'Philadelphia' Jack O'Brien and collapsed, vomiting blood, in round 13. Two years later he was knocked out by the menacing black heavyweight Jack Johnson. The old warhorse had his last contest in 1914 at the age of 51. In a test case his licence was revoked. The New York State Athletic Commission said he was too old to box; Fitz filed suit, claiming an infringement of civil liberties, but a court upheld the decision.

By now, Fitzsimmons was on his fourth marriage. Rose had died in 1903. Within 14 weeks he had met and married Julia Gifford, a pretty young actress. She couldn't handle his frequent drinking bouts and they parted after eight years. 'When the whisky got to him it was evil and frightening,' she said. 'We could have had a wonderful life together if it had not been for the whisky.' Bitterness was partly the cause. Fitzsimmons often complained he had been jobbed out of money he should have earned. It was mainly his own fault. Throughout his career he followed poor advice and was easily swayed. Fitzsimmons occasionally tackled his financial problems with the same directness he had in the ring. In 1915 a bailiff who arrived to repossess his 47-acre New Jersey farm left quickly nursing a bruised jaw and ribs. Fitzsimmons was fined $10 for assault.

His boozing was stopped by his fourth wife, Russian-born divorcée Temo Slomonin, who called herself 'The Countess'. She persuaded him to join her as a travelling evangelist, a role into which he threw himself with customary zeal. While on a tour in Chicago he was stricken with double pneumonia. He died on 22 October 1917, and was buried in Chicago's Graceland cemetery. According to Temo, his last words had been, 'I'm taking off the gloves and putting them on you. Keep fighting sin and remember, good fighters never lose.'

A number of contenders vied to fill the vacuum when Fitzsimmons left the middleweight division. Prime among them were Tommy Ryan, Tommy West, Kid McCoy, Dick O'Brien, Jack Bonner, Frank Craig and Dan Creedon. On 14 October 1895 a contest was billed for the world title at the National Sporting Club, London, between Craig, an American negro known as the 'Harlem Coffee Cooler', and Creedon, the last man to challenge Fitzsimmons. Creedon won on points over 20 rounds and was presented with a championship belt. His claim, however, was very much disputed. Tommy Ryan, not Craig, was deemed the best American.

The man to emerge as Fitzsimmons's successor was Charles 'Kid' McCoy. He was one of the most unusual and complex individuals ever to step into a boxing ring. McCoy's life was masked by myth, a tangle of half-truths, scandal, lies and tragedy. His own grip on reality was tenuous. The trade paper *Boxing News* said he 'was probably the first national sports figure anywhere to be publicity-created. He lost his own identity in trying to live up to what was expected of Kid McCoy.' Even his name was fake. While probably responsible for the phrase 'the real McCoy' — meaning the real thing — which is still used today, he was in fact born Norman Selby. There are several versions of why he changed his name, one being that he took it after seeing a melodrama starring Kid McCoy and Spike Hennessy, two infamous burglars whose exploits were also described in a dime novel.

A conman in gloves, he would pull any stunt to win: fouling, feigning illness, cheating. He sometimes boxed when drunk. He was just as shameless in his private life and was married ten times to eight women (one wed and divorced him three times). Tall, skinny and flat-chested, he had a languid air and foppish manner, with 'the lean and pallid face of an undernourished poet', according to author Chris Greyvenstein. He also had bags of charm, unfettered by scruple.

He was born on 13 October 1872 in Moscow, Indiana, to Frank and Mary Selby. His mother was part-insane and his sister Mabel also went mad. His deeply religious father owned a store. McCoy left home in his teens and once claimed to have spent five years as a hobo, almost certainly an exaggeration. He ended up as a cash boy in a department store in Louisville, Kentucky, where he suffered taunts as an out-of-towner. He went to the local YMCA to learn self-defence and showed a natural aptitude for the subtleties of ringcraft.

Boxing as Kid McCoy, he won his first pro bout at 18 in 1891 against Peter Jenkins. He then compiled a three-year unbeaten streak, according to records, until he lost inside one round to Billy Steffers in 1894. McCoy always learned from defeats and improved enough to outpoint Steffers 15 weeks later. In his next contest he received what he called his 'first boxing lesson', but still managed to eke out a decision over Shadow Maber, another talented Australian. McCoy had become a 'road' fighter, travelling from town to town, boxing in small halls, barns and railroad camps. And the McCoy legend was growing. After Maber he met Jack Wilkes, and allegedly wore stage make-up into the ring. Wilkes, fooled by his opponent's ghastly appearance, though he was ill and expected an easy win. McCoy beat him in two rounds.

In the winter of 1895, McCoy sailed to England seeking a fight with title claimant Dan Creedon. Instead he met Ted White, a leading English middleweight. The American had lost only one of 37 recorded bouts and was supremely confident, but White taught him the value of a good left jab and won on points. It was a different story two months later when McCoy dismantled the highly-rated Tommy West in two rounds in New York. He sought a fight with Tommy Ryan, who claimed the world welterweight title. McCoy had once served as Ryan's sparring partner and had not forgotten the beatings he took. Ryan initially treated his challenge as a joke but accepted the purse put up by the Maspeth AC in New York. Apparently McCoy promised he would do whatever Ryan told him during the bout. Another, highly unlikely, story is that McCoy persuaded Ryan to fight him by pretending he was suffering from consumption and desperately needed money.

They met on 2 March 1896. To Ryan's painful surprise, he was outboxed, outpunched and, in the 15th round, beaten. Alexander Johnston called it 'a classic example of the double-cross'. Although Ryan's welterweight title was not at stake, McCoy now had a strong case for claiming the middleweight crown. However, many thought Fitzsimmons was still the best. McCoy had once worked as a sparring partner for the former champion and was told by his wife Rose, 'You're going to beat a lot more than beat you, but you'll never lick Bob. That's for certain, and if you try you'll only get hurt and I wouldn't want to see you beaten up. So forget it.' They never fought.

McCoy next beat 'Mysterious' Billy Smith on a foul. In 1896 he sailed to Cape Town, South Africa, under the name Harry Egan. With typically devious intent, he planned to masquerade as a third-rate American boxer. He intended to look bad in a few bouts, then to challenge the national champion, when he would turn the burners full on and hopefully clean up the betting. His fame preceded him, however, and he was quickly recognized. Instead, he challenged Billy Doherty, an Australian import acknowledged as the best middleweight in South Africa. Their bout would be for the 'world' middleweight title and a side wager of $500. McCoy trained in secret to cause rumours that his form was poor. He then postponed the bout, claiming typhoid fever. It all served to push the odds to 5–1 in Doherty's favour.

They finally met on Boxing Day 1896, in Johannesburg, ostensibly for the vacant title. Doherty was brave but outgunned. He later wrote of McCoy: 'He introduced a kind of punch I had never seen or heard of before — a species of corkscrew delivery that wound like a snake through my guard . . . with bewildering rapidity.' The Australian was knocked out in the ninth round and was unconscious for nearly 30 minutes. McCoy's corkscrew punch, a penetrative hook in which the wrist twisted inwards at the moment of impact, became much celebrated. He once claimed to have got the idea from watching a kitten swiping at a ball of string. On another occasion, he said it came from the rifling inside a gun barrel.

With gold recently discovered in the Transvaal, McCoy stayed a while in Africa. He travelled with a circus and took on all comers, offering £20 to anyone who could stay four rounds (only one did).

Returning to the US, he beat the likes of Dick O'Brien, Jack Bonner and Dick Moore and whipped old George LaBlanche in one round. On 17 December 1897, he stepped into the ring in Long Island City to meet Dan Creedon in a bout to decide the middleweight supremacy outright. It was scheduled for 25 rounds, but Creedon failed to answer the bell for the 16th.

McCoy never bothered to defend the title after this. His eye for the main chance led him to the money and fame of the heavyweight class. He outpointed the huge Gus Ruhlin and another heavy, Joe Goddard. But in January 1899 his lack of weight and strength were exposed by Tom Sharkey, the granite-jawed sailor, who bludgeoned him to defeat in ten rounds. McCoy returned with four wins, including an impressive victory over Joe Choynski, after which a newspaper proclaimed, 'Now you've seen the real McCoy!'

His career never ceased to be eventful. In August an unknown called Jack McCormick knocked him stiff in one round. McCoy extracted revenge later that year, giving McCormick an awful beating in eight rounds. In 1900 he conspired with gamblers to lose a New York bout with Peter Maher. He was warned off by 'Big Tim' Sullivan, a powerful political boss and architect of the Horton Law, and instead he won in five rounds. The same year, on 30 August, to took on former heavyweight champion Jim Corbett in New York in what was the last bout under the Horton Law. There were sweeping rumours that McCoy had agreed with a bunch of gamblers to lie down in the fifth. When the fateful round arrived, he suddenly fell from a blow to the stomach and flopped around in an unconvincing display of agony. Referee Charley White wasted no time in stopping the fight. Corbett insisted it had been legitimate.

McCoy boxed next in December 1901 in England. On one remarkable night, he knocked out two boxers and beat the third on a foul. Six months later, he was saved from a knockout by Kid Carter in Philadelphia when the timekeeper deliberately rang the bell a minute early while McCoy was being counted out. He recovered to last the distance. In 1903 he lost a ten-round decision to Jack Root for the fledgling light-heavyweight title. The next year he defeated his biggest-ever opponent, Henry Placke of Holland, who weighed 241lb and stood 6ft 5in (McCoy was 5ft 11 and 163lb). Placke fell for the oldest trick in the book: McCoy pointed to Placke's feet, then punched him as he looked down, knocking him out in the second round.

His career gradually petered out. There was a comeback in 1908, another in 1911 that took him to Paris, and a last fight in 1916. In between were several brushes with the law. After retiring, he went to Hollywood, appearing in Mack Sennett silent movies and D. W. Griffith's famous *Broken Blossoms*. Mixing with starlets helped add to his ever-growing collection of ex-wives, which had started years earlier with Lottie Piehler, a washerwoman's daughter. A woman was to prove his downfall.

McCoy lived with Teresa Mors, a wealthy woman he hoped to marry. She and her husband had divorced but wrangled over the division of their fortune. In August 1924, she was killed by a single shot through the head in the apartment she shared with McCoy. The boxer then entered the Mors' antique shop, where he shot and wounded three more people. As customers came into the shop, McCoy held them at gunpoint and robbed them. He was eventually arrested. At his subsequent trial for first-degree murder, McCoy emotionally testified that Mors committed suicide after he told her he was planning to leave town for a few weeks. He was convicted of the lesser charge of manslaughter and sent to San Quentin prison for one-to-ten years.

McCoy was freed in 1932 and found a position as a security guard at the gardens of the Ford Motor Company in Detroit. He married again and lived quietly. But his turbulent soul wouldn't let him rest. On 18 April 1940, in a trough of depression caused by the war in Europe, the man who once announced he intended to live until he was 150 took an overdose of sleeping pills and died. He left a note, which ended, 'I wish you all the best of luck. Sorry I could not endure this world's madness.' It was signed 'Norman Selby'. The real McCoy.

While McCoy tussled with giants, Tommy Ryan continued quietly on his way, taking over his mantle as middleweight champion. Ryan was a master boxer, an expert in every facet of the game who later became an expert trainer. Without the flamboyance of his predecessors, he let his fists do the talking and compiled an enviable record. He was born in Redwood, New York, on 20 March 1870, and christened Joseph Youngs. His father was French, his mother English. He began boxing in 1887, in the twilight years between bareknuckles, driving gloves and Queensberry rules. The grit of the prize ring never left him.

Ryan served a hard apprenticeship. His formative contests included 33 rounds with Dick England, 46 rounds with a brawler named Mike Shaughnessy and 57 rounds to a no-contest with Jimmy Murphy. He continued unbeaten in 1890, winning all five fights by knockout. In February 1891 he met Danny Needham, a good welterweight, at Minneapolis. After 76 gory rounds, Ryan won because he could lift his hands into a fighting position and the half-dead Needham couldn't. For the next three years, Ryan fought when and where he could, dodging arrest to ply his trade.

A hard-nosed pug with the name Mysterious Billy Smith had come east claiming the welterweight title. After holding him to two six-round draws, Ryan challenged him for the title in July 1894 in Milwaukee. Ryan won the 20-round decision, but Smith protested loudly. They fought again at Coney Island in May 1885. Police stopped the bout in the 11th, when Ryan was on the floor about to be counted out. Inexplicably, they then let the contestants continue until round 18, when Smith was on the verge of defeat. The bout was called a draw. Between these two bouts, Ryan dished Jack Dempsey in three rounds. He started to claim the middleweight title, but then was beaten by McCoy.

Ryan defended his welterweight title four times. On 24 October 1898 he outpointed Jack Bonner in 20 rounds at Coney Island for the vacant world middleweight championship, according to the *Ring Record Book*. McCoy was no longer interested in the title. To prove his right to it, Ryan systematically took on all his top contenders. In September 1899 he mastered Frank Craig, the Coffee Cooler, in ten torrid rounds at Coney Island. Craig was a cutey who entertained outside the ring as an 'eccentric dancer', but Ryan wore him down with a body attack.

In 1900 Ryan lost a non-title bout to McCoy — only his second defeat. Ten months later, in March 1901, he was challenged by Tommy West. They clashed at the Southern Athletic Club in Louisville, Kentucky, which had become a boxing stronghold. West, square-jawed and stocky, hailed originally from Cardiff, Wales. He had lost a welterweight challenge to Ryan three years earlier but had since crunched a number of top fighters and was even stronger at the higher weight.

They should have held it in a dogpit; it was one of the bloodiest fights ever seen. West forced the early rounds with his powerful jab, cutting Ryan's face. In the second he dropped the champion for 'eight' with a right. A promoter, Jack Curley, later wrote:

> In the fourth round West butted Ryan in the mouth, splitting his tooth, and Ryan, turning to Tim Hurst, the referee, mumbled, 'What do you call that, Tim?'
>
> Tim looked at him blandly. 'You've got a head too, haven't you, Tommy?' he asked.
>
> Ryan took the tip and in the fifth round butted West in the mouth, splitting his lips and dotting the canvas with his broken teeth. After that he ripped West's lacerated mouth with his left wrist and forearm whenever they went to close quarters and at times the floor of the ring was so wet with blood that between rounds employees of the club mopped it with towels to provide a dry footing for the fighters.

In the ninth, a police captain tried to stop the fight. Tim Hurst persuaded him that the men were not as badly hurt as they appeared and the battle continued. Only West's great pluck kept him going; in the last three rounds he was virtually helpless. His second, Terry McGovern, threw in the sponge in the middle of the 17th round. It was later found that West had a broken nose and Ryan a broken left hand. Unbelievably, West was back in action ten days later, when he was knocked out in 16 rounds by Marvin Hart.

Later in the year, Ryan lost for only the third time, on a foul to George Green. He later gained revenge by a knockout. He defended his title just twice more, beating Johnny Gorman in London in June 1902 and Kid Carter in Fort Erie, Canada, three months later. Before the Carter bout he was ill and came in at 142lb for a contest set at 158. The promoters wouldn't allow postponement. Carter pursued him to the ropes in the sixth but was caught by an uppercut and counted out.

By now Ryan had earned a well-deserved reputation as a trainer and tactician. He had already been credited with helping Jim Jeffries win the world heavyweight title by teaching him a defensive crouch. He boxed on until 1907 when, having drawn with Hugo Kelly, he retired, nominating Kelly as his successor. He devoted himself to training, running a gym in Syracuse, New York State, and became a respected man-about-boxing. One of the few pugilists to retire at the top, his record showed just three defeats, two by McCoy, in well over 100 contests. He died at Van Nuys, California, on 3 August 1948.

At the height of his fame, in 1903, Ryan had beaten an opponent called John Willie in the town of Butte, Montana. It is said that he also boxed exhibitions there against the local copper miners. One in particular, a boy of 16, startled him with the force of his punches and afterwards Ryan predicted great things for the youngster. His name was Stanley Ketchel.

2

The Michigan Assassin

STANLEY KETCHEL lived by whim. 'He was a creature of emotions,' wrote Alva Johnston, 'and could be a lamb or a devil, according to which emotion happened to be stirred up.' By turns wild, lovable, treacherous and amiable, his dominant trait was violence. He once shot his trainer in the leg for waking him from a nap. He brutalized opponents and sparring partners alike and took pleasure in cruel practical jokes. Such disdain for others endeared him to the fight mob; here was a man after their own hearts, a firebrand who hit hard, drove fast, chased women and toted a gun. They called him the 'Michigan Assassin'.

Everyone noticed his eyes. Slanted behind high cheekbones, they were cold and piercing. One look could chill an opponent. His face was coarsened by bathing in salt brine, an old fighters' trick to toughen the skin. He had unruly brown hair parted at one side, a sullen face and taut, set lips. His body was hard rather than muscular, his fighting weight around 154lb. Only 5ft 9in tall, he was self-conscious about his height and wore Cuban heels to look taller. He sported silk shirts and Fifth Avenue suits and cultivated the insolent poise of the gunslinger.

Contemporaries called Ketchel the greatest of all middleweights. His lust for destruction accompanied a numbing punch, sharp reflexes and raw resilience. With alley-cat caginess he would loll, flat-footed and listless, before springing forward with what one foe called 'tumultuous but ill-directed ferocity'. His favourite move was 'the shift', in which he would throw a punch to the jaw then suddenly shift his feet and hook with all his weight to his opponent's body. For all that, his boxing style was unrefined. He was easy to hit and bled freely. Ketchel was equally reckless out of the ring, and knew it. He often said he would die before he was 30, a prediction inaccurate only in its optimism.

His real name was Stanislaus Kiecal and he was born on 14 September 1886 in Grand Rapids, Michigan, of mixed German and Polish ancestry. His father Thomas was a farm labourer; his mother Julia doted on her children, and in later years Ketchel would stoke up hate for rivals by pretending they had insulted her. He was an unruly child with a vicious temper, defying his father's beatings to lead a juvenile gang called the West Sides. His adolescent ambition was to be a Wild West outlaw, to ride and shoot like Jesse James and Billy the Kid. Years on, he would boast of his friendship with bandits like Emmet Dalton and Cole Younger.

According to his biographer, Nat Fleischer, Stanislaus ran away from home at the age of 12 to become a cowboy. He sneaked onto a freight train and reached Chicago, where he met an ex-boxer named 'Socker' Flanagan. Flanagan, who owned a lunch-counter, gave the young urchin a job, taught him a few boxing moves, and anglicized his name to Ketchel. Other writers say Ketchel left home at 15. Either way, in his mid-teens he became a hobo, joining the vast army of transients that ghosted across turn-of-the-century America. Most were migrant labourers seeking work; others were winos, bankrupts, con artists, runaways and thieves. They travelled by hiding in rail wagons or 'riding the rods' — clinging to two metal bars under the carriages — and slept rough in makeshift camps known as 'jungles'. Food was pooled and cooked in communal pots.

The camps were dangerous. 'Here,' wrote Alexander Johnston, 'where fighting is purely a survival of the fittest, this Michigan farm boy learned to battle for his life, and later he carried the flaming intensity of these life-and-death battles into the prize ring.' Ketchel scrounged food and turned his hand to any job that came along. He panhandled through Minnesota, harvested corn in the Dakotas, trod logs at a British Columbia sawmill and criss-crossed the Canadian border. In 1902 he wandered, penniless and hungry, into the town of Butte, high in the Montana Rockies. His fortunes were about to change.

Butte, centre of the largest copper mining region in the States, was known as 'the richest hill on earth'. According to boxing writer Nigel Collins it was 'a wide-open, freewheeling town, crawling with miners,

cowboys, gamblers and prostitutes; the kind of frontier outpost that
gave the American West its rowdy reputation'. Ketchel loved it. He
found work as a waiter-cum-bellhop at a dive called the Copper
Queen and soon replaced the resident bouncer after pummelling him
in a fight. For $10 a week, the skinny 16-year-old kept drunken
pitmen and lumberjacks in line, a job he executed with vicious glee.
'Ketchel had the soul of a bouncer,' said fight manager Dan Morgan,
'but a bouncer who loved his work.' He was encouraged to box by
Maurice Thompson, a fighter working in the mines, and was hired by
the Casino Theatre to meet all comers for $20 a week.

Ketchel had dozens of unrecorded fights at the Casino, similar to
the booth fights that flourished in Britain. His first professional bout
on record came on 2 May 1903 against Jack 'Kid' Tracey, a hard-
hitting welterweight offering $10 to anyone who could take him four
rounds. Ketchel flattened him in the first. Legend has it that Tracey
was slugged with a sandbag by a friend concealed behind a curtain at
the back of the ring, the slugger mistaking his pal's head for
Ketchel's. Stanley won his next fight in 24 rounds, then began 1904
by drawing with Rudolph Hinz and losing to Maurice Thompson, his
former mentor. Thompson, a brute, gave the teenager a hiding, but
he gamely lasted the six-round distance.

Thereafter, Ketchel's climb through the professional ranks was
spectacular. He fought 12 more times that year, winning ten inside
the distance and losing again on points to Thompson, with whom he
also drew. Through 1905 and 1906, he fought 25 times, mainly in
Montana, scoring 23 knockouts and two draws. His opponents were
limited but his electrifying style drew crowds of woodsmen and
miners from the camps to watch. Ketchel acquired a manager, a
photographer called Joe O'Connor, and became a man to be reckoned
with, if not avoided, in Butte. His ability with his fists gave him status
in such a muscular town. His purses went on gambling and
prostitutes and he started to carry a gun.

But horizons, sporting and otherwise, were limited in Montana.
Political persecution of prize fighting in America's southern and
eastern states had driven it to the West Coast, where its technical
illegality was often ignored. California had become the centre of the
boxing world; every heavyweight title fight since 1901 had been
staged there. In 1907, Ketchel moved down the coast. He picked up
something called the Pacific Coast championship by beating Mike

McClure in seven rounds, then stopped Benny Hart in eight. In May, he took on George Brown in Sacramento. Brown, a clever black boxer, was preparing for a fight with the highly regarded Joe Thomas. He mistakenly underestimated Ketchel, and was knocked unconscious by an uppercut in the third.

Victory earned Ketchel a fight with Thomas. At 20, they were the same age, but Thomas, from Beverly, Massachusetts, had already beaten some of the best welterweights and middleweights in the country. A slick, durable boxer, he was widely tipped as a potential champion. The two young contenders fought in Marysville on the Fourth of July and put up a lively contest. Ketchel knocked his opponent down in the 11th and pushed him to the limit. Neither side was satisfied when the referee declared a draw after 20 rounds.

Tommy Ryan had recently announced his retirement as champion. With the title vacant, the California boxing writers were prepared to ignore the claims of Hugo Kelly and Jack 'Twin' Sullivan and accept the winner of a Ketchel–Thomas rematch as the new champion. Jimmy Coffroth, the state's leading promoter, signed them to meet on 2 September at Colma, a small town south of San Francisco which permitted 45-round contests. Coffroth, known as 'Sunny Jim' for his luck with good weather at open-air shows, had been one of the first to benefit when the no-decision law was introduced in New York, driving the big fights to the west. He was to promote some of Ketchel's most important bouts. Against Thomas, Ketchel was so confident that he asked for a share of his purse in advance to bet on himself. Both men weighed under 150lb.

The battle began at 3pm and lasted for more than two hours; referee Billy Roche called it 'the greatest fight I ever saw'. For round after round Ketchel attacked, ripping hooks to the body. Thomas met him head-on with straight-arm jabs and crosses. Ketchel scored the first knockdown in the ninth; both hit the canvas seven or eight times after that, but neither would stay down. In round 29, Thomas caught Ketchel coming in with a tremendous right cross and dropped him in a heap. The contest appeared to be over, but at 'seven' Ketchel was on one knee and at 'nine' he was up. Sick and groggy, he instinctively tottered forward, flailing punches, and his bravado broke Thomas's resolve. In round 32, a one-two to the stomach and head draped the exhausted New Englander over the ropes, where he lay motionless, suspended from the bottom strand. His seconds threw in the towel.

Ketchel had emerged from obscurity to claim the world title. Reports of the wild hobo with a punch like a mule kick spread across the country. Thomas, however, was not done. He demanded another chance and a third bout was arranged for 12 December in a huge circus tent erected on an old San Francisco baseball park. On the night of the fight a terrible storm broke. Thunder rumbled over the city and wind and rain battered the marquee. A hole was torn in the canvas directly above the ring; water poured in and the makeshift electric lights began to fail. According to Fleischer, the boxers fought in eerie shadows, 'the place being lighted only by one incandescent lamp and the occasional flashes of lightning. The two fighters and the referee looked liked phantoms struggling in the twilight of the world.' It was another bloody encounter. Ketchel pounded Thomas early on, dropping him in the first and cutting his left eye, but the challenger rallied and the initiative see-sawed. From rounds 15 to 19, Thomas took a beating, his face swelling alarmingly, but in the 20th and final round he knocked Ketchel down with a left. Both men were exhausted at the end. Ketchel got the decision.

With his fighter's fame spreading, O'Connor's control slipped. Rival managers circled like sharks. The sharpest was Willus Britt, a dapper young chancer who once sued the city of San Francisco for letting the 1906 earthquake damage his property; when the city administration pointed out that it was an act of God, Britt said it couldn't have been, because churches were damaged. He already managed his brother Jimmy, a popular lightweight, and had the connections and savvy to make the deals that counted. He allegedly spirited the champion out of the window of a hotel room in which O'Connor had locked him for safe keeping, then wooed him in 'Frisco's clubs, bars and bordellos. Ketchel was hooked. He didn't even mind too much when Britt asked him to sign a contract handing over 40 per cent of his earnings. The money was going to pour in.

However, there remained two obstacles between Ketchel and universal acceptance as champion. Jack and Mike Sullivan were twins, born to Irish immigrant parents in Cambridge, Massachusetts in 1878. Both became fighters, Jack at middleweight, Mike at lightweight and welterweight. They were identical both in appearance and ring style: balding, hairy-chested men, good boxers without a telling punch. Their mannerisms were comically similar. One would often finish a sentence the other had started and they both loved nothing better than a roistering sing-song. They established their reputations in the west before travelling east. By 1907 Jack was a veteran of more than 100 fights, including a win over Tommy Burns shortly before the Canadian won the heavyweight title. In May he claimed the vacant middleweight crown after a draw with Hugo Kelly.

Ketchel now challenged him to settle the matter. Sullivan airily replied, 'Beat my brother first.' Mike, who already held California's version of the world welterweight title, accepted the challenge. They met in Colma on 22 February 1908 in a contest scheduled for 20 rounds. It lasted just four punches. Ketchel floored Sullivan with his first blow, a left hook. On rising, Sullivan was put down again with a right. He staggered up a second time, but a powerful one-two knocked him senseless. A gold crown smashed from his mouth lay on the canvas and referee Billy Roche mumbled, 'My goodness, he's dead.' He wasn't, but it took longer to revive him than the 108 seconds the fight lasted.

Jack Sullivan, who had been in Mike's corner, challenged Ketchel there and then, threatening, 'Things will be different next time.' Less than ten weeks later, on 9 May, his chance came to prove it in the same ring in a bout to settle the middleweight supremacy. Sullivan kept pace with Ketchel for the first few rounds, avoiding serious trouble, but by the eighth was beginning to suffer. By the tenth, the 'Assassin' was well on top, but Sullivan was cagey and stubborn and it wasn't until the 20th and last round that Ketchel landed his favourite combination to the jaw and belly as his foe came off the ropes. Sullivan was counted out.

With the heavyweight title held by the uninspiring Tommy Burns, Ketchel was now the most exciting fighter in the world. He had won 42 of his 50 recorded bouts inside the distance, one on points, and had lost just twice. He was still only 21. But there was no shortage of hard young men eager to take his crown. The hardest was Billy Papke, a heavy-fisted ex-miner born three days after Ketchel. They were to engage in a blood feud that gave the sport four of its greatest contests.

Despite its pretty name, Spring Valley was a mining town, one of many dotted above the great Illinois coal seams. Almost every male out of childhood worked down the pits. William Herman Papke was no exception. Born to German–American parents on 17 September 1886, his main pursuits as a boy were baseball, fighting and working. When barely into his teens, he ran errands for a grocer and drove a delivery van. Soon he was toiling beside his father at the coal face. It was hazardous work. Deaths and injuries were common, safety measures negligible. The heavy labour filled out Papke's already sturdy frame, building slabs of muscle in his shoulders and thighs. He had a pleasant, farm-boy demeanour, with crew-cut blond hair, fair skin and an open face. But his pale blue eyes were icy and suspicious. Naturally reticent, he did not make friends easily.

In the evenings the miners would box, often to settle personal disputes. Papke had been good with his fists since the age of six and excelled in these roughhouse contests. On the advice of workmates, he turned professional in November 1905, and fought draws in New York and Boston. His manager, Tom Jones, was a businessman from Streeter, Illinois, who trawled the mines for strong boys to make into boxers. He later managed the giant heavyweight champion Jess Willard. Papke went unbeaten over the next 18 months, fighting mainly in Peoria and LaSalle, then small towns where Chicago boxers came to pick up a few purses. One, Tony Caponi, held Papke to two draws, but he beat most of the others inside the distance. He developed into an relentless pressure fighter, stalking forward in a crouch, ready to take a punch to land one. 'I had many hard fights in those early struggles for recognition,' he said in 1911, '. . . and if I did not lose any contests it was because I could hit harder and oftener than the other fellows.' He wasn't fussy about the rules and would hit low or on the break, bore in with his head and use his elbows and forearms.

Papke's breakthrough came in November 1907: he won a 'newspaper decision' over Pat O'Keefe, a former British champion, knocked out Caponi in two rounds, then stopped two men on the same night in Boston. He rounded off the year by drawing with Hugo Kelly. In January 1908 he won in Boston, then outpointed Kelly over 10 rounds in Milwaukee in March. Now unbeaten in around 30 fights, he was beginning to live up to his nickname coined by sports reporter Ed Smith: the 'Illinois Thunderbolt'.

Papke and Ketchel collided at Milwaukee on 4 June 1908. It is unclear whether Ketchel's title was at stake; both weighed 154lb, inside the weight limit, and Papke would have claimed the crown had he won. Ketchel made his customary fast start, flooring his opponent immediately with a left hook, Papke later claimed the punch landed while he was holding out his glove for the customary pre-fight handshake. Enraged, he jumped up and waded in. For once, Ketchel was facing someone as nasty as himself. Papke never took a backwards step. Ketchel seemed to be getting on top in the seventh, landing heavily to the body, but the Illinois brawler showed his grit in the eighth, standing toe-to-toe with the champion in a furious exchange that had the fans on their feet. They kept up the pace to the final bell, when Ketchel was declared the winner. Papke complained about the first-round incident but was ignored. He went away nursing an abiding animosity.

In July Ketchel defended his title in San Francisco against Hugo Kelly. The Italian drew blood from the champion's mouth before walking into a left hook in the third. He was counted out. Less than three weeks later, in the same Coliseum ring, Ketchel took on Joe Thomas for the fourth time. His old foe was now a spent force, flabby and under-trained. A right to the eye dropped him at the end of the first and an uppercut finished him in the second. Thomas was out for several minutes and was never as good again. He retired in 1912, made a futile comeback in 1921, and died aged 39 in 1926.

Papke, meanwhile, kept in the frame by repeating an earlier feat, beating two men in one night. He knocked out Johnnie Carroll in two rounds, then faced Frank Mantell, a young German living in the States. Mantell was no slouch. He had tangled with some of the world's best welterweights, beating Honey Mellody but losing inside the distance to Harry Lewis. Papke knocked him out inside a round. He was clearly the leading contender and a second bout with Ketchel was arranged for Labor Day, 7 September.

The venue was the James J. Jeffries Athletic Club at Vernon, a Los Angeles suburb. Jeffries, the former heavyweight king, had converted an old barn into an arena, but demand for the fight was so high that a larger stadium seating 7,000 was erected. The bout was due to start at mid-afternoon, the worst possible time. The temperature soared into the low 80s and many spectators wore cardboard visors to shield their eyes from the sun. Ketchel was a wide betting favourite.

The champion entered the ring first. Papke followed and made a point of going to his rival's corner to shake hands. At the bell, Ketchel advanced to the centre of the ring and held out his glove to shake once more. Instead, Papke struck him with a booming right to the face. As Ketchel staggered, Papke followed up with a thumping left, rushed his opponent into a corner and floored him with a volley of hooks. Ketchel pulled himself up but was dropped twice more before the bell saved him.

The champion was hauled back to his corner bleeding and dazed, his eyes already closing. He was still unsteady at the start of the second and another mighty blow sent him reeling across the ring. But the over-eager challenger couldn't land a finishing punch. Though Ketchel's face was smeared with gore, he managed to clinch and survive the round. Cornerman Pete Stone lanced one of his eyes to restore his sight and in the third he gave a memorable display of bravery, taking the fight to his opponent.

But defeat was only a matter of time. By the fourth, Ketchel's left eye was shut tight. Papke slowed in the heat but continued to attack and a wicked left to the solar plexus nearly ended it in the sixth. By the ninth both of the champion's eyes were closed. He lurched sightlessly around the ring, holding when he could, and was shaken repeatedly by uppercuts. Blood was everywhere. Papke waved triumphantly to the crowd at the end of the tenth and in the 11th side-stepped a Ketchel rush to jolt him with a right and left. Spectators yelled at Jeffries to stop it, but the old 'Boilermaker' refused. Papke went for the kill, a left setting his opponent up for a series of blows that sent him through the ropes onto the pressmen at ringside. They pushed him back as the gong sounded. The ghastly-looking champion staggered out to start the 12th and was felled by a fast right. He somehow rose, to be dumped again by a right smash to the jaw. Amazingly, he was struggling to his feet when Jeffries stopped the count at 'nine' and signalled Ketchel's handlers to come and pick him up. It was over.

Papke's first-round sneak-punch became a by-word for boxing treachery. After the fight, he revealed why he had done it: 'When we met in Milwaukee, we shook hands as the gong sounded. Ketchel not only held my hand in a vice-like grip, but pulled me toward him and hit me flush in the face with a hard left, breaking a tooth and knocking me down. Right then, I decided to get even for that trick, and this was the main reason why I made the match with him here at Vernon. I could have finished Ketchel much sooner, but I figured he deserved an extra dose of punishment.' From then on, boxers shook hands during the referee's instructions, not after the first bell.

The ex-champion retreated to a ranch to lick his wounds. Coffroth knew a third, deciding bout between them would sell out, and set it for his arena at Mission Street, San Francisco, on Thanksgiving Day, 26 November. Ketchel, his natural aggression now fuelled by a sense of grievance, trained harder than ever before. Meanwhile, his followers spread rumours that he was out of condition and drinking heavily. The tales reached Papke at his training camp, apparently inducing over-confidence in the new champion.

Mission Street was packed as the two bitter rivals climbed into the ring. There were no handshakes this time; Ketchel was in a cold fury and threatened Papke before the start. He set about the former miner from the opening bell. Papke was in serious trouble as early as the fourth, was rescued by the bell in the eighth and was driven around the ring in the ninth. Ketchel eased off in the tenth, hurt Papke at the start of the 11th with a body punch, the floored him with a short left hook to the jaw. Papke fell heavily, face forward. He took a long count and tried to cover up. Two more rights and a hard left to the stomach sent him down again. He fell on his hands and knees, then rolled onto his back. He struggled up, but just failed to beat the count, rising as referee Jack Welch tolled 'eleven'. Ketchel had become the first middleweight to regain the title.

Britt planned to exploit his fighter's awesome performance with a publicity campaign in the east. He kitted out Ketchel in a cowboy outfit and they hit New York. Reporters loved the colourful Ketchel, or 'Steve' as they called him. He was great copy. The champion became a fixture on Broadway, hanging out with the boys, smooching with chorus girls and acquiring a taste for champagne and cigars.

Boxing in New York was governed by the Lewis Law. Fights took place in members-only clubs and no decisions were allowed (see Introduction). Ketchel's first bout was at the National, a former horse mart, against Philadelphia Jack O'Brien, world light-heavyweight champion and a survivor of nearly 100 battles against the likes of Bob Fitzsimmons, Tommy Burns and Marvin Hart. At 31

O'Brien was fading, yet his skill gave him the better of the early
rounds as he found his opponent impossible to miss with straight
lefts. By the seventh blood was running down Ketchel's legs. But the
older man tired and in the ninth he fell from a body shot. He made it
to the bell, needing to last just one more round to take the 'newspaper
decision'. In the tenth he took two long counts. Then, with just
seconds left, a right from Ketchel caught him under the chin, lifting
him off his feet and sending him crashing into his own corner, his
head resting in a resin box. O'Brien was unconscious but, as the
referee reached 'four', the bell went, ending the fight. Newspapers
were split over who deserved to win, probably one of the few
occasions when 'no decision' was a fair result.

The inconclusive ending did no harm to Ketchel's reputation and a
rematch was arranged. In the meantime he fought a no-decision
six-rounder against Kid Hubert in Pittsburgh, then defended his title
against Tony Caponi in Schenectady in June. Poor Caponi was
treated like a human punching bag. He was knocked down once in the
second round and four times — the last for the full count — in the
fourth. Ketchel blew almost his entire purse on silk shirts.

The return with O'Brien took place a week later in Philadelphia.
The veteran's eye was cut in the first and he was dropped twice in the
second. He was still dazed at the start of the third and Ketchel
virtually ran across the ring to catch him with an avalanche of
punches. O'Brien slumped to the floor and the referee stopped it.
Some years later, O'Brien claimed he threw the fight to make Ketchel
appear a credible opponent for the new heavyweight champion, Jack
Johnson; curiously, Ketchel sent a victory telegram to his father
before the fight. Some historians say Ketchel won O'Brien's light-
heavyweight title but it was not a claim he pursued.

The 'Assassin' now set his sights on Johnson. Before negotiations
could be completed, Coffroth arranged a fourth bout with Papke for
his 10,000-seat Colma arena on 5 July 1909. The Illinois fighter had
remained in California after his brutal beating from Ketchel and had
shown remarkable powers of recuperation by boxing a 25-round draw
with Hugo Kelly just three weeks later. He followed it with a ten-
round no-decision against 'Fireman' Jim Flynn and a dramatic one-
round knockout of Kelly in May, and was at his peak as a fighter.

Ketchel did not really want to box Papke again but the prize was a
bout with Johnson. The champion scowled as he faced his adversary

before another packed stadium. Papke looked fit and confident, his face and arms burned brown by the California sun. Ketchel started fast and in the second forced Papke to the ropes with body punches. As they came out of a clinch the challenger landed a right to the nose and drew first blood. Then, in a mid-ring exchange, Papke broke a bone in his right hand. Ketchel pressed fiercely but Papke wouldn't buckle. The champion extended his lead through the fourth with some wicked body punching and by the fifth Papke was looking ragged. Red welts around his ribs and chest showed the accuracy of Ketchel's attack.

However, the challenger was in top condition. He came on in the sixth, helped when Ketchel broke *his* right hand, and in the seventh the champion dislocated his left thumb. By now, there was little clean boxing; both fighters were hampered by their hand injuries and spent much of the time mauling. Heads bumped dangerously, laces rubbed in faces. The middle rounds were even until the tenth, when Papke nearly dropped from a right cross. He held on desperately and was unsteady as he walked to his corner.

Ketchel came out looking for a knockout in the 11th but walked into a big right that kept him quiet for the rest of the round. The battle continued in fits and starts. Both were arm-weary. In the 18th two short left hooks and two follow-up rights put Ketchel in trouble on the ropes, and he was glad to hear the bell. The bout degenerated into wrestling. The fighters grinned and tapped gloves at the end of the 19th, a sign of mutual respect. Both tried hard in the last round but they were too tired to swop more than a handful of blows. Referee Roche lifted Ketchel's arm at the end, though Papke's supporters claimed their man had done enough to win.

Ketchel's desire to win the heavyweight title was fuelled partly by racism. Jack Johnson, the first black titleholder, was detested by white America. His victory over Tommy Burns in 1908, in which he taunted the white champion as he beat him, and his subsequent behaviour outraged conservative politicians and newspaper editors. So began the quest for a Great White Hope to take his crown. It was, wrote Randy Roberts, 'like the search for the origin of the Nile, full of false hopes, preposterous characters, tragic deaths, and excessive newspaper coverage'. It was also a desperate search. Johnson was a great boxer, a telling counter-puncher with a tight defence. A remarkable and imposing man, with his shaven head gleaming, gold teeth flashing in a famous grin, he stood over 6ft 1in and weighed more than 200lb. Yet Ketchel, three stones lighter and four inches shorter, was convinced he could beat him.

There was bitter irony in Ketchel's pursuit of Johnson. For the middleweight champion refused to risk his own title against another black boxer. Sam Langford, the son of a sailor from Weymouth, Nova Scotia, had been chasing Ketchel for a year. Although only 5ft 7½in tall, the 'Boston Tar Baby' was a master technician and ferocious puncher, probably the best pound-for-pound fighter in the world. Like many negro boxers of his time, he was forced to accept the short end of purses and to box far heavier men. Still he chopped them down by the score. Many experts thought he was better than Ketchel. They nearly fought in New York in September 1909 but the city governor intervened, forbidding the contest. Langford accused Ketchel of 'knowing more about it [the cancellation] than he cares to admit'.

Coffroth matched Ketchel and Johnson for Colma on 16 October. The preamble to the bout reeked of duplicity and has been the subject of conjecture ever since. The most likely story is that Ketchel's manager Willus Britt offered Johnson a deal. He knew Ketchel had little chance in a fair fight, so he asked Johnson to let his man go the whole 20 rounds. This would provide a full-length movie which could be exhibited throughout the States for a substantial sum. The fight was expected to take around $40,000 at the gate and Britt promised the film revenues would be equally attractive. There would be no decision, so Johnson wouldn't lose his title. As a further inducement, a rematch over 45 rounds may have been offered. Strapped for cash as usual, Johnson agreed.

What is certain is that, as Ketchel stepped through the ropes, he had no intention of holding back. Urged on by the duplicitous Britt and a partisan crowd of 10,000, he was going for a knockout. From the start he loaded up for the one haymaker which might flatten the champion. One connected in the second and Johnson, angered, bundled his opponent to the ground. In the fourth, he showed his strength by picking Ketchel up and carrying him across the ring. In the sixth, he broke the smaller man's nose.

By now, the double-cross must have been apparent to Johnson, but

he didn't seem to care. He outboxed Ketchel easily. Then came the
12th — and sensation. As they circled, Ketchel leapt forward with a
looping right. Johnson tried to duck but was caught on the temple and
went down. The spectators leapt to their feet. Johnson, however, was
unhurt and had broken the fall with his hand. He rose and waited for
Ketchel to attack. As the Michigan man came in, winding up another
huge right, Johnson exploded in a blur of punches, culminating in a
deadly right uppercut. Ketchel fell backwards and Johnson, carried
by his own momentum, sprawled over him. The black champion was
quickly up and stood by calmly while Ketchel, spreadeagled, was
counted out. The crowd stood in stunned silence. Later, in his
dressing room, Johnson allegedly found two of Ketchel's front teeth
embedded in his right glove.

Surprisingly, given the racial overtones of the fight, Ketchel and
Johnson became friends. They were kindred souls. Both bucked
conventional mores and they shared a passion for high living and
sports cars. In his autobiography Johnson called Ketchel 'a fine
fellow' and 'one of my best friends'.

Ketchel was burning out. His loss to Johnson and his parting from
Willus Britt soon after sent him into a depression. He fell more and
more under the influence of Wilson Mizner, a dissolute friend of
Britt's from their days as Klondike gold prospectors. Mizner was now
a Broadway playwright and celebrated wit. He encouraged Ketchel's
worst excesses, adding opium smoking to his considerable list of
vices. They set up headquarters at the Woodlawn Inn on the outskirts
of New York; it became a magnet for Mizner's smart-set literary
crowd and a procession of hangers-on, hacks, conmen and painted
ladies. At the end of the year Ketchel renounced his title, declaring he
could no longer make the weight limit. Papke saw his opportunity and
on 19 March 1910 beat Willie Lewis in three rounds in Paris in a bout
advertised for the world title.

Four days later Papke's pretensions were forgotten as Ketchel
returned to the ring. His opponent was Frank Klaus, a powerful
23-year-old who was unbeaten in more than 60 bouts and had won a
'newspaper decision' over Papke. They fought in Pittsburgh, Klaus's
home city, and in the first round Ketchel broke his left thumb on his

opponents forehead. 'You bashed your hand that time, didn't you, Stanley?' taunted Klaus. The struggle continued at close quarters, which favoured Klaus's in-fighting skills. Ketchel missed often, causing later rumours of a fix, and many thought Klaus had done enough to win at the end of six rounds. No decision was given.

A month later, Ketchel finally met Sam Langford in Philadelphia. It was another six-round no-decision contest and took $18,750 at the gate, a record for the city. Some accounts say it was a tremendous fight, with Ketchel on top at the end. But there were persistent and probably accurate rumours that Langford 'carried' Ketchel. Certainly there was booing in the early rounds when Langford seemed to hold back. The bout was intended to whet appetites for a 45-round match later in California. A few years before his death in 1956, Langford told a friend that he had agreed to pull his punches so as not to jeopardize the second bout.

In May 1910 Ketchel knocked out Porky Flynn in three rounds in Boston. As Flynn lay unconscious, the champion threw a bucket of water over him. Next came a title defence against Willie Lewis at New York's National Athletic Club in May. Lewis came from the city's Gas House district, an awful slum. He was a friend of Ketchel's, a perennial contender who had lost to Papke in Paris. Some sort of deal was struck before the bout, but Lewis departed from the script when he stung Ketchel with a right-hander in the first round. He was summarily despatched in the second.

In June 'Westchester' Jim Smith surprised a New York crowd by hitting the champion at will in the opening round and driving him around the ring. For the next two rounds Smith more than held his own and in the fourth he won over the fans when, after taking some wicked shots, he blasted back to stagger Ketchel with a right to the jaw. Ketchel opened up in earnest in the fifth and a crushing right dropped Smith. He tried four times to rise, but couldn't beat the count.

Coffroth now announced that the long-awaited Ketchel–Langford title fight would go ahead at Colma on 2 July. But once again Langford lost out: the bout was cancelled. In August Ketchel pulled out of a match with Australia's Bill Lang, claiming a sore foot. Lang said it was called off because he (Lang) wouldn't accept a bribe to 'throw' the fight. Ketchel's one goal now was a return with Jack Johnson. He also needed to put the brakes on his runaway life. In September he was reported to be 'resting' in Grand Rapids and contemplating giving his title to Hugo Kelly. He told a newspaper, 'I'm through with fighting in the middleweight class. I'm working for Johnson. I don't want money if I lose but will give it to charity. I'm in the game no longer for the money. I'm going on a ranch to gain weight to meet Johnson.' On 11 October he arrived at the farm of a friend, Pete Dickerson, at Conway, Missouri, where he intended to lick himself back into shape. Four days later, he was dead.

On 12 October a couple calling themselves Mr and Mrs Hurtz were taken on by Dickerson as ranch hand and housekeeper respectively. The name Hurtz was an alias; their real names were Walter A. Dipley and Goldie Smith. Dipley was a Navy deserter travelling with false papers. Smith had been married four times, the first when she was 12. She had known Dipley for years and joined him on the run. They moved about aimlessly, working here and there, dodging the law.

Ketchel was in good spirits, having accepted a $30,000 offer to fight Sam McVey in Paris. But he took an instant dislike to the scrawny Dipley and was soon bullying him. His feelings for Smith were more ambiguous. Some time on Friday, 14 October there was an 'incident'. Smith later claimed in court that Ketchel made advances and raped her when she tried to resist. She said she told Dipley that night and they decided to leave the next day.

At 6.30 the following morning, as Smith served Ketchel his breakfast in the screened porch, Dipley walked in with a .22 Marlin rifle. The boxer's .44 Colt revolver was in his pocket, as usual, but he never had a chance to use it. Dipley shot him in the back, the bullet entering below his right shoulder blade and rising through his chest. Ketchel collapsed in a pool of blood. As his attacker fled, the dying boxer was tended by a doctor, then taken to the hospital at Springfield, Missouri, where surgeons operated to remove a build-up of blood. After showing brief signs of recovery and calling, 'Where's Pete?' he died just after 7pm. He was 24 years old.

Dipley was soon brought in by the owner of a farm where he had sought shelter. Smith was already in custody. Ketchel's body was returned to Grand Rapids to be buried by his parents. The whole town turned out to watch a Polish military band lead the white hearse, with young girls scattering flowers along the way. Ketchel's 'fiancée', a Miss Jewell Bovine, tried to kill herself in rather melodramatic fashion by swallowing carbolic acid. She was stopped by Dickerson.

Both defendants were charged with first-degree murder. The trial

was held in Springfield and attracted wide media attention.
Dickerson, a big wheel in the Missouri Democratic party,
undoubtedly wielded an unfair influence on the proceedings. Despite
the defence claim of rape, Dipley and Smith were found guilty and
sentenced to life imprisonment. Smith was paroled after 12 years and
faded into obscurity. Dipley served 24 years, then returned to
Missouri, even visiting the Dickerson place occasionally on his
rounds for a gas company. There were threats that Ketchel's old
friends would seek him out and kill him, but he died of natural causes
five years after his release.

Damon Runyon observed that 'the memory of Ketchel prejudiced
the judgement of anyone who was ever associated with him. They can
never see any other fighter.' He has fascinated boxing fans for decades
and his lurid legend endures to this day, his bloody death only
enhancing his notoriety. Indeed, Ketchel has come to epitomize the
turn-of-the-century American fighter: lawless, pitiless and amoral.

At the time of his murder his lifestyle had taken its toll and his best
boxing days seemed to be over. He had been treated for syphilis, was
strongly rumoured to be hooked on drugs, and had had several
brushes with the law. His reputation was damaged by fixed fights and
his dodging of Langford, and his earnings were squandered.
According to the Grand Rapids Probate Court, he was worth only
$500 when he died — not much for a boxer who regularly earned
five-figure purses.

Still, his record was impressive. Of 66 bouts, he won 50 inside the
distance and three on points, drew five, lost four, and fought four
no-decisions. Despite the question marks and contradictions,
Ketchel's courage and fire have never been surpassed. Wilson
Mizner, who had a phrase for everything, summed up the sentiments
of fight fans all over the world when, informed by telegram of his
friend's death, he cabled back: 'That darling kid can't be dead. Start
counting over him and he'll get up.'

3

The Search for a Champion

TEN DAYS after Stanley Ketchel's death in October 1910, the *New York Times* named its four leading middleweight contenders: Billy Papke, Frank Klaus, Eddie McGoorty and Hugo Kelly. Papke, as a former champion, headed the list. Kelly made a career out of claiming the title, while Klaus and McGoorty were the brightest prospects in the division. Lurking, unmentioned, was Sam Langford. With Ketchel gone, his title prospects were dimmer than ever. Papke had declared he would never fight a black man; the others were equally reluctant. Despite repeated challenges to his white rivals, Langford never got the chance he deserved. As he grew older, he gained weight and went after the heavyweight title. That quest, too, was doomed to failure. Perhaps the finest boxer of his time, he would never fight for any world championship.

Over the next few years, the division went through chaos. Along with the four named by the *Times*, a whole stream of contenders claimed the crown, including Johnny Thompson, Frank Mantell, Leo Houck, Jack Sullivan, Bob Moha, Buck Crouse, Harry Lewis, Jimmy Gardner and Jack Dillon. With no international governing body, there was no consensus between countries. The muddle was compounded when different claimants appeared in different parts of the world. For a time the United States dwindled in importance as the best boxers converged first on France, then Australia, to settle their differences. Not until 1917 would a single champion gain worldwide acceptance.

Papke heard of Ketchel's death in Australia. An enterprising antipodean promoter, Hugh D. 'Huge Deal' McIntosh, was anxious to exploit the interest in boxing in his country and had signed up some top US boxers to fight there. Papke and his new wife Edna joined ringmen Jimmy Clabby, Ray Bronson and Johnny Thompson and sailed in October for Sydney. There, Papke declared, 'The claim of Hugo Kelly to the title is not recognized by competent sporting authorities, for I beat him once in a ten-round bout . . . then knocked him out in a round. As champion of the world I will be ready to defend my title against all comers.'

Papke failed, however, to cement his claim. He neglected training and his form was indifferent. He won his first bout in Sydney but was thrown out of his next for landing a low punch on Dave Smith, a leading Australian, in an over-the-weight match. On 11 February 1912 he entered the ring in Rushcutter's Bay, Sydney, against 'Cyclone' Johnny Thompson, another of the visiting American party. Thompson, from Ogle County, Illinois, was ten years older than Papke. After campaigning in the States at lightweight, he had recently put on weight, and at only 5ft 4in was built like a little bull. He traded on strength. 'Every time I step into the ring I expect to take a beating,' he said, 'but I always bank on my reserve powers and endurance to bring me victory in the end.' They were enough to beat Papke, who was in poor condition. He had trouble breathing through his nose and flagged at crucial moments in the fight, giving Thompson the 20-round decision.

The controversy started afterwards. Thompson saw a chance to take the title and took the unusual step of weighing in *after* the fight. He claimed to be 10st 13¾lb, well inside the limit, though he must have lost weight in the heat of the contest. Papke had certainly been well over the middleweight maximum; furthermore, it had not been billed as a title bout. Thompson sailed back to the US two days later, claiming the title, but was never taken seriously. Over the next few months he lost several 'newspaper decisions', outgrew even the middleweight class and faded from view.

Papke simply ignored the defeat. After a revenge win over Dave Smith, he sailed halfway around the world to accept an offer from McIntosh, now in England, to fight Jim Sullivan, the newly crowned British champion. It was billed as a world title fight. The venue was the famous Palladium music hall and the fight, on 8 June, was unique for two reasons: the contestants wore white gloves, and their respective corners were on the same side of the ring, which was mounted onstage. Both weighed inside the British middleweight limit of 160lb, two pounds above the American limit.

Sullivan, from the East End of London, had a straight-up British style, in stark contrast to the crouching, swaying Papke. For eight rounds, Sullivan dabbed out his left and crossed his right in the text-book manner, winning points and polite applause. Papke, primed in the bloodbaths of the California ring, sneered contemptuously. His blond hair was spiked with sweat and his chest heaved with exertion, but his fists still carried power. In the ninth, miles behind on points, he trapped Sullivan on the ropes and dug a left and right to his gut. The Londoner gasped and collapsed. The bell rang at 'nine', stopping the count, but Sullivan's cornermen couldn't revive him for the tenth round.

Once again, Papke was hailed as champion and once again he failed to consolidate. Returning home, he antagonized the authorities by announcing that he would fight in future at 160lb, the British limit. In August he fought a no-decision bout against Sailor Burke in New York. He lost clearly over ten rounds, was booed from the ring, and later apologized, saying he had hardly trained. Worse followed. On 31 October he met Bob Moha, a sawn-off brawler known as the 'Cave Man'. The fight, in Boston, was dreadful: barely a decent punch was landed, and many of the 3,000-strong crowd were convinced it was a fake (it was not the first time a Papke fight had been questioned; his contest against Joe Thomas in 1910 was a blatant fix). Moha won the decision at the end of 12 rounds. Papke claimed he had broken his right hand in the first round and declared he was through with boxing.

His retirement was brief. On 22 February 1912 he returned to the ring against a man he had already knocked out in one round. Frank Mantell (real name Mintell) was born in Brandenburg, Germany, in 1886 before his family emigrated to Pawtucket, Rhode Island. A boxer since 1906, he had scored some useful wins but had been knocked out by Harry Lewis, Papke and Klaus. Beetle-browed and dogged, he was described by one paper as 'a bandy-legged, long-armed, powerful fellow'. He fought Papke in a ring pitched in Buffalo Park, Sacramento. The Thunderbolt's decline was obvious. Mantell cut his right eye and bloodied his nose and mouth, forcing him to clinch persistently. Mantell easily won the 20-round decision. The bout was not advertised for the title, but Mantell still claimed it. He was not initially recognized outside California. In March he beat Jack

Henrick over 20 rounds in a fight billed as for the title but, despite more wins that year and a draw with Johnny Thompson, his claim fizzled out. He lost five times in 1913, drew with Jess Smith for the 'title', then lost to Pat O'Keefe.

Papke had lost four of his past seven fights — lousy credentials for a would-be champion. He sent manager Tom Jones a telegram saying, 'Consider all business connections between us off.' Jones cabled back, 'Tickled to death.' He was replaced by Al Lippe. In May Papke knocked out a police chauffeur called Billy Leitch. Then he sailed for France. While the Illinois man was discredited in his own country, he was respected in Europe for his victory over Jim Sullivan. The slightly higher weight limit was also to his liking. There was no sanctuary, however, from one implacable foe. Frank Klaus was hewn from the same Neanderthal rock as Papke. Like rivals in some primitive power struggle, they would meet to settle their differences in a far-off place.

'Hell with the lid off' was one observer's description of 19th-century Pittsburgh. The iron and steel capital of America was a fertile, if tormented, breeding ground for fighters. Waves of mainly German immigrants flooded its clotted tenements to live in smoke-stack squalor and swelter at the huge blast furnaces or toil in the nearby coal mines. Sport was one of the few escape routes. The Smoky City youth were a tough lot; none was tougher than Frank Klaus. Born on 30 December 1887, he was built like a block. Everything about him was square, from his huge chest and shoulders to his jutting jawline and shock-proof head. He was the archetypal in-fighter, strong as an ox and impervious to punishment. Georges Carpentier said he 'seemed to be made of wood'.

Klaus started fighting around 1904, at the age of 16. He boxed locally for four years before manager George Engel found him matches in New York and Philadelphia. By 1909 he was fighting on level terms against the likes of Harry Lewis, Hugo Kelly, Papke and Joe Thomas. Most of his fights were limited by Pennsylvania law to six rounds, but they allowed him to develop the techniques which were to serve him so well. In his book *The Art of In-fighting* he wrote: 'In-fighting is the artillery of pugilism, as continual pounding at the

walls of the enemy's defence gradually reduces him to capitulation.'
He would punch opponents on the arms or funny bone to incapacitate
them and claimed to have once knocked out a well-defended
opponent by punching the man's own gloved fist into his jaw. They
called him the 'Pittsburgh Bearcat'.

In 1910 he burst into the rankings by outpointing Jack Sullivan and
Jimmy Gardner, won a 'newspaper' nod over Ketchel and kayoed
Frank Mantell. However, like Papke he lost fights at crucial times.
Just as he was emerging as the best at the weight, he dropped
decisions to Gardner and Kelly. In 1911 he scored an important win
over Leo Houck, belted Willie Lewis and mauled Johnny Thompson
in a fight some regarded as a title eliminator. By March 1912, with
Papke in temporary retirement after his defeat by Mantell, the title
picture seemed to be clearing. Eddie McGoorty won a 'newspaper
decision' over Hugo Kelly and three days later Klaus outpointed Jack
Dillon over 20 foul-filled rounds in California. Jim Coffroth
announced that Klaus and McGoorty would meet in April for the
vacant world title and ordered a belt for the occasion. It was not to be.
The boxers argued over the time of the weigh-in, and the bout that
could have cleared up the middleweight confusion never came off.

Instead, Klaus pursued the come-backing Papke to France. There
two rival organizations, the Fédération Française des Sociétés des
Boxe (FFSB) and the Fédération Française de Boxe Professionelle
(FFBP), were prepared to sanction world title bouts. Big purses were
on offer. The FFSB recognized Papke as world champion and said his
bout with French champion Marcel Moreau on 29 June would be for
the title.

The FFBP beat them to it with its own world title fight between
Klaus and Georges Carpentier. They met on 24 June at Dieppe.
There was the now-commonplace chicanery before the start. The
boxers weighed-in on a machine supplied by Carpentier's manager,
François Deschamps. Both were shown to be comfortably under the
limit; in fact, both were over it. Carpentier, the 18-year-old European
champion, fought well, but took a battering about the body. In the
19th round Klaus split Carpentier's lip, which spouted blood.
Thinking his boxer was badly hurt, Deschamps jumped into the ring
and Carpentier was disqualified.

Five days later Papke and Moreau put on a frantic fight for the
FFSB version of the title in Paris. Moreau attacked with panache and

floored Papke in the first. The American repaid the compliment in the second and dropped Moreau again in the eighth. The Frenchman bravely fought on until the 15th, when he fell from sheer exhaustion. His corner threw in the sponge.

After a brief return to the States, Papke fought Carpentier in Paris in October. It was supposed to be a title bout and a gold belt and ivory plaque by the sculptor Paul Vaultier were on offer to the winner. But Papke was slightly over the weight limit and the French commission decreed the title could not be at stake. There were rumours that Papke would lie down in the fourth and, when that round arrived, the American suddenly claimed he was blinded. Carpentier was found to have ointment on his gloves. Papke was offered the fight on a foul but declined. He was given five minutes to recover. The young Frenchman was drained by weight-making and was disqualified in the 17th round, his manager again intervening to save him from punishment. Papke received the belt and in December took on George Bernard, the latest French hopeful, in a title fight at the Cirque de Paris. Bernard was knocked down twice in the sixth round. At the bell, he returned to his corner and promptly fainted. He remained unconscious for two minutes and later claimed he had been drugged. The fight was awarded to the American.

Meanwhile Klaus fought Moreau at Vichy in September for his version of the title. The Frenchman was badly outclassed, was dropped several times and in the third round resorted to hitting Klaus low. On the second such occasion, the American snarled, 'Just wait a minute. I'll bash your brains out.' Before he could, Moreau fouled again and was disqualified. A Klaus–Papke contest was now inevitable.

The fight the boxing world had been waiting for since Ketchel's death took place on 5 March 1913 at the Cirque de Paris. It was scheduled for 20 rounds, with four-ounce gloves. There was considerable bad blood between the two, and the contest wasn't pretty to watch. Denzil Batchelor wrote: 'Their fight must have been a satisfaction to both, for it was one of the most terrible in history. Klaus was a caveman . . . while Papke was a snarling hooligan. The two butted each other, bashed each other with their elbows, kicked, kneed, thumbed each other in the eyeball, and repeatedly launched colossal blows that landed below the belt.'

Klaus waged war at close range, shouldering Papke onto the ropes to deny him punching room. The 'Bearcat' was dominant by the sixth, and in the seventh put Papke down with two heavy rights. He was up immediately and stalled for the rest of the round. Klaus continued to crowd; while Papke's punches were more accurate, Klaus was clearly stronger. As the fight slipped away from him, Papke tried a new tack, rushing his foe at the beginning of each round in the hope of catching him unguarded. He was punished heavily each time. In the 13th Klaus thumped Papke's head back repeatedly with uppercuts. In the 15th Papke was cautioned for butting. The fighters fell into a clinch and, as they pulled apart, Papke deliberately butted again. He was disqualified. Klaus was the champion.

Defeat spelt the end of Papke as a fighting force. After two more bouts and an optimistic attempt to claim the light-heavyweight title, he hung up his gloves at the end of 1913, reputedly with a $300,000 fortune. He returned for one fight in 1919, then quit for good, with a record of 38 wins and nine losses in 64 bouts. The most dramatic event of his life was to come.

Papke settled down in Altadena, California, with Edna and their three sons, one of whom, Billy Jnr, became a boxer. He owned real estate and a citrus grove. But life turned sour. Papke had been raised in a close-knit Germanic community where the man ruled the home; he was jealous of his wife's new friends and found himself brooding. Finally, she left him. He threatened to kill her but she told friends, 'Bill will never hurt me.' They divorced in August 1936 and Papke turned to drink. On one occasion he pulled out a gun at her apartment at Balboa Island, but his sons took it from him. Edna finally decided to go to Los Angeles the day after Thanksgiving to ask the courts for protection.

Thanksgiving Day, 26 November 1936, was a poignant day for Papke. It was 28 years exactly since he had lost his title to Ketchel. His marriage was over. He drank heavily at Fireman Jim Flynn's cafe and beer parlour in Los Angeles, where he worked as a celebrity host and which bore a poster saying, 'Meet Billy Papke, your host. Enjoy the personality and simplicity of a great fighter.' Just before 5pm owner Ben Rosenberg remarked he would be going home for a turkey dinner. 'I'll go too,' said Papke, and left abruptly. He drove the 25 miles to his wife's apartment, entered and pulled out a .38 revolver. He shot his wife three times, then shot himself twice in the chest. Both died; he was 50, she 46. He left property valued at $75,000.

After the tragedy H. B. Murray, a former fight manager and friend of Papke's, told a newspaper: 'Billy Papke was a one-woman man and because he never loved, or even paid attention to, any other woman, he killed his wife and then took his own life. The same stubborn will which took him to heights in the prize ring made it impossible for him to accept defeat in their domestic affairs. He once told me after they separated, "I'll get her back if I have to use a gun on both of us. She's not going to leave me. And no man is ever going to boast he took Billy Papke's wife to a dance."'

Paris gave Frank Klaus the title: it also ruined him. The life-or-death conflict with Papke was bad enough; the temptations of Paris night-life did the rest. In America there was still dispute over the championship. A bout in May 1913 between Eddie McGoorty and Jimmy Clabby was advertised for the world title. It ended in a draw. Later that month, the new International Boxing Union, based in Paris, said it would prepare final rules for all world title fights and decide all disputes. It was a promising move, but the National Sporting Club in London was the first influential body to back away from it.

Most people were prepared to recognize Klaus as champion. He returned to America, where he fought a couple of unimpressive no-decisions and beat Jimmy Gardner in three rounds. In June, he lost a clear 'newspaper decision' to McGoorty, who said he hoped their next fight would be for the title, as he had beaten the Australian and British champions, Dave Smith and Jack Harrison, and Klaus had beaten Papke and the European champ, Carpentier.

On 11 October 1913, Klaus met George Chip in a routine six-rounder in Pittsburgh. He was already looking forward to a planned trip to Australia for a lucrative series of fights. His opponent, a heavy-set man with a bulldog jaw, was not expected to spring any surprises. But Klaus found it hard to get near him in the first round and in the second he was caught repeatedly as he tried to rush in to close-quarters. The champion had more success in the third, but was picked off again in the fourth. He won the fifth on sheer persistence. They shook hands before the start of the sixth, then swapped punches. Suddenly Klaus, the indestructible, was knocked down by a right to the solar plexus followed by a right to the jaw. The US correspondent for England's *Mirror of Life* reported:

Klaus, lifted from his feet, lay prone while referee Tom Bodkin counted nine. Then, hanging on to the ropes of the ring, he clambered painfully to his feet. Chip swung, and Klaus, dazed as he was, had sense enough to again hunt the floor. Once more he was forced to rise at the count of nine, and as he did so Chip, measuring his distance and taking careful aim, shot a powerful right to the point of the jaw.

Crash! landed the miner's powerful fist, propelled by all the strength in his mighty shoulders. Still the 'Bearcat' refused to loosen his hold on the ropes. Then, as Chip was setting himself for another swing, referee Bodkin rushed in front of him and pushed him away, at this moment signalling the beaten pugilist's seconds that it was over.

George Engel tore at his hair as he stared at his beaten fighter. His reign was over.

The new champion's real name was George Chipulonis. He was born on 25 August 1888 of Lithuanian–American extraction. His family lived in Madison, a hamlet near Irwin, Philadelphia. They were a pugnacious bunch: Chip's brother Joe became a good-class middleweight and there were two other brothers who could fight. Chip, who built his strength as a mine blacksmith, turned pro in 1909, beating pugs with names like Thunder Boltless and Punched Eagle. Within a year, he was fighting men of the calibre of Buck Crouse, Jack Abbott and Jack Dillon. Crouse was one of only three people ever to knock him out. He was a solid but ponderous boxer. *Mirror of Life* said, 'Chip is a fighter in every sense of the word, and he is a formidable one at that. He is one of those rugged, stockily built lads who keeps ploughing in after his opponent every second of the fighting time. He likes to swop punches, for he has confidence in his ability to outslug any man of his weight.'

It is impossible to gauge Chip's true ability. Most of his fights were no-decisions. Those that weren't, he lost — to Jack Dillon in 1911 and Jeff Smith in 1912. After his shocking victory over Klaus, it became clear that the no-decision law was going to protect him. He couldn't lose the title unless someone knocked him out. Though floored and

well-beaten by Leo Houck in his next contest, he lasted the distance
— and saved the title. In December Chip met Klaus in a six-round
rematch in Pittsburgh. Klaus was a 10–7 favourite but Chip led in the
first four rounds and in the fifth he slugged his tired foe at will. The
'Bearcat' retired at the end of the round.

It was Klaus's last real fight. He was only 25. In 1918 he went six
rounds with fellow Pittsburgher Harry Greb in a charity exhibition to
buy tobacco for US servicemen in the war. Two years later, it was
reported that he had undergone an operation to graft rejuvenating
monkey glands onto his body and was considering offers to fight in
England and Belgium. Instead he went into the hotel business and
dabbled occasionally in boxing management. In middle age he was
asked why his career, which promised so much, had ended so
abruptly. 'Ah,' he said, 'being the toast of the Paris boulevards didn't
help.' He died of a heart attack on 8 February 1948 in Pittsburgh.

Chip began 1916 with three fights in two weeks: two no-decisions
and a knockout. On 6 April he journeyed to Brooklyn's Broadway
Sporting Club to stand in for his brother Joe, who had been forced by
injury to pull out of a contest with a local club fighter called Al
McCoy. No one thought McCoy, who was only 19, stood a chance
except his manager, 'Three-Fingered' Jack Dougherty. Even
McCoy's father, a poultry farmer, bet fellow chicken fancier Toby
Irwin 'all the chickens you want' that his son would be knocked out.

Chip was in a hurry to end it and rushed McCoy into a corner from
the bell. The Brooklyn southpaw wriggled away and was then
pursued to the ropes. This time he blocked the champion's swings
and even smiled as he made the champion miss. Chip, angered,
plunged in again to trap McCoy in a corner. This time, instead of
slipping away, McCoy met him with a huge left. It caught the
champion on the point of the chin and sent him crashing, his head
banging on the floor. He was counted out after just 45 seconds. It was
the shortest world title fight ever, the first time a championship had
been lost in a no-decision bout in New York and the first title bout
won by the first and only blow thrown by the winner. Chip received a
purse of just $800; a week earlier his manager Jimmy Dime had
turned down a reported $50,000 for five fights in Australia.

The new champion was virtually unknown outside the small fight
clubs of Brooklyn. He was born Alex Rudolph in Rosenhayn, New
Jersey, on 23 October 1894. While he was still a boy his Orthodox

Jewish family moved to the tough Brownsville section of Brooklyn. His father opened a poultry market on Pitkin Avenue. Al, after his share of street fights, had his first pro bout as a bantamweight at the age of 14. He knocked out his now-forgotten opponent in two rounds. He changed his name to McCoy, probably after Kid McCoy, to hide his activities from his family, who at that time disapproved of prizefighting.

McCoy was a southpaw with a decent left cross and an unwieldy but effective defensive technique. He hadn't been stopped in 100 fights and so, given the no-decision law, was technically unbeaten. Apart from that, he was not much good. Fans called him the 'cheese' champion, a derogatory term first coined by the lightweight Battling Nelson to describe his great rival Ad Wolgast. Until someone could knock him out, the title was effectively in abeyance. The attention of the boxing fraternity turned instead to Australia, where the finest middleweights in the world had gathered.

★ ★ ★

The Australian boxing boom fostered by Hugh McIntosh continued under his sidekick Reginald 'Snowy' Baker, a promoter who later became a film industry pioneer. With large purses on offer and excellent domestic boxers to tackle, a number of US middleweights crossed the Pacific, including Eddie McGoorty, Jeff Smith and Jimmy Clabby. The resulting concentration of talent, and the frustration at America's no-decision law that protected second-rate champions like Chip and McCoy, led to the instigation of an alternative, Australian version of the world title. Though the men who won this never gained worldwide currency as champions, they were all top-notch fighters.

The ball started rolling on New Year's Day 1914, when McGoorty met Aussie hero Dave Smith before 16,000 fans in the Rushcutter's Bay stadium, Sydney, in a fight advertised as for the world title. McGoorty had beaten Smith in one round 16 months earlier and had no trouble repeating the feat, putting him down four times and out within two minutes.

For the 24-year-old American (real name Eddie van Dusart) it was recognition of sorts after nine years of professional boxing. Born in Eureka, Wisconsin, he had fought in cities as far apart as Dublin,

Belfast, London, New York, New Orleans, Denver and Sydney. A
favourite with crowds across the globe, he had a great deal of natural
talent and knew the game inside out. In February he defended his
new crown by outpointing Pat Bradley in 20 rounds. Next he met
another classy American, Jeff Smith (real name Jerome Jeffords), two
years his junior. He too had boxed around the world and was known
as the 'Globetrotter'. On 14 March before a Sydney crowd of 12,000,
they put on a fast, hard-fought bout. McGoorty was given the
decision, but the fans, sure that Smith had won, rioted. Stadium
manager Harry Keesing took it upon himself to reverse the decision
and Smith was proclaimed the new champion.

Smith beat Pat Bradley in his first defence. His second, a points
win over fellow-countryman Jimmy Clabby, again provoked a near-
riot, with police forced to restore control. Nonetheless, Smith was
presented with a $2,500 title belt from Theodore Vienne of the
Wonderland Club in France, a leading light in the International
Boxing Union. Five months later, on 28 November, it was Australia's
turn to celebrate as national champion Mick King took the title from
Smith over 20 close rounds in Sydney. King, a 21-year-old knockout
specialist, went down in the first round but came back to hurt the
American with a spectacular 20-punch barrage in the eighth and
withstood a late surge to win.

King's reign lasted just four weeks. On Boxing Day Smith took his
title back on points. In January he defended against a 19-year-old
blacksmith called Les Darcy, who had been causing a stir in local
sporting circles. Darcy surprised the American with the vehemence
of his attack, and in the fifth Smith punched him in the groin. Darcy
doubled up in agony but managed to survive to the bell, when his
seconds demanded Smith be disqualified. The referee refused and, in
the subsequent confusion, with Darcy unable to continue, awarded
the contest to Smith. He was the last man to beat Darcy. Smith made
one more successful defence, against Mick King in Melbourne,
before he was matched against Darcy again in Sydney on 22 May
1915. Darcy gave him such a chasing that the champion again
resorted to punching low. He was disqualified in round two, and the
finest fighter Australia ever produced was crowned champion.

Les Darcy's life was one of sport's great tragedies. A genial, slow-
speaking lad, he found a barbarous eloquence in his fists. Darcy the
boxer was capable of anything, a remarkable mix of speed, strength,

Jack 'Nonpareil' Dempsey, the first internationally acclaimed middleweight champion.

Bob Fitzsimmons, the British-born former blacksmith who won world titles at three weights.

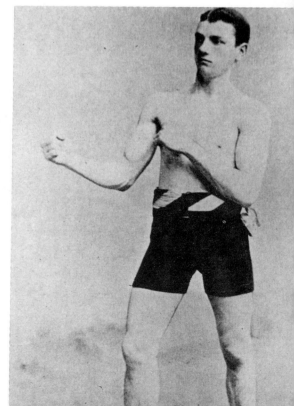

A young Kid McCoy. He married ten times, served a jail term for manslaughter and finally committed suicide.

The great Stanley Ketchel squares off against his sworn rival, Billy Papke. Both died violently.

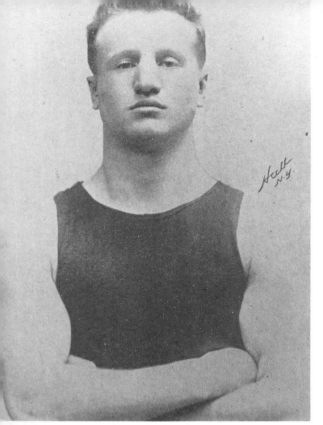

Al McCoy displaying the badges of his profession – a broken nose and cauli-flower ears.

Johnny Wilson and Bryan Downey before their controversial second bout in Jersey City in 1921. Note the sticking plaster on Downey's nose.

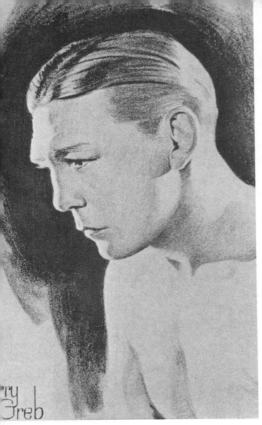

(*Above left*) A portrait of the legendary Harry Greb by fellow boxer Joe Shannon.

(*Above*) Tiger Flowers was the first black middleweight champion. Like Greb, he died prematurely and mysteriously after a routine operation.

(*Opposite*) William 'Gorilla' Jones, who kept a pet lioness on a lead and was managed by Mae West.

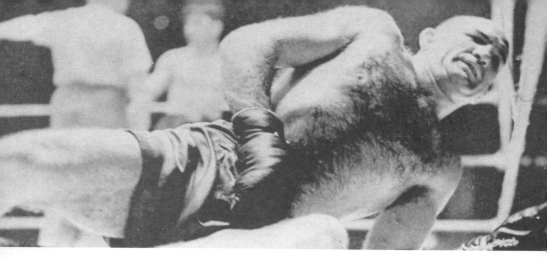

Frenchman Marcel Thil retains his title against Lou Brouillard while lying on the canvas clutching his groin in this 1936 fight.

Two smart boxers, Ken Overlin and Billy Soose. Soose took the title on points over fifteen rounds in New York in May 1941.

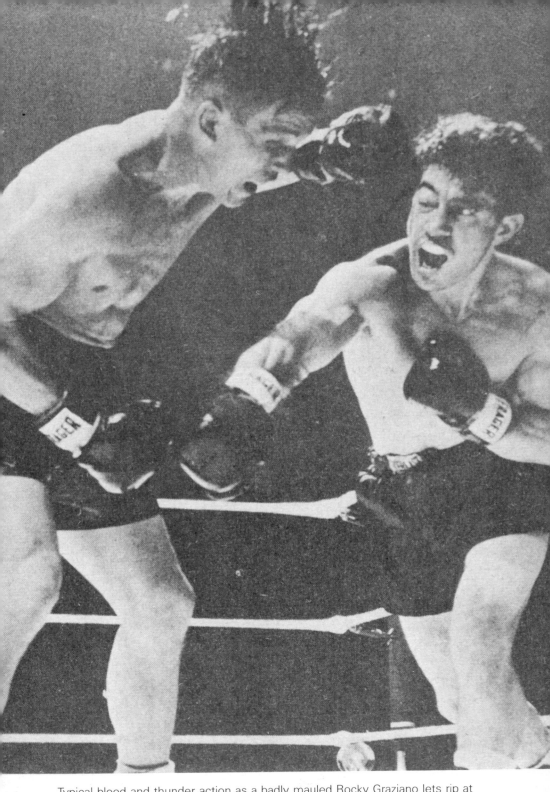

Typical blood and thunder action as a badly mauled Rocky Graziano lets rip at
Tony Zale, the Man of Steel.

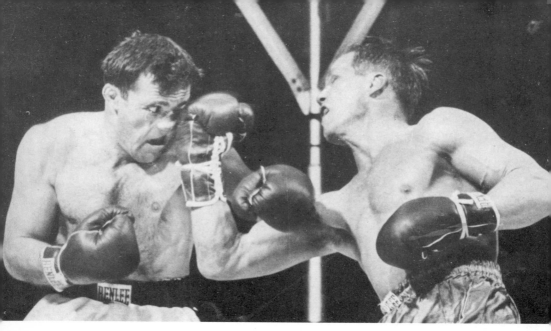

Marcel Cerdan bludgeons Tony Zale into retirement in Jersey City in 1948.

Cerdan on the floor against Jake LaMotta. The Frenchman injured his shoulder in the fall and was later forced to quit.

toughness and skill. A prodigy, he was boxing 20-rounders at 17 and beating heavyweights at 20. He was undoubtedly the best middleweight of his day and beat the best America had to offer before his 21st birthday. Only three men ever defeated him; each was subsequently beaten.

He was born in Woodville, on the Hunter River in New South Wales, on 31 October 1895, one of six brothers and five sisters in a farming family. At the age of 12 he spent money he was given for boots on a pair of boxing gloves. By the time he was 16, farm work had given him the strength of two men. Though he was only 5ft 6in, he weighed 11st at his peak and had a 73½in reach. He won amateur contests around Sydney and turned pro in 1910 by beating a railway ganger. He became a favourite at the Maitland Stadium, with a huge following among local miners. Apprenticeship to a blacksmith increased his vigour.

His first loss was in 1913, to Bob Whitelaw in a match for the Australian welterweight title. Four months later, he demolished Whitelaw in five. His first American opponent was Fritz Holland, who won on points. Two thousand of Darcy's miner fans set fire to the arena and hurled bottles. The lights went out and someone fired a pistol. A return bout attracted 16,000 to the Sydney Stadium. Darcy fought well but was disqualified for a low blow in the 18th round. In January 1915 he finally overcame Holland on points over 20 rounds.

Darcy made eight defences of the Australian world title he won from Jeff Smith. Australian rival Mick King said Darcy was afraid of him; King's corner threw in the towel in the tenth to save him from further torture. In July 1915 it was Eddie McGoorty's turn before 15,000 people in Sydney. The American was felled four times in the 15th round before the police stepped in to save him, the first time he had lost inside the distance in almost 100 fights. McGoorty said afterwards: 'Darcy will beat any middleweight in the world, and most of the heavyweights too.'

Another American, Billy Murray, lost every one of 20 rounds to Darcy. Welsh welterweight Fred Dyer was outclassed until his trainer threw in the towel — which Darcy caught and held aloft. Jimmy Clabby was almost stopped on several occasions and lost by a wide points margin. A puny Romanian called Alex Costica should not have been allowed in the same ring; he was knocked down in the second, third and fourth rounds before the police intervened. Clabby

was outpointed again; and on 30 September 1916, Darcy met former
champion George Chip. Since losing his title to McCoy two-and-a-
half years earlier, Chip had boxed 19 times (13 no-decisions), losing
three, and had knocked out some hard opponents. But his best
punches just bounced off Darcy, who smiled in return. In the ninth
round Chip was knocked unconscious by a right hand and had to be
carried to his corner.

Between title defences Darcy found time to take the Australian
heavyweight crown from Harold Hardwick. It was a bitter contest.
Hardwick, a stone heavier, broke off two of Darcy's teeth but was
dropped three times and his corner threw in the towel. Darcy had the
teeth riveted back by a dentist. Outstanding among his other
performances was a frightening two-round knockout of the
experienced Buck Crouse.

Voices in Darcy's ear were now telling him to go to the US.
Manager Jack 'Doc' Kearns, who had travelled to the States with
boxer Billy Murray, was one of those urging Darcy to cross the
Pacific. There would be huge purses, he promised.

Al McCoy's reign had been a farce. Its tone was set by his first
showing after winning the title. He knocked out a man called George
Pearsall in one round. Pearsall was later revealed to be 'Soldier'
Johnny Shaw, previously knocked out twice by McCoy under his real
name. The champion next displayed little more than a strong instinct
for survival in losing two 'newspaper decisions' to Billy Murray. His
reaction was to sack his manager, Jack Dougherty. A run of several
more no-decisions, including a beating from Joe Chip, was broken by
a knockout of the fading Willie Lewis.

In all McCoy fought 42 times while he held the title. He won four
inside the distance and two on points; all the rest were no-decisions.
Some were probably fixed so that McCoy would lose the 'newspaper
decision' but would not be knocked out. Other fighters genuinely
tried to flatten him. Typical was his bout with a talented Britisher,
Young Ahearn, in September 1915. McCoy was jeered by his own
Brooklyn crowd even before the bout began. By round six, spectators
were chanting, 'McCoy, you're a bum.' He finished with a cut eye and
a split nose. One report said: 'Being knocked out was about the only

thing that did not occur to McCoy in the ten rounds and maybe at times a knockout might have been a relief for him.' But he kept the title. Meanwhile the weight limit of 160lb, accepted by most of the world, was adopted by New York.

★　★　★

On 31 October 1916, his 21st birthday, Les Darcy was due to report to the military authorities in Australia for enlistment. Australian soldiers were serving with immense bravery in World War I; thousands had died in the bloody Gallipoli campaign in 1915. Darcy had said he would enlist when he was 21. He first planned to go to the States. Passports were not issued to people of military age unless they had been exempted from service, and Darcy's applications were twice denied. Instead, he sailed illegally on a tramp steamer under the name Dawson. He was excoriated in the newspapers back home, not entirely from noble motives. Hugh McIntosh, who owned two of the most vocal papers, was furious that he and Baker had lost their hold on the fighter.

Darcy said he needed money to support his invalid father and his young brothers and sisters, and fully intended to join up when he had earned it. He was matched to fight Al McCoy in April in New York, with a second bout to follow against Mike Gibbons, the best boxer in the US. This would have decided the title. But he was barred from boxing in New York State by the governor. A proposed 'world title' fight with Jeff Smith in New Orleans also fell through when the governor of Louisiana barred Darcy 'for the public good' and said he should go home and join the army.

On the day the US entered the war, Darcy enlisted and was placed in the reserve aviation corps of the US Army at Memphis, Tennessee. He was given furlough to fight Len Rowlands of Milwaukee but, while out running, he collapsed. He complained of sore teeth, stiff and painful joints and a sore throat. His infected tonsils were removed but he was stricken with blood poisoning and pneumonia. During his delirium, he was heard to say, 'The count is seven but you'll never count ten on me.' He died on 24 May. His body was shipped back to Australia, and on 30 July was interred at Maitland. Tens of thousands lined the funeral route. It was probably the largest funeral ever seen in Australia. People said he died of a broken heart.

4

Only the Ring Was Square

ST PAUL, Minnesota, occupies a unique place in American history. In the first quarter of the 20th century, it was the vacation spot of the criminal underworld. Bank robbers and gangsters from all over the country came to rest, play and scheme, free from arrest so long as they behaved inside the city limits. This immunity, known as the 'layover' system, was guaranteed by an all-powerful pair of political bosses, John and Richard O'Connor, and brought criminal loot flooding into the local economy. Entertainment of all kinds, from brothels to boxing, boomed.

In the same period St Paul boasted a second claim to fame: it produced three of the best middleweight boxers in the world. Just as Pittsburgh spawned German fighters, so St Paul's large Irish community bore in turn Mike Gibbons, the 'uncrowned champion', Mike O'Dowd, who won the world title, and Jock Malone, who claimed it. O'Dowd, in particular, was the darling of the Irish. Few sportsmen have ever made such a blatant appeal to ethnic support. His nickname was the 'Fighting Harp', his trademark a green dressing gown embroidered with golden harps. Wherever he boxed his fellow countrymen turned out in droves to yell him on. Even Irish–American opponents complained that he seemed to have the whole of Eire in his corner.

He was born on 5 April 1895 and was imbued with fighting spirit in the cradle. 'I guess it was born into me,' he once said. 'My mother and father are from a part of Galway where they fight at the drop of a hat, like all the game Irish. I was born and brought up in a part of St Paul called Frogtown, which is full of the fighting Irish. Boxing was very popular among the boys, so I just fell into the game. Another reason . . . was our dislike for the mob of Germans over in Goosetown, another part of St Paul. There was always considerable scrapping going on between the young fellows of Frogtown and Goosetown. So, of course, I had to do my share of it.'

After school O'Dowd climbed telegraph poles as a lineman. He first fought with gloves at the age of 18 'against a big Dutch [Deutsch = German] fellow in a blacksmith's shop on a Sunday morning. We had a grudge against one another and we agreed to fight it out in a regular ring. The Hun was some forty pounds heavier than me but that didn't cut any ice. All the sports from Frogtown and Goosetown were there to bet their dough. The big Dutch guy was the favourite in the betting because he towered over me. But he was not fast enough and I knocked him flat as a pancake in the second round. I think I got a couple of dollars for winning — a dollar a round. The fight changed my whole life and I became a regular fighter.'

O'Dowd soon made his name as a crowd-pleasing welterweight, a crowding, two-fisted scrapper who was also called the 'St Paul Cyclone'. He carried a stiff punch but was more likely to wear opponents down than blast them out. He had craggy, rather battered features, steely eyes, prominent ears and was inordinately tough. By 1915 he was holding his own with hard men like Billy Miske, Soldier Bartfield and the deaf-mute Silent Martin. In June 1916 he challenged the new welterweight champion, Jack Britton, in Boston, but lost on points over 12 rounds.

By 1917, O'Dowd was boxing at the rate of once a fortnight against the best around, men like Britton, Soldier Bartfield and Frank Carbone, and was beating most of them. He was rarely in an easy fight. One bout in August, against the iron-boned Britisher Ted 'Kid' Lewis, was said to have resembled 'a rough-and-tumble on the waterfront'. By November O'Dowd had more than 60 contests under his belt. Some had been in Brooklyn, home of world champion Al McCoy, who O'Dowd was trying to force into a title fight.

14 November 1917 was the last night of the Frawley Law in New York. The act had been repealed and boxing in the city was about to enter another phase of illegality. On the same night O'Dowd stepped into a Brooklyn ring to fight Al McCoy. The champion, who had

somehow clung to his title for three-and-a-half years, was fresh from a rare victory over Montana Dan Sullivan. As usual, he simply had to stay on his feet to retain his title. McCoy senior offered $1,000 to $200 that his son would last the distance.

The fight was one of the weirdest in all of boxing. Bob Edgren of the *New York Evening World* reported that whispers of a fix were so prevalent, many regular gamblers refused to bet. The rumours grew stronger when odds were offered that O'Dowd, not a big puncher, would stop McCoy, who had never been knocked out. Expectations of a theatrical ending were further increased by the presence of three film cameras mounted on ringside platforms. McCoy was at least a stone over the title limit and was said to have trained for just one day. O'Dowd was just inside the limit.

The bare facts of what followed are that McCoy was floored repeatedly before his corner threw in the towel in round six. But the facts don't begin to tell the story. Edgren claimed the first round was cut short by six seconds, the second round by 12 seconds, the third by 18 seconds and the fourth by 40 seconds. In the fourth McCoy was knocked down four times and O'Dowd twice, although neither was on the deck long enough to take a count. 'The knockdowns,' wrote Edgren, 'looked "stagey" and not particularly well-rehearsed at that. Both fighters went to the floor when apparently only half hit.' The confusion was exacerbated by O'Dowd's rowdy and intimidating supporters, who made a deafening din. Several fistfights broke out during the contest, including one involving McCoy's father and a free-for-all after McCoy's cornermen threw water on their man as he lay on the floor.

In the sixth McCoy went down from a short right. In the act of rising, he was dropped again by a right. Once more, he was up without a count. O'Dowd set about him and put him down a third time for nine seconds. McCoy was dropped again for a count of 'three', then a final right felled him for the fifth time. He was sitting, seemingly listening to the count, when his corner threw in the towel at 'seven'. Edgren said McCoy 'showed no sign of being dazed or weakened by punishment either before the blow was struck or after the towel was tossed into the ring'. O'Dowd's hysterical followers swarmed through the ropes and chaired the new champion shoulder-high.

Not every ringside reporter agreed with Edgren's version of events.

Some claimed the fight had been genuine and said only the losing gamblers complained. Time has blurred the truth. This was perhaps the most crooked period in the history of boxing. So many bouts were bent that even legitimate contests were dismissed by cynics as fixes. It seems this was one of the occasions when only the ring was square.

The jubilant O'Dowd promised to be a fighting champion. He ended fighting in uniform. In the spring of 1918, after winning a 'newspaper decision' from Harry Greb, a leading contender, he joined the army, sailing to Europe with the American Expeditionary Force as the only current world champion from the US to take part in active service. After the armistice he boxed in a forces tournament in London before returning to St Paul in May 1919 to a hero's welcome. In June he cropped up in Rome, where he knocked out Al Norton in one round.

On 17 June O'Dowd was matched again with McCoy in a ten-rounder in St Paul. The fight was as farcical as their first. McCoy had lost five in a row, including 'newspaper decisions', since surrendering his title and made little attempt to compete. In the first round, his corner threw in the towel. The referee kicked it out. The same thing happened in the second. Finally, after hitting the canvas for the seventh time, McCoy decided to stay down for the full count in the third.

It was the 'cheese' champion's last fight. A brave and durable fellow, he could not be blamed for the boxing laws of the day. His record showed 144 bouts, of which over 80 were no-decisions. He lost only three official decisions and was stopped just twice, by O'Dowd, despite the efforts of the hardest hitters in boxing. In fact, given the no-decision law, he was technically unbeaten in his first 136 bouts! Dan Morgan, who took over from Jack Dougherty as his manager, said, 'I always liked McCoy. He was a likeable chap outside the ring, and he was courageous inside the ropes. He just couldn't fight, but nobody was knocking him out.'

Settling in Los Angeles with his wife Ruth, McCoy played bit parts in movies and worked as a trainer, manager and general gopher for his brother Babe, matchmaker at the Olympic Auditorium. He was seriously injured when hit by a car in 1954 and lost his job in 1956 when Babe's licence was revoked and he was indicted on fight-fixing

charges. In 1964 he barely escaped alive when a fire destroyed his
modest frame house, incinerating his precious mementoes and
newspaper cuttings. He told reporters, 'This ruins me. I got nuttin'
left.' He became chronically ill, was confined to a Los Angeles
nursing home, and died there on 22 August 1966, aged 69.

It's hard to be certain how many, if any, of O'Dowd's 24 bouts over
the next 12 months were legitimate title defences. Most were no-
decisions and in many he exceeded the middleweight limit, though in
those days that wouldn't necessarily have stopped the title changing
hands. The accuracy of so-called 'newspaper decisions' was also
debatable. Apart from the prevalence of get-to-the-wire-first
merchants (see Introduction), many papers took their national sports
reports from the Associated Press agency, whose boss was Irish and
widely believed to encourage pro-O'Dowd bias.

Results were mixed in his most significant fights. Four days after
beating McCoy for the second time, he stopped Young Fisher in
three. But in August his limitations were exposed when he received a
neat lacing from his nemesis, Jack Britton, the masterful welterweight
champion. O'Dowd had difficulty landing a punch and retained his
title only because the eight-round bout, in Newark, New Jersey, was a
no-decision. His other results included a 'newspaper' win over Kid
Lewis, a 'newspaper' loss to Augie Ratner, and several stoppage wins.

One question about O'Dowd's reign remained. Was he the best
boxer in his home town? For years that accolade had gone to Mike
Gibbons, the 'St Paul Phantom'. Now 32, eight years older than
O'Dowd, he had been a pro since 1908. He peaked during the tenures
of Chip and McCoy, never getting a title fight though he won
'newspaper decisions' over both. According to Alexander Johnston,
'If referees had been allowed to render a decision, Mike could have
taken the title from McCoy any night of the week.' A superlative
defensive boxer with a baby face and snub nose, he elevated the sport
to a science, keeping a book of written notes on all his potential rivals.
His one fault was a tendency to over-caution and some of his bouts
against other defence-minded boxers, such as Packy McFarland,
ended in dreary stalemate.

Gibbons was also smart outside the ring and worked in league with the Minnesota promoters. They paid him 65 per cent of gross takings on his fights, out of which Gibbons would pay his opponent. This highly questionable arrangement raises serious suspicions that some of his bouts were not on the level. In November 1919 he persuaded O'Dowd to accept one of these peculiar promotions to settle their rivalry in St Paul. The champion was tempted by the fact that Gibbons had lost back-to-back 'newspaper' verdicts to Harry Greb and Jeff Smith and appeared to be slipping. Gibbons took 80 per cent of the $40,000 gross receipts, out of which he paid O'Dowd $15,000. The remaining 20 per cent was split between the club and the state. Gibbons also received 75 per cent of the picture rights. He was clearly well-rewarded for his efforts, but it was O'Dowd who won the close 'newspaper decision'. Gibbons announced his retirement.

In the first half of 1920 O'Dowd hit the best form of his life. He scored a string of inside-the-distance victories and, by the time he accepted a title defence against Johnny Wilson in Boston, had stopped 11 of his last 15 opponents. O'Dowd was a 10–3 favourite to beat Wilson. However, a decision would be allowed at the end of the fight and he didn't want to take any chances. So O'Dowd's manager, Paddy Mullins, insisted that his cousin, Hector McInnis, be referee. His demand was granted and the bout went ahead on 7 May.

O'Dowd launched his usual charge. But eight fights in two months had wearied him. He was nonplussed by the challenger's southpaw stance and couldn't avoid the right jabs and left crosses coming his way. He even suffered the indignity of a knockdown in round two. Even so, Mullins and O'Dowd were startled at the end of 12 rounds to see McInnis raise Wilson's hand. They complained loudly that they had been robbed by their own referee, but the result stood and Wilson was the champion.

His real name was John Panica and he was born in the close-knit Italian ghetto of East Harlem, New York on 23 March 1893. It was a poor but vibrant neighbourhood, haunted by crooks. One of Panica's boyhood friends was a young thug called Francesco Castiglia; later, as Frank Costello, he became the czar of organized crime in America. Another acquaintance, a Brooklyn boy called Al Brown, moved to Chicago and changed his name to Capone. These criminal connections would taint Wilson's boxing career.

After leaving school he worked for Western Union, running messages to night clubs. He started boxing in the New York clubs and received $2.25 for his first fight. Frank Costello introduced him to his first manager, Vincent Morello, one of a clan of murderous hoods said to be the first Mafia family established in the US. Morello was known as the 'Artichoke King' because he controlled the local sale and pricing of artichokes, a staple of Italian cooking. He eventually passed Wilson's contract on to Sam Golden, a Harlem 'sportsman', and the notorious John 'the Barber' Reisler, described by Randy Roberts as a 'boisterous, obnoxious parasite . . . noted for his heartless use of boxers'.

Wilson had a mixed record in dozens of club bouts in New York before the repeal of the Frawley Law forced him to practise his trade elsewhere. He moved to Charlestown, a waterfront suburb of Boston, and signed a management contract with Marty Killilea, a former baseball pro. He developed into a cagey, puzzling southpaw who made opponents look bad. Old photographs reveal a sneaky-looking character with oiled hair and a prominent, slightly mis-shapen nose. He won and lost against the formidable Leo Houck, beat Augie Ratner and lost on a foul to Frank Carbone. He was generally too good for the Boston opposition. In 1920 he stopped Billy Murray and out-pointed Pal Reed and was hailed as the champion of New England. Whatever his faults, he worked hard. 'I always believed in religious training,' he told Peter Heller. 'I'd go to bed at nine o'clock at night, I'd be up at eight. I'd have a glass of hot water with a little salt in it, you know, so that would wash all the fat that's hanging inside of your stomach.'

He had trained especially keenly for his challenge to O'Dowd. Fifty years later, he told Heller that the champion 'became furious, like a bulldog. That I loved. I didn't have to do much. All I had to do was wait for him to come in and just jab, counter, hook. As the fight went along I started weakening him with left hooks to the stomach. I was more of a body puncher, I never believed in hitting a man on the jaw because I thought it was a little bit too hard. You break your hands on them.'

In May 1920, boxing in New York took a step forward with the enactment of the Walker Law, allowing bouts to go 15 rounds to a decision under the supervision of the New York State Athletic Commission (NYSAC). It became the model for the rest of boxing. In January 1921 the sport's first large-scale governing body was formed, the National Boxing Association, with delegates from 15 states. New York, however, refused to join, saying it would not subordinate its functions under the Walker Law to 'an outside unofficial body'. Massachusetts adopted the same position.

While these changes were taking place, Wilson had six fights, including a 'newspaper decision' over George Chip, whose roundhouse blows he dodged in what was classed as a title defence. It was the veteran Chip's last chance to regain the crown. He retired in 1922 and lived to the age of 72, dying in New Castle, Pennsylvania, on 6 November 1960. Like most ringmen of his day, it is impossible to assess his true worth because of the large number of no-decisions on his record: 97 in 155 bouts.

Mike O'Dowd was pressing hard for a rematch with Wilson, and he was granted his wish at New York's Madison Square Garden on St Patrick's Day, 17 March 1921. The Irishman had shown impressive form in 11 fights since losing the title and there was enormous interest in the bout. Wilson was to receive $40,000 and O'Dowd $22,000. Most of the 12,000 spectators were hoping to see O'Dowd regain his crown; but they were disappointed. His blows had little effect on the champion. Wilson repeatedly landed fierce shots to the stomach, despite breaking his left hand in the third. He took at least ten of the 15 rounds, but won only by split decision on the casting vote of the referee. O'Dowd later had an operation on a hernia caused partly by the body punches he took.

On 28 July in Cleveland, Ohio, Wilson engaged in a title fight which for controversy put even the O'Dowd–McCoy bout in the shade. His opponent was Bryan Downey, a 24-year-old of Irish–German stock from nearby Columbus. Downey had fought nearly 100 times, starting as a featherweight, and had officially lost twice, to Jack Britton and Jock Malone. He was on a winning run, with victories over the likes of Augie Ratner, Frank Carbone and Joe Chip. A plodding, pugnacious sort — 'of the rushing, aggressive type whose aggressiveness amounts almost to recklessness', according to one observer — he was not expected to win. They fought at catchweights, with an obviously under-trained Wilson weighing 172lb, while Downey was 154lb. The title, therefore, should not have been at stake. Wilson refused to go into the ring unless his own nominee, Jimmy Gardner, was referee. The Cleveland Boxing Commission agreed to this but placed observers at ringside to watch for sharp practice.

Downey floored Wilson in the third, but the champion recovered
and the match was even going into round seven. Then Downey
dropped Wilson with a terrific right. Timekeeper Art Foote later
testified that Wilson was on the floor for nearly 14 seconds, but
Gardner only counted 'nine'. Wilson was dropped again, this time for
11 seconds, and again Gardner counted only 'nine'. Wilson pulled
himself up by the ropes but was hammered down again. At this point,
Marty Killilea jumped onto the ring apron and grabbed Wilson,
apparently trying to help him up. Jimmy Dunn, Downey's manager,
shrieked in protest, and with that, Downey lost his head and landed a
glancing blow on Wilson, who was still on his knees. Gardner, who
had counted up to 'seven', promptly disqualified Downey. The
stadium erupted. Scores of people rushed the ring and started a
massive brawl. Gardner was punched and kicked and it took a
concerted police effort to restore order. The Cleveland commission
announced it was rescinding Downey's disqualification and declared
him the new champion.

Two days later, safely back in Boston, Killilea gave his own version
of events. He claimed that when Wilson went down the second time,
one of Downey's seconds grabbed his leg. Wilson got up and kicked
backwards at the second, turning his head, and Downey came in and
knocked him down again. He claimed Wilson was resting on one knee
when Downey pushed the referee aside and rushed him, grazing his
head. The Massachusetts commission backed Wilson. New York, the
leading commission, remained neutral.

Tex Rickard, the greatest promoter of the 1920s, secured a quick
rematch at Boyle's Thirty Acres in Jersey City, New Jersey, on Labor
Day, 5 September. Jim Savage, an ex-heavyweight of impeccable
reputation, was referee. Rickard timed the bout for 4pm and 30,000
spectators turned out; by the end, they wished they hadn't. The fight
stank. Downey, willing but crude, did little more than strike
threatening poses and flounder about. He staggered Wilson twice in
the first round, but there the excitement ended. In one round alone,
the referee broke 24 clinches. A band aid on Downey's nose, legacy of
their first fight, was not dislodged until round four. The bout went its
12-round course with no decision allowed under the Hurley Law
governing New Jersey.

Rickard was furious. He saw Wilson's performance in particular as
a slur on his match-making and withheld his purse money of $35,000.

Downey received his end, a healthy $27,500, while the New Jersey Boxing Commission investigated whether the boxers had been trying. One commissioner said he had heard Wilson's corner telling him to 'take things easy and carry off the bacon'. Referee Savage testified that 'Downey fought hard but awful and Wilson fought as hard as could be expected of a champion of his calibre'. He said he would have abandoned the fight if it hadn't been for the title.

In his defence Wilson testified, 'I gave the best that was in me. I was hit on the jaw in the first round and I didn't know where I was for five rounds.' He said Downey had fooled him by adopting a crouch. When told he had led off only 11 times during the fight, the champion replied, 'That is more leading than I have done in my other bouts. I'm strictly a defensive boxer.' The commission, under pressure from Rickard, concluded that Wilson had made an unsatisfactory showing but that there was no evidence of collusion or dishonesty. His purse was held pending a final decision by the district attorney.

Rickard said he would release the money if Wilson signed to defend his title against Harry Greb. Wilson agreed, signed, took the money, then pulled out. On 3 January 1922 the NYSAC suspended him indefinitely for breach of contract. Killilea argued that they had been forced to sign the contract under duress but Massachusetts joined the ban and the NBA, consisting of most of the other states in which boxing was legal, suspended both of them until September for 'conduct unbecoming a fighter and his manager', a charge which caused some amusement.

So the champion of the world was unable to fight and the division entered another period of chaos. In Ohio Downey was hailed as champion. He defended his esoteric version of the title by beating Frank Carbone and Mike O'Dowd on points, then lost it by decision to Jock Malone in September. Meanwhile, on 20 June the NYSAC said Wilson had forfeited his right to the title but would be allowed to keep it if he fought Greb, the top contender. Three days later, the commission said Wilson had failed to agree terms and Greb would now contest the vacant title with the number two contender, Dave Rosenberg of Brooklyn.

Greb failed to accept offers for the fight. His manager said they were too busy fulfilling other engagements. For such ingratitude Greb was suspended indefinitely in New York. The commission now decided that the first middleweight to post a forfeit of $2,500 would be matched with Rosenberg for the title. The opportunity was snatched by Phil Krug of Harrison, New Jersey, who had recently won a 'newspaper decision' over Rosenberg. New York also told Wilson that he could have his licence back if he agreed to challenge the winner.

Rosenberg, 21, was a former amateur star who had officially lost only twice as a pro, to Mike Gibbons and Italian Joe Gans. Krug was a nonentity. Yet such was the popularity of boxing that their bout attracted 12,000 fans to the New York Velodrome on 14 August. Rosenberg won all 15 rounds. Krug was bludgeoned about the body and in the last third of the fight was staggered repeatedly with left hooks, his face covered in blood. He survived through bravery and his opponent's inaccuracy. The *New York Times* concluded, 'Rosenberg has a well-developed body but lacks the ability to fight at long range. He frequently missed when he stood off his opponent.'

Rosenberg didn't stay in favour for long. In October he was suspended for breaking a contract to box Mike O'Dowd. William Muldoon, chairman of the NYSAC, now attempted to clear up this unholy mess. He announced an elimination tournament to find a challenger for the temporarily suspended Rosenberg. Muldoon invited eight boxers to take part: Lou Bogash, Bryan Downey, Tommy Robson, Tommy Loughran, Jock Malone (who still held the Ohio 'title'), Mike O'Dowd, Augie Ratner and Pal Reed. He said, 'The middleweight situation now existing is deplorable. The division itself has lost the appeal to the public which it once held.' In a familiar refrain, Muldoon continued, 'There are no Ketchels today, nor any boxers who come near comparing with some of the old timers.'

Bogash, a fast and tricky boxer, quickly eliminated Reed and Downey, but it was O'Dowd, now 27 and the loser of his last two bouts, who got the shot at Rosenberg. They fought at the Rink Sporting Club, Brooklyn, on 30 November. Rosenberg had a swollen left hand but Muldoon refused his pleas for a postponement. The injury was a crucial handicap. O'Dowd was able to walk through Rosenberg's jabs and floor him in the third. By round eight, the Brooklyner was desperate and landed a low right which left O'Dowd writhing in agony. Rosenberg was disqualified. It took ten minutes for O'Dowd to be assisted from the ring. Rosenberg said forlornly, 'I'm sorry. I've had a hard time as a professional boxer. Everything has been done to discourage me.' He was suspended again and his purse was confiscated.

New York now recognized O'Dowd as world champion. But his days were numbered. He was suffering recurrent pains that affected the use of his legs. On 16 March 1923 he met Jock Malone, the third of the trio of famous St Paul middleweights. Malone knocked him out in less than one minute of a ten-round no-decision bout, adding the New York version of the title to the Ohio one he already held. O'Dowd quit the ring and was found to be suffering from primary lateral sclerosis of the spinal cord. He recovered sufficiently to lead an active retirement and died in his beloved St Paul on 28 July 1957, 11 months after Mike Gibbons. Malone, who met the best boxers around in 15 years as a professional, strangely never pursued his title claims, which lapsed. He is not considered to have been a true champion. He did, however, have a gift for publicity, once jumping fully-clothed from Boston's Charlestown Bridge as penance for losing a fight.

Johnny Wilson had now been inactive for almost a year. By right of succession he was the true champion, but he was isolated by suspension. He needed to get back in the ring. To this end, Frank Marlowe replaced Killilea as his manager and applied for Wilson's suspension to be lifted. Marlowe had influential friends; he was a close associate of mobster 'Big' Bill Duffy and a pal of Al Capone. Suddenly there came the announcement that Wilson had been reinstated and was to defend his title against Greb at the Polo Grounds on 31 August 1923.

The *New York Times* was sceptical about the quality of the two protagonists. 'Neither man is of the type which places its main reliance on science and boxing skill. Once Wilson gets started he is likely to hit anything that is inside the ropes, including the referee, and Greb has long been known as the human windmill,' it sneered. Wilson opined, 'Greb can't stand body punishment. After a few rounds he will lose his steam. I will win in ten rounds.' Greb, for his part, predicted a win in eight.

Greb won the decision after 15 rounds. According to the *Times*, he 'completely baffled Wilson with a swirling attack which started in the first round and did not end until the bout ended. Greb won every round except the first and the last. When the final bell ended the hostilities, Wilson was a sorry sight. The bridge of his nose was cut from a blow in the second round, his mouth was bleeding, his lips were puffed and raw, he had a slight growth under his right eye, and his left was almost closed.' Wilson hit the challenger low several times, but Greb was a master of the black arts and was warned repeatedly for hitting and holding, punching on the break and thumbing.

Titleless, Wilson returned to Boston. He won three bouts and in 1924 challenged Greb in New York. He again lost over 15 rounds. By now Wilson was fronting the Silver Slipper, a Broadway night club, for Bill Duffy and his cronies. He continued to box, beating Pal Reed again, losing to Tommy Loughran and knocking out Jock Malone in a fierce grudge fight. As the batteries ran down he was stopped in three by Tiger Flowers and lost a non-title fight to Greb. In 1926, after two points defeats by Maxie Rosenbloom, he retired.

Wilson continued to 'manage' the Slipper through Prohibition and into the Depression, mixing happily with bootleggers and gunmen like 'Legs' Diamond and Owney Madden. He was also involved in clubs in Boston. He promoted boxing and marathon dancing, owned a cigar store and managed the tassle dancer Sally Keith. Wilson lived out his retirement in Boston where, he told Peter Heller, he once had 'six rooms, a maid, governess for my child, and I had a chauffeur for my wife and kid, and I had a seventeen-thousand-dollar Lincoln. They were cars, they were cars.' He died in hospital on 8 December 1985 at the age of 92, after contracting pneumonia while recovering from a broken hip.

5

The Roaring Twenties

'HE WAS something to see. He had this beautiful silk dressing gown. His hair was parted down the middle in a pompadour style and his face was heavily powdered. At first glance he could have been mistaken for a dude in another line of work. But once the bell sounded, such doubts were washed away. Everything went with Harry. He would miss a man with a hook and catch him on the way back with his elbow. He would step on his opponent's toes in the clinches, butting him in the self-same moment. He would rough up a fellow's face with the laces and no one in the business was more adept at thumbing his opponent's eye. To Greb, it was all part of the game . . .'

Larry Gains, who penned this description in his book *The Impossible Dream*, was one of a generation of boxers in awe of Harry Greb. He was the fighter's fighter. His flat nose, craggy brows and frozen gaze spoke of lessons learned in the hardest rings. Some, like Gains, copied his centre-parted, brilliantined hairstyle. None could copy his lifestyle. In the words of one critic, Greb 'fought like a wild cat and lived like an alley cat'. Dames, dance halls and dust-ups were his domain. He was said to have sex in his dressing room before bouts, to train in bordellos and night clubs. His outlook was simple: 'Prize fighting ain't the noblest of arts and I ain't its noblest artist.'

Some of the stories were exaggerated. Though he loved the night life, Greb rarely drank. And he boxed so often he didn't really need to train. Greb's record, probably incomplete, shows 299 pro contests, putting him in the all-time top ten. Incredibly, he lost only seven, though many of his fights were no-decision bouts. He often fought once a week, engaging in hard ten- and 12-rounders in towns and

cities across North America, arriving on the morning train and
leaving on the sleeper — unless there was a girl willing to share her
bed. Usually, there was.

His boxing method was unique. 'It was as though someone had
opened up the ceiling and dumped a carload of boxing gloves on me,'
said Pat Walsh, trounced by Greb in 1925. The man himself told
Colliers magazine, 'I never think along defensive lines. My plan is to
start an offensive rush from the first second and keep both gloves as
busy as my arms can drive them. I like to fight as often as I can, for
that keeps me in shape. I also like to tackle the big fellows around 200
pounds, for they are slower and easier to hit than the little fellows.
The bigger they come, the easier they generally are when they have to
face speed.' They called him the 'Iron City Express' and sports writer
Ed Hughes dubbed him the 'Human Windmill'.

Greb was born in a streetcar on 6 June 1894 in the Garfield district
of Pittsburgh to a German father, Pius, and an Irish mother, Anne.
Christened Edward Henry, he took the name Harry from an older
brother who died. As a child he wanted to be a baseball player, but he
was better with his knuckles than the bat. He first used his fists to
protect friends from neighbourhood bullies. His father remembered
the time four thugs tied the young Greb to a wagon wheel. He broke
free and licked them all. A restless, energetic boy, he was strong for
his size and impervious to pain. At ten he would stand on a box in the
basement and proclaim himself champion of the world.

He left home in his early teens because his father didn't approve of
him boxing. Sportswriter Grantland Rice said he won the amateur
welterweight titles of Pennsylvania and Ohio in 1913 and then turned
pro, aged 18. He joined the hard-boiled crowd at George Engel's
gym, where sparring with the likes of Buck Crouse soon earned him
the sobriquet 'Flat Nose'. He lost once in his first year as a pro.
Overmatched against George Chip's brother Joe, he was knocked out
in two rounds. In 1914 he had 17 bouts, winning one on a foul and
getting the 'newspaper verdict' in all but one of the rest. Most went
six rounds, the limit allowed in Pittsburgh.

By 1915, his third pro year, he was mixing with the likes of Jack
Blackburn (who later trained Joe Louis), Billy Miske, Tommy
Gibbons and George Chip. He ended the year by breaking a bone in
his left arm against Ted 'Kid' Graves and had to quit after two
rounds. It was the last time he would fail to finish a contest. For the

next six years Greb moved like a cyclone through America's middleweights, light-heavyweights and even heavyweights. He would fight anyone, anywhere. He boxed 19 times in 1916, 32 times in 1917, 26 times in 1918, an incredible 44 times (420 rounds) in 1919, and 25 times in 1920. His opponents were a who's who of boxing: Chip, Mike and Tom Gibbons, Jeff Smith, Frank Klaus, Mike O'Dowd, Jack Dillon, Mike McTigue, Eddie McGoorty, Leo Houck, Battling Levinsky, Bill Brennan and dozens more of that ilk.

Greb first tried to claim the middleweight title in 1917 after a close no-decision with Al McCoy. His best results that year included first-round knockouts of Young Ahearn and Frank Mantell and 'newspaper decisions' over Jeff Smith and Jack Dillon. In 1919 he won several 'newspaper' verdicts over Battling Levinsky, who claimed the light-heavyweight title (Greb would beat ten world champions in his career). He also won the scribes' nod over Mike Gibbons before the largest crowd to watch boxing in Pittsburgh up to that time.

Greb's exploits would fill a book. There was the time in Ohio when gamblers chloroformed him in the dressing room. He recovered to win his bout. In a match with Soldier Jones he was knocked down six times in the first two rounds but came back to win the 'newspaper' decision. He was in several car crashes and newspapers were forever preparing his obituary. His long-running dispute with referees — he called them 'cops' — included threatening to throw one, the retired heavyweight Marvin Hart, out of the ring. For that he got away with a fine. He was usually in trouble with one commission or another, though it is said he never engaged in fixed fights. Incredibly, he was only partially sighted during his finest years. He lost the vision in his right eye when thumbed by Kid Norfolk in a bout in 1921.

While waiting for a title fight with Johnny Wilson (see preceding chapter), Greb decided to take on the light-heavyweights. In one four-month spell he beat three of the world's best: Tom Gibbons, Gene Tunney and Tommy Loughran. The Tunney fight, for the vacant American light-heavy title, was perhaps his greatest performance. He beat the bigger man to a pulp. Tunney later wrote, 'In the first round . . . I sustained a double fracture of the nose which bled continually until the finish. Towards the end of the first round my left eyebrow was laid open four inches.' Somehow he lasted 15 rounds, the canvas drenched with gore. Four years later, Tunney

would take the world heavyweight title from the great Jack Dempsey.
Greb was the only man ever to beat him.

Greb always wanted to fight Dempsey himself and it was probably
this that made him reject his first chance at the middleweight title
against Dave Rosenberg in 1922. Engel said his boxer had prior
commitments but he was probably trying to get his man a
heavyweight title bout. As it turned out Greb and Dempsey never
met, apart from one hectic sparring session. Dempsey called him 'the
fastest fighter I've ever seen'. In disappointment, Greb left Engel in
November and hooked up with James 'Red' Mason.

In mid-1923 Greb was absent from the ring for six months. His
wife Mildred had TB. He took her to warm resorts to ease her
condition, but it deteriorated and she died. Greb was left with a
toddler daughter, whom his family helped raise. Friends said his
womanizing did not start until after Mildred's death.

His first bout after she died was for the title. Johnny Wilson was
allowed back from his New York exile to defend against Greb in
August 1923. It is said that on the eve of the bout Greb conned a
group of powerful gamblers, including Sam Boston (once Wilson's
manager) and Arnold Rothstein, by collapsing 'drunk' in front of
them outside Lindy's restaurant. It was an act. He won easily (see
pages 71–2) and even in a world title challenge, couldn't resist a bit of
mischief. In round six he thumbed Wilson in the eye. When the
referee demanded to know what he thought he was doing, Greb
replied, 'Sticking my thumb in his eye. What does it look like?'

Greb's first defence is listed as a ten-round win over Bryan
Downey in Pittsburgh, which now allowed decisions. But according
to the *New York Times*, Greb was a pound over the weight limit. He
was to make five more defences, the next a January 1924 re-match
with Johnny Wilson. Greb won clearly in a bruising slog and Red
Mason celebrated with a handspring in the middle of the ring.

His match with Fay Keiser in Baltimore two months later was a
murky affair. Greb was heavily overweight but the commission
wanted it to be a title bout, so it was agreed to announce his weight as
159lb. Greb was also worried about being disqualified and brought
his own referee, but the local commission insisted on its own man.
They settled on a compromise — Benny Franklin, the promoter.
Keiser, who had fought Greb eight times before, was no match for the
champion. He was floored heavily by a left hook to the jaw in round 12

and was helpless, with Greb pummelling him in a corner, when Franklin apparently stopped the fight. Keiser's handlers claimed their man was floored and Franklin straddled him while he was counting so he couldn't get up. Greb was run out of town that night by two gunmen. A few days later, Franklin told the state commission that he had been approached before the fight with an offer of $3,000 to give any decision to Keiser.

Welsh middleweight Frank Moody, who fought Greb at this time, gave a graphic description of what it was like to be in the ring with him:

> He came tearing out of his corner at the first bell, leapt at me and started swinging both arms. I took most of the punches on my shoulders and arms, then he was close in and hooked away with lefts and rights in an unceasing bombardment. Greb was never in one place for more than half a second, and the swift lefts I shot at him hit the empty air as he bobbed and weaved, then jumped in to clutch me with one hand and whirl away with the other.
>
> Each rush was followed by a spell of in-fighting, with Harry pulling and pushing, punching under and over, here, there and everywhere. My arms were plastered with leather and although I jabbed, hooked and uppercut, it was like fighting a dozen men or an octopus with gloves on. Midway through the opening round Greb butted me under the chin and as my head went back he gave me the laces of his left glove and finished the stroke by jabbing his thumb into my right eye. The pain was deadly.

Moody was counted out in the sixth and couldn't see out of his right eye for two weeks.

In June, Greb made his fourth defence against Ted Moore, another Britisher campaigning in the States. Fifty thousand filled New York's Yankee Stadium for what was the annual Milk Fund Show. Moore, as hard as nails, refuted the soft reputation of British boxers by matching the champion punch-for-punch. It was so close that the crowd waited in silence for the decision. Greb got it, and took a rare two-month break. After 12 years in the ring, he should have been showing signs of wear, but on his return he won more than a dozen non-title bouts and fought several no-decisions.

His most famous bout was his next: a title defence against Mickey

Walker, the world welterweight champion. Walker, 24, was a
compact slugger known as the 'Toy Bulldog' for his belligerent style.
A huge crowd of 60,000 packed the New York Polo Grounds on a
steamy night on 2 July 1925. Walker attacked from the bell and won
the early rounds. Then Greb got working. Both fists flew at lightning
speed. It was so wild that referee Eddie Purdy was twice knocked
over. The younger man wilted first in the heat. Greb called on his
limitless energy to paste Walker over the final stretch and win the
decision in one of the best bouts ever seen in New York. Walker called
him 'the greatest fighter I ever fought'.

The two men allegedly fought again that night. Walker said they
met in a New York club and, after arguing, fell to blows on the
sidewalk outside until separated by a burly cop. Walker claimed he
won the second fight by hitting Greb as he was removing his jacket.
Others said it never happened. More amazing than fiction is the fact
that, after one of the toughest fights in history, Greb crammed in four
more bouts before the end of the month.

His next defence, against Tony Marullo in New Orleans, was
relatively uneventful, Greb winning on points. On 26 February 1926
he gave a shot to Tiger Flowers, a Georgia southpaw. Flowers was
only the second black man ever to be allowed to box for the
middleweight title. He had an all-action style similar to Greb's and
together they attracted a record indoor gross for New York of
$105,134. Greb looked pale and was hurt in the first by a body shot.
He tried the usual rough stuff but Flowers had seen it all before and
punched back. For once the 'Windmill' seemed to tire, with Flowers
taking the last round and the split decision. Only referee Gunboat
Smith, once kayoed by Greb, voted for the champion.

Not everyone agreed with the verdict. Journalist Charles W.
Wilcox wrote that it provoked two ladies, supporters of Greb, to rush
'screaming down an aisle, as each, grabbing a chair' violently
assaulted a reporter they had mistaken for a boxing judge. Six police
officers were needed to restrain them. William Muldoon, chairman of
the NYSAC and an alleged racist, said Greb had won 'but the
decision will stand. If we reversed it, the negro people might think
they were being discriminated against.' Reporter George Underwood,
however, thought, 'Harry Greb was beaten on the Broadways of the
world. The candle that long has been burning at both ends, finally
burned out.'

They met in a return in New York on 19 August. Greb tried hard, roared on by several hundred travelling fans from Pittsburgh, but the old fire was gone. The *New York Times* described him as 'listless' and the event as 'one of the worst championship fights we have ever seen'. Tiger won on points.

Greb retired. Thirteen years of boxing and nearly 300 fights had taken their toll. Several weeks later, however, his car left the road and rolled over an embankment. Greb broke his much-flattened nose. To ease his breathing, he decided to have an operation and entered hospital in Atlantic City, New Jersey, on 21 October 1926. The operation was started under local anaesthetic, then continued under gas. But about 13 hours after leaving the operating table, Greb's heart began to fail. At 2.30pm on 22 October 1926, he died. A girlfriend, Naomi Braden, was at his side. His death was attributed to 'heart failure superinduced by shock of the operation combined with injuries received in a car accident'. He had never fully come round from the anaesthetic. He was 32.

Theodore 'Tiger' Flowers could not have presented a greater contrast to Harry Greb: quiet, devout, church-going. And black. As with Greb, it is hard to know how much of Flowers's image was real and how much was concocted. He was an intelligent man and well knew the obstacles facing black athletes. In the post-Jack Johnson years, the idea of a black champion was anathema to many whites. Harry Wills stayed number one heavyweight contender for years without getting a title shot. It needed someone with the right image — humble, modest, indeed saintly — to be accepted by whites. A negro from the Deep South — Flowers was from Camille, Georgia — had a radar for such things. Flowers's behaviour could almost have been the model for the 'rules' drummed into heavyweight Joe Louis a decade later to make him acceptable to whites.

When Flowers first boxed in New York in 1924, the cynics thought his 'Georgia Deacon' tag and Bible-carrying persona was a promotional gimmick. Before each fight, he was said to recite the beginning of the 144th Psalm: 'Blessed be the Lord my strength which teacheth my hands to war and my fingers to fight.' He was, however, genuinely religious and a steward at a Methodist church. 'I am a professional pugilist because I believe God meant me to be just what I am,' he said. 'It's not wrong, the Bible tells me, for a man to fight for his livelihood, and it's right to pray for what you fight for.'

He was born on 5 August 1895 to a family of poor but devout Southern farmers and grew to be an active, wiry boy with a sad face. He first boxed at the age of 15, probably in local bootleg bouts. During World War I he enlisted in the government's ship-building corps and was sent to work as a carpenter at the Hog Island shipyard in Philadelphia. At a Liberty Loan rally hosted by former champion Jack O'Brien, Flowers joined in some sparring exhibitions. He looked promising and O'Brien advised him to turn pro.

Flowers's first recorded bout was a knockout of Bill Hooper in Brunswick, Georgia, in 1918. Hooper's manager was an Atlanta promoter and gym owner named Walk Miller, who invited Flowers to join his stable. In the next two years he won all 13 fights, six by knockout. He was then overmatched and was knocked out by hardened warriors such as Panama Joe Gans, Kid Norfolk, Sam Langford, Lee Anderson and Jamaica Kid. They were the iron men among America's black fighters and often met each other because whites were too scared to fight them. Tiger also boxed several times in Mexico, where one bout ended with his opponent, Frank Carbone, being thrown in jail after fouling Flowers and causing a riot.

In 1924 Tiger fought 36 times without defeat. He avenged himself on several of those who had knocked him out, gave Harry Greb a torrid time in a no-decision encounter and stopped former champion Johnny Wilson. Wilson said, 'He didn't hurt you or nothing. The only thing he did that made it look good, he throws a million punches. But there's no steam behind it. And it looked one-sided and the referee stopped the fight. He was throwing all the punches and I was just doing the blocking.' Others said Flowers could really bang when he wanted, but often held back. He told one writer, 'I hate to knock a man out. What if he shouldn't come to again? What then?'

In January 1925 Flowers met Jack Delaney at New York's Madison Square Garden. It was a contest between two of the top contenders. Flowers started at his usual fast pace but in round two was up-ended by a beautiful right uppercut. He rocked himself to get in a sitting position but his legs wouldn't respond and he was counted out. The next day, Walk Miller complained to the boxing commission that Delaney had carried 'Irish confetti' (a metal slug) in his glove.

A rematch was ordered. This time, Delaney dropped Tiger for a count in the fourth, then struck him as he went to his knees to avoid a second blow. *Boxing News* said, 'The referee disqualified Jack, but changed his mind when the crowd became hostile. Calling the two men to the centre of the ring, he told them that as Delaney had struck Flowers when he was down, and as the Tiger had gone down without taking a punch, it was obviously a "double foul" and he was going to wash out the fourth round and they would have to start it again. So they re-started the fight, but it only lasted 65 seconds. The Tiger had been really tamed by the previous knockdown, and soon left an opening for Delaney's deadly right. It flashed home, and this time they counted "ten" without the coloured man moving a muscle.'

Black men got no favours. At the end of the year Flowers fought Irish favourite Mike McTigue on the understanding that the winner would get a title fight with Greb. Following complaints about the previous quality of officiating at Madison Square Garden, something special was arranged for the big pre-Christmas show. New York businessman Bernard Gimbel and a prominent banker were made judges. Quite why Tex Rickard did this is unknown. Ringsiders gave most of the ten rounds to Flowers, but the new judges blithely awarded the bout to McTigue. There was uproar at ringside, but Flowers shook McTigue's hand and afterwards Walk Miller said, 'The deacon says it was God's will and let it go at that.' The next day, Rickard announced that Flowers, not McTigue, would meet Greb.

Flowers's conquest of Greb has already been described (page 78). Frank Moody, who fought him around this time, described his style: 'He had long arms and that right lead of his came in from all angles. He thrust it out, jabbed it and jumped in with it and it never stopped. How he managed to avoid my punches was a mystery. He seemed to be made of grease, for no matter what I threw at him he slipped them with astounding ease.' Moody, who hurt a hand early in the bout, said Flowers could have knocked him out on several occasions, but instead let him recover. Afterwards, he asked him why. 'I never punish a man more than I can help,' was the reply.

After beating Greb in their return, Flowers travelled to the Chicago Coliseum to cross swords with Mickey Walker on 3 December. Chicago was the most lawless city in America and rumours circulated that Flowers wouldn't be allowed to win. Charlie

Rose, a well-known British boxing figure, said so many referees rejected the bout that Jack Kearns, Walker's manager, turned in despair to a prominent artillery captain. The military man told him, 'I'll act if you allow me to station my company around the ring . . . fully armed.' Walker dropped Flowers with his first right hand but the champion came back with good jabs to cut Walker's eye in the fourth. He piled up the points and landed three punches to every one he took. In the ninth Walker dropped him again but again he was up without a count. At the bell to end the tenth and final round, the referee and sole judge, Benny Yanger, gave the nod to Walker.

Nat Fleischer in his book *Black Dynamite* wrote, 'The decision was given to Walker after ten bloody rounds, but it was one of the worst ever handed down in a ring, and caused the Illinois Boxing Commission to hold a special meeting the following day to investigate the verdict.' The commission contemplated reversing the decision, but didn't. Walker recollected, 'I went the limit and my hand was raised after the fight. Flowers was a great guy, a swell fellow, and a great fighter.' Flowers's contract had a return fight clause but it was ignored.

A story told about Flowers's next bout in Chicago, against Maxie Rosenbloom, gives some indication of the atmosphere prevalent there at the time. According to Graham Nown in his book *The English Godfather*, Rosenbloom was waiting to be called to the ring when five hoodlums entered his dressing room. They 'offered' him $10,000 to lose.

'Me and the boys kinda like the nigger,' said one. 'We figure he'll take you this time. But it's close — too close for our money. We'd feel more comfortable if we had your co-operation.' Rosenbloom refused. After a phone call to his friend, the New York mobster Owney Madden, the Chicago gang agreed to switch bets. Perhaps fortuitously, the result was a draw.

Flowers fought Rosenbloom again that year, this time in Detroit, a city almost as corrupt as Chicago. Again, the verdict was a draw. Three days later he beat Leo Gates in Harlem, and four days after that, on 16 November, he entered the private New York hospital of Dr Wilfred Fralick for the removal of scar tissue from above his right eye. He expected to be out of action no more than three weeks. Several hours after the operation, however, he collapsed, and he died within minutes. Dr Fralick said death was due to a condition of the lymph glands; but, as with Harry Greb, suspicions remain over the anaesthetic dose.

Gene Tunney gave a moving eulogy for the ex-champion: 'I am proud to have called Tiger Flowers my friend . . . as a man he showed to the world that he could carry and keep his religion in the pursuit of the profession of boxing. He was deeply religious, but he did not parade it . . . he was an inspiration not only to the youth of his race, but to all boys and young men — to live cleanly, speak softly, trust in God, and fight hard and fair.'

Less than a year after Flowers was buried, Walk Miller shot himself in his training camp near Kingston, New York. He was only 39. He had been worried about recent bad investments, and it was said he had never recovered from Flowers's death.

There is an old film of Mickey Walker in his training camp, belting the heavy bag while dancing the Charleston. Fighting and fun: that was Walker. He was a Runyonesque character, a playboy, a rogue, a gambler, a rake. He moved through the big dirty business of boxing with a permanent little-boy grin, loving every minute, perfectly complemented by his larcenous manager, Jack 'Doc' Kearns. Inside the ropes he was one of the toughest, bravest men in the business. Outside, he lived the life of speakeasies, clubs and girls. No fighter more epitomized the Roaring Twenties.

Edward Patrick Walker was born on 13 July 1901 in Keighry Head, the rough Irish section of Elizabeth, New Jersey. His mother had wanted a girl and set his hair in curls. Little 'Mickey,' however, was naturally pugnacious and learned to fight against freight-yard hobos at Cooper's Corner, a neighbourhood hangout. 'You had to learn how to fight down there, because if you couldn't fight, you couldn't be around the corner,' he told Peter Heller.

After leaving school he worked briefly for a firm of draughtsmen but was fired after punching another office boy. He then went to the boiler shops of the New Jersey Central Railroad. After drifting into St Michael's Lyceum, a local gym, he decided to be a boxer and turned pro in 1918. In his eighth fight he was knocked out in the first round by Phil Delmont, the only time he ever took the full count. 'It was the best lesson I ever had,' he said. 'From that time I learnt to bob and weave as I attacked, making me hard to tag with a good punch.' He signed with a local matchmaker called Jack Bulger and in 1920 his star began to rise after he kayoed Newark's Banty Lewis in the seventh round.

Five days after his 20th birthday, he gave welterweight champion Jack Britton a hard ten rounds in a no-decision contest. Soon after, he beat the capable Dave Shade inside the distance. In mid-1922, he lost four out of seven bouts but still managed to clinch a title bout with Britton. Walker knocked the great champion down and won easily on points. Despite the emphatic manner of his victory, however, some said Britton had sold his title. According to journalist Paul Gallico, Bulger as promoter took 50 per cent of the net and paid Britton a guarantee of $30,000. Since the gross amounted to $49,000, this left Walker $10,000 short. But he got the title.

Writers nicknamed Walker the 'Rumson Bulldog' (Rumson, New Jersey, was a town where Walker had a home), for his short (5ft 7in), stocky build and tenacious spirit. This was altered by publicist Francis Albertanti to the more famous 'Toy Bulldog'. He beat Dave Shade on a split decision in defence of his title, but often neglected training and made heavy work of matches he should have won easily. Morrie Schlaifer almost knocked him out, and against Jimmy Jones he was ruled out for not trying and given a three-month suspension. In 1923 Bulger, his friend and mentor, died.

Walker would be handled for two years by Joe Diegnan, but it was Jack Kearns, who took over his affairs in 1925, with whom he is most closely associated. Kearns's life reads like a fanciful Hollywood script. He learned to box as a young gold prospector in the Yukon and was managed for a while by Wyatt Earp. Kearns discovered it was less painful to be a manager himself. He handled several leading pugs and during World War I he travelled to Australia, where he played an inglorious role in the disgrace of Les Darcy (see page 58). Back in the US he stumbled across heavyweight Jack Dempsey, who became the most sensational fighter of his era and made Kearns rich. He was a big spender. After falling out with Dempsey, he homed in on Walker, immediately ballyhooing him into a fight with Mike McTigue for the light-heavyweight title in January 1925. It went 12 rounds without a decision. Six months later he secured Walker a challenge against Harry Greb. The smaller man performed heroically but lost.

In August Walker was due to meet Bermondsey Billy Wells, a very good British fighter, for his welter title over 15 rounds in Chicago. Two days before the bout Wells was cooling off after a workout when three men with bulging jackets came into the locker room and announced, 'The Big Fella wants to talk to you.' Wells recalled: 'The Big Fella was Al Capone. And, in Chicago, bigger men than I would ever be would have to listen to him. But Al had sat ringside for most of my fights and was one of my chief supporters. I was always winning him a few more dollars he could add to his millions.'

Wells was taken by Cadillac to a huge apartment building, where he was brought before the gang boss, a 'short roly poly guy with hard eyes and a smile that would chill a man sun-bathing on the Equator.' Wells told Capone he was a cinch to win and he should bet on him.

Capone slowly shook his head. 'I got other plans, Billy,' he said. 'Walker has gotta win.'

Wells protested, but Capone was adamant. 'Be wise,' he said. 'There is too much dough for you to beat Walker and the wise guys think that you are a good bet. I'll get you another shot. But this time you lose. And no capers. Good luck, kid.'

Wells was ushered out and caught the train to Los Angeles that night. He never fought for the title and he never went to Chicago again.

Crooks couldn't help Walker when he ventured to Scranton, Pennsylvania, in May 1927 to fight local coalminer Pete Latzo. Latzo took his title on points. A month later Walker was stopped by Joe Dundee. It was to be his last bout in New York for almost five years, owing largely to problems between Kearns and the local commission. Freed from the constraints of having to make 147lb, Walker compiled a marvellous record in 45 fights over the next six years, losing only to Tommy Loughran. The extra weight gave an even bigger kick to his punches. 'Even with 12-ounce gloves on his hands, his sparring partners kissed the canvas, and had to like it,' said Charlie Rose.

He was a particular favourite in Chicago, where he took the middleweight title off Tiger Flowers. Like many pugilists of the time, he mixed freely with the likes of Capone and 'Machine Gun' Jack McGurn, enjoying their hospitality and no doubt receiving and returning favours. His win over Flowers left a rotten smell. According to Paul Gallico, Walker took a beating but 'was awarded one of those mysterious and wholly undeserved decisions that happen every so often in the sweet-scented game.'

Kearns and Walker pulled off a great scam in his first defence, at Olympia in London against Scotland's Tommy Milligan. The bout was promoted by C. B. Cochran, the theatrical impresario, who paid Walker the then-enormous sum of £22,000. Kearns, only half in jest, requested that the Prince of Wales be referee. Milligan was the 3–1 favourite and the Americans laid down several large bets. In fact, the Scot was no match for Walker and was kayoed in ten rounds after a very game challenge. Cochran, who pitched the ticket prices too high, lost £15,000.

With all that cash burning holes in their pockets, Walker and his entourage slipped over to Paris, where they spent a riotous few weeks until the money was gone. This was the start of Walker's second career, as a serious playboy. He was divorced soon after by his first wife, Maude, who testified, 'He has made our home a clandestine meeting place for married men and women. This has resulted in three divorce suits already. . . . Mickey threatened me, beat me, threw me out of the house. He started to go wrong when he went to Paris. When he returned, he just kept chasing booze and women . . .' Walker was to marry six times altogether.

Walker was now struggling even to make middleweight. He beat two of the best light-heavies of the day, Mike McTigue (in one round) and Paul Berlenbach, before defending his title for the second time in Chicago in June 1928. His opponent was a feral Nebraskan, Ace Hudkins, of whom William Muldoon once said, 'He is, pure and simple, an animal. He has not yet learned the code of ethics.' No quarter was asked or given and at the end of ten rounds many thought Hudkins had won. But this was Chicago, and Walker got the decision. He admitted, 'I was lucky.'

Walker beat Hudkins again in October 1929 in Los Angeles in his last defence of the middleweight title. The National Boxing Association was tired of his failure to meet worthy contenders and stripped him, installing Dave Shade above him in its rankings. There was talk of the 'Toy Bulldog' going back to London to defend against Len Harvey, but they couldn't agree terms. Walker formally relinquished his title on 19 June 1931.

Walker's career now entered its extraordinary third phase: he went after the heavyweight championship. He beat opponents inches taller and often stones heavier than himself, including Paolino Uzcudun, King Levinsky, Johnny Risko, Jim Mahoney and Salvatore Ruggirello, and he boxed a draw with future champion Jack Sharkey. His hopes were ended when he was battered almost out of recognition by Germany's Max Schmeling and retired before the start of the ninth round. Paul Gallico wrote: 'Walker was a study in pain in that last round. Can you imagine how he must have hurt? His mouth was cut. Both eyes were shut. One of them was cut, his lips were mashed. He had nothing but a smear on his face and into that smear Schmeling kept driving his fists . . .'

Walker dropped down to light-heavy and fought one last title bout, losing to Maxie Rosenbloom in 1933. He struggled on for two more years until stopped by Eric Seelig after an accidental butt. In retirement he opened the Toy Bulldog Tavern, a successful restaurant and bar on New York's Eighth Avenue which became meeting place for the fight crowd. He also worked as sports columnist for the *Police Gazette* and even trained women boxers for a spell.

Later in life, Walker took up painting and became known for his primitive art. His work was accepted by the Associated American Artists' gallery. He beat a drink problem and briefly did a nightclub comedy routine. By the mid-1970s the money and the wives had all gone. One day Walker was found unconscious in the street. A victim of Parkinson's Disease, he had wandered away from friends, fainted, and hit his face on the kerb. He was taken to a Brooklyn Hospital and was found to have amnesia and anaemia. A charity fund was started for his care. He died on 28 April 1981, in Freehold, New Jersey, at the age of 79.

6

The Muddleweights

THE BOXING world fragmented in the 1930s. Its governing bodies realized their power and began to wield it. Three organizations, the National Boxing Association, the New York State Athletic Commission and the European-based International Boxing Union, came into conflict. Each chose its own 'world' champions. By the end of the 1920s, the NBA had decided to break the NYSAC boxing department's title monopoly. Its members were disenchanted with the NYSAC's apparent preference for New York-licensed boxers. Meanwhile the IBU was fed up with America's pathological reluctance to allow titles to go overseas. The muddle was made worse when the NBA withdrew from the IBU in the early 1930s.

If a title fell vacant the different organizations each sought their own champions, a situation resolved only if two 'champions' fought each other. There were also occasions where one controlling body would declare a title vacant because the champion failed to meet its nominated challenger, while another would continue to recognize the same champion. The result was predictable: between 1932 and 1941 there were at least 15 claimants for the middleweight title. Sometimes there were three champions at once. According to American historian Jeffrey Sammons, 'Mediocre boxers, archaic rules, foreign [sic] invaders, a rash of foul fights, and criminal dealings all came to characterize boxing in the early thirties.'

Mickey Walker had already been stripped of his title by the NBA when he gave it up in 1931. First the NBA, then New York, announced loosely structured elimination tournaments to find successors. From these, two parallel lines of succession emerged. In the first, the subject of this chapter, the mantle was passed between

Gorilla Jones, Marcel Thil, Fred Apostoli, Ceferino Garcia, Ken
Overlin and Billy Soose. The second, which involved Ben Jeby, Lou
Brouillard, Vince Dundee, Teddy Yarosz, Eddie Risko, Freddie
Steele, Al Hostak and Solly Krieger, is dealt with in chapter seven.

It was a long journey for William Jones: from a poor home in
Tennessee to Hollywood and the bed of film star Mae West. He paid
his dues along the way. Being black meant starting at the bottom in
Memphis, where Jones was born on 12 May 1906. He grew into a
healthy, pleasant-looking lad with a smooth complexion and big
brown eyes. He received little schooling, having to work as soon as he
was able so as to help support his family. He worked for a spell as a
handyman at the Atlanta gym of Walk Miller, manager of Tiger
Flowers, and later did chores around a Memphis barber shop
operated by the father of a boxer. These influences encouraged him to
box. It has been claimed that he was given the cognomen Gorilla
because he had long arms. In fact, the name was that of an old black
boxer in Memphis who had once fought the great Flowers.

A promoter called Stephen 'Suey' Welch heard about Jones's
amateur prowess and offered him money to turn pro. Jones caught
the next train out of Memphis. He won his first bout by knockout in
January 1928 and by the end of the year had boxed 24 times as a
welterweight, losing just once. His best results included a no-decision
with leading welterweight Tommy Freeman and a win over Bucky
Lawless, one of a pack of good black boxers struggling for
recognition. Jones trekked all over the country, building a reputation
as a formidable boxer. In June 1929 he claimed the 'coloured'
middleweight title after beating Jack McVey in Boston. Four months
later he took world welterweight champion Jackie Fields to a tight
decision in a non-title fight. His good showing denied him a title
chance.

In December Jones and Fields were thrown out of the ring on a
charge of faking at Boston Garden. It was not the only time this would
happen to Jones, and calls into question some of his performances.
Sixteen months later he was disqualified for not trying against
Frankie O'Brien, for which he was suspended in Massachusetts, and
there was a scandalous contest against Ben Jeby in 1933. Some

blamed his cautious style. According to *The Ring*, 'He never was known to rush in madly, head-on, intent only on putting his man away. If anything, he sometimes spent too much time for the patience of the spectators sizing up an opponent before cutting loose.' Like Tiger Flowers, Jones found it prudent to disguise his true ability for reasons of colour. He often carried opponents. Noble Chisell, a contemporary boxer, said, 'Gorilla was not a killer. If he had a guy in a bad way he would not try to kill him. A lot of hometown boys he could have beat or knocked out but as long as the fight was going fine . . . all he wanted to do was win.'

Many white boxers avoided him, so Jones found himself pitted constantly against fellow blacks. He fought Bucky Lawless seven times altogether; other rivals included Roy Williams, Harry Smith, Jack McVey and Tiger Thomas. Boxing in opponents' backyards brought the occasional raw decision. In 1930 and into 1931 Jones continued to box once a fortnight. He developed into a superb boxer with a solid punch in reserve, though he was only 5ft 6in tall.

A draw with Chick Devlin and victory over Paul Pirrone levered him into the NBA tournament to find Mickey Walker's successor. For reasons political, it didn't contain the best fighters in the division: Dave Shade, Vince Dundee, Len Harvey and Ben Jeby were conspicuous by their absence. A win over classy Tiger Thomas took Jones a step further and on 25 January 1932 he found himself facing Italy's Oddone Piazza for the vacant NBA championship in Milwaukee. Piazza, a former amateur star, was out of his depth. Jones won four of the first five rounds and in the sixth hit Piazza so hard that he reeled across the ring on his heels before sprawling in a corner. The referee stopped it seconds later. Jones was presented with the NBA's title belt.

In April Jones outpointed Young Terry in 12 rounds to retain the crown. His trappings of success included a pet lioness which he walked on a lead. In June he was tempted to Europe by the influential promoter Jeff Dickson. Marcel Thil of France had proved himself the best boxer on the continent and was duly matched with Jones for the title on 11 June in Paris. Thil was an extremely hard man to beat and was ahead on points when Jones hit him low in the 11th round. The American was disqualified.

By rights this should have made Thil the undisputed champion. But New York had other ideas and promptly announced its own elimination tournament. For some reason the NBA also decided not to recognize Thil. Instead it sanctioned a bout between Jones and Sammy Slaughter on 30 January 1933. Jones ducked and blocked for a few rounds, then opened up in the seventh and put Slaughter down for the full count with an uppercut. On the same night, in the same ring, Ben Jeby, who had won New York's title, kayoed Paul Pirrone.

There were now three champions: Jones (NBA), Thil (Europe–IBU) and Jeby (New York). In April 1933, Jones met Jeby in a non-title bout in Cleveland to settle who was better. For five rounds the two 'champs' indulged in little more than a gentle wrestle. Referee Fred Block warned, 'You'll have to fight,' but this had little effect, and in the sixth Block stopped the bout and declared it no contest. The 8,000 spectators were furious. A chair was hurled into the ring and security guards had to form a cordon around the ring as the boxers cowered in their corners, protected by their seconds. Five squads of riot police hustled the fighters to their dressing rooms.

The purse money was suspended and the Cleveland Boxing Commission launched an immediate investigation. Its chairman, Al Sutphin, said he 'couldn't understand why a fighter like Jones who hits straight and hard, should suddenly turn up as a roundhouse puncher'. Mayor Ray Miller called it an 'apparently fake fight'. He added: 'I should prefer to see boxing eliminated in Cleveland rather than see a repetition of last night's feeble performance.' The boxers' purses were withheld and both were suspended by the Ohio Commission for a year, a ban effective in all 32 NBA states.

Jones retreated to the West Coast for the next few months. Though still notionally the NBA titleholder, his claim fizzled out after a disqualification loss to Vearl Whitehead. He started to lose as many as he won. A brief resurgence in 1936, including two knockouts of Tait Littman, earned him a final fling at the title. Freddie Steele was by now recognized as champion by New York and the NBA. In January 1937 he beat Jones on points. The Gorilla chugged along in good company until a final points loss in the town of Kellogg, Idaho, persuaded him to hang up his gloves in 1940. In 140 bouts, he was never stopped inside the distance.

Jones settled on the West Coast. Suey Welch was a good friend of Mae West, the Hollywood sex bomb famed for her risqué one-liners. She had a soft spot for well-muscled boxers and Welch would introduce her to any she took a fancy to. One was Jones. According to

Jet magazine, West became his manager and financial adviser and 'made it possible for him to avoid ending his career as a broken boxing bum'. Sometimes he worked as her chauffeur or bodyguard. His mother became her maid and would entertain West with old negro spirituals. Jones once rejected a $250,000 offer to film his life story, showing him to be Mae's lover. He declined, saying, 'That would be lie because she was just my manager and friend.' Those who knew them knew better.

Jones taught boxing for several years at the Boys' Club in Watts, but his eyesight gradually deteriorated until he was virtually blind. He could still be seen hanging out at Cauliflower Alley, a club for old-time boxers and wrestlers, sporting a bad toupee and a natty line in suits. In his seventies he was stricken with a severe stomach ailment. He weighed just 102lb when he was found dead on 4 January 1982, at the age of 72. Reporter Patt Morrison in the *Los Angeles Times* wrote:

> He died in his home near MacArthur Park surrounded by cherished memorabilia of his glory days — photographs, cards, newspaper stories — in the small grace-and-favour house with the little gorilla nailed outside, over the street numbers. He lived there rent-free, thanks to the actress Mae West — 'my lady', the benefactor whose bodyguard and chauffeur Jones had been, and from whose death 15 months ago he never really recovered.

A neighbour said, 'After she passed on, he just changed, he went down. I think he just gave up.'

Marcel Thil looked like cheap muscle from a 1930s B-movie. One could imagine him scowling at the door of some dingy back-alley dive or brawling in a waterfront saloon. With his battle-damaged face, narrow-set eyes, bald head, cauliflower ears and huge, hairy chest, he intimidated many opponents even before the opening bell. Thil was a close-range operator with an unbending will. He liked to move in and slug and would coat his body in oil so opponents couldn't wrestle him off. 'There was nothing very spectacular about his technique,' wrote Peter Wilson. 'There's nothing very spectacular about running smack dab into a telegraph pole.' He was the bona fide champion for much of the decade and was recognized as such by all but the governing bodies of US boxing.

Thil hailed from Saint-Dizier in France, where he was born on 25 May 1904. Enthused by the boom years of French boxing, he became a professional boxer in 1925 with a first-round knockout, but then met with little success. By the end of 1927 he had lost almost as many as he had won, including points defeats to British stylists Len Harvey and Jack Hood in London. In 1928 Thil discovered he could punch. Seven short wins in eight fights brought him a crack at the French middleweight title, and he took it in style from Marcel Thuru in the first round. Six months later he won the European title from a man who had previously stopped him, Leone Jacovacci. He lost that title in his second defence, but continued to box with success.

As with many boxers, Thil's career turned on one big win. In 1931 Jeff Dickson, the Paris-based American promoter, brought leading US contender Vince Dundee to Europe. The plan was for Dundee to beat the best French and British boxers and then return home with an unanswerable case to succeed Mickey Walker. Thil wrecked the script by outpointing him over 12 rounds. After more wins, he licked another American, Jimmy Tarante, then cut Jack Hood's eye to stop him in seven rounds in an eliminator for the world title. By beating Gorilla Jones in June 1932 (see page 90), Thil was accepted by most commentators as the true champion.

The Frenchman defended his title nine times in five years. His best win was probably his first, against Len Harvey in London. Thil lost the first three rounds and his right eye was closed. But he would not be denied. He walked indomitably through Harvey's shots to pin him on the ropes, pounding his torso before switching to the head. The Englishman couldn't understand the interjections from the French-speaking Swiss referee and was warned several times for unknown infringements. He took more punishment than in any previous fight and was well beaten at the end of 15 rounds.

Kid Tunero, a muscular Cuban who had beaten Thil in a non-title fight, was granted the next shot. The challenger had won 48 of 51 contests, but was ground down and outpointed. Other defences included two decisions over Spain's Ignacio Ara, a lucky draw with fellow Frenchman Carmelo Candel and a stoppage of Vilda Jacks. In between Thil boxed a stack of non-title fights, beating the best boxers from all over Europe and taking the continental light-heavyweight title. The one European boxer he never risked his title against was

Britain's fearsome Jock McAvoy. They did fight, but McAvoy had to weigh over the limit so the championship could not be at stake. Thil won anyway.

Thil seemed to improve with age. Despite his loss of NBA recognition when that organization withdrew from the IBU, he continued to be rated the best in the world. In January 1936 he put his crown on the line against Canada's Lou Brouillard, a short, blocky gladiator and one of the few ringmen who could match Thil in close. It wasn't pretty as they mauled and banged away. In the fourth, Thil dramatically crouched to the floor, clutching his groin. Brouillard was disqualified. Later scrutiny of a film of the fatal round failed to show a low punch. They fought again in February 1937. Brouillard was giving the champion all the trouble he could handle when again he was disqualified for a low blow, this time in the sixth. Brouillard claimed he was cheated and many in the crowd agreed.

Thil had lost just once in 46 fights, but was tiring of boxing. He was contemplating retirement when he received an offer to appear in a unique event. New York promoter Mike Jacobs was staging a Carnival of Champions at the Polo Grounds on 23 September 1937. It featured an unprecedented four world title fights on one programme: Lou Ambers v Pedro Montanez (lightweight), Sixto Escobar v Harry Jeffra (bantam), Barney Ross v Ceferino Garcia (welter), and Thil v Fred Apostoli (IBU middle title). Jacobs had hoped that New York would also recognize the middleweight contest, but it refused to allow the bout unless both boxers signed an agreement stipulating the title would not be at stake, no matter what the weight. Jacobs had both men come in over the weight limit.

Thil–Apostoli was first. Thil came in low, looking to get inside and leading to the body. Apostoli's efforts to check him were crude, but he kept throwing rights that made the Frenchman's knees buckle. The fight was evenly balanced when, in the ninth, a heavy left swing caught Thil above the right eye and opened an inch-long gash. Apostoli made it a target in the next round and it became so bad the referee was forced to call a halt. Apostoli could not claim the title because they were overweight, but Thil relinquished his claim soon after and the American gained some recognition as champion. Incidentally, the show lost $70,000.

Thil, who never lost his title in the ring, retired. During the war he worked with the French Resistance. He was captured and tortured, which he apparently bore with the same stoic fortitude he showed in the ring. He died in Cannes in August 1968 after a long illness complicated by injuries suffered in two separate car accidents the previous year. He was 64.

The orphanage wasn't so bad. The priests even let you box. For a nine-year-old, fighting with those huge padded gloves wasn't easy, but Fred Apostoli didn't mind. He loved to scrap. Life had been a fight, one way or another, since he was born in North Beach, San Francisco, on 2 February 1913. His family was dirt-poor. Then his mother died when he was seven. His father couldn't cope with four children, so they were sent to live with their grandmother. Two years later, Fred and his brother John wound up in a Catholic orphanage.

The dark, handsome Italian kid with olive skin and a dimpled chin was farmed out at 15 to work for a family on a ranch. A year later he returned to San Francisco to live with his re-married father, working part-time as a hod-carrier to support himself through high school. With America in the grip of the Depression, jobs dried up, so Apostoli joined the National Guard. There he started boxing again and won the welterweight championship of his camp. He was working as a hotel bellhop when he met a jeweller, Joe Niderost, who took him to the Olympic Club to learn boxing properly. Apostoli won a string of amateur awards, culminating in the 1934 national AAU middleweight title in St Louis.

He turned professional with Niderost and won six fights before he was stupidly rushed into a contest with Freddie Steele, a battle-hardened contender. Steele stopped him in ten. Niderost handed Apostoli over to Larry White, who handled Young Corbett III, a former welterweight champion and Apostoli's idol. By 1936 he was beating people like Babe Risko and Lou Brouillard and moving up the ratings. He had every quality: punch, skill, speed, guts. He never realized how good he could have been: 'I wasn't a boxer or a fancy dan. I liked to wade in and bang hard to the body. Fortunately I could take a belt. Punchers seldom hurt me.' His one weakness was a suspect temperament; if something upset him, he seemed to sleepwalk.

In January 1937 he debuted in New York. It was no disgrace to lose a close decision to tricky Ken Overlin and he soon made amends with five impressive wins. Then came the Carnival of Champions contest with Thil (see above). It had originally been planned to match Apostoli with Freddie Steele, now the NBA–NY champion, but Steele's manager didn't like Apostoli's manager and 'had other plans', even though Jacobs offered him $40,000. Jacobs therefore matched Apostoli with Thil. His win made him champion in the eyes of most fans.

Steele consented to fight Apostoli, but was careful to make it a non-title match. In a brutal, bloody brawl, Apostoli cut loose in the ninth round — one writer counted 165 punches he threw — and the referee was forced to stop it. The New York commission, which had ignored Thil for so long, now ordered Steele to defend against Apostoli within 30 days. When he ignored it, he was stripped. Apostoli outpointed Glen Lee in another close punch-out on 1 April 1938, and New York and some other states joined Europe in recognizing him as the true title-holder. In November he defended against his former hero, Young Corbett III. Apostoli worked him over and won in eight rounds. But he blew hot and cold. In the first two months of 1939 he lost two decisions to Billy Conn. Conn told Peter Heller, 'You couldn't make a mistake with him because he could box real good and he could punch real good. I thought he was really great. He was a real good-looking fellow. There wasn't a mark on him. I wound up in hospital for five days he busted me up so bad in the second fight. I won both of them. I don't want to win too many fights like that.'

Mike Jacobs had faith in the champion and even intimated that if he put on weight he could fight Joe Louis for the heavyweight title. Apostoli told him to forget it. He won four non-title fights after the Conn losses, then risked his crown against Ceferino Garcia in New York. It was one of his off nights. Apostoli took a fearful hiding and was knocked down three times in the seventh round before the fight was stopped. 'Nobody could have missed my chin that night,' he rued.

An insight into his psyche was given by trainer Whitey Bimstein: 'Fred was a good fighter, but he was a very high-strung boy who had to be handled carefully.' In a bout with Melio Bettina, Apostoli was knocked down three times in the first three rounds. Years later, Bimstein remembered, 'Fred took a beating through the first four rounds and when he came back to the corner after the fifth round, he started to cry like a baby. I was so surprised that I wasted five of my precious 60 seconds just watching the tears roll down his cheeks.'

Bimstein asked him what the matter was. 'I just can't fight, Whitey,' sobbed Apostoli.

Bimstein responded in the time-honoured manner. 'I yanked him off the stool and smacked him across the face. It was a simple shock treatment, and it worked. His eyes grew as big as silver dollars and his mouth flew open. "Now get in there and fight," I yelled at him.' Apostoli battled back to drop Bettina in the tenth and take a split decision. In a return, however, Apostoli was stopped and needed hospital treatment for fever and exhaustion.

Apostoli took a break before coming back under new management. He won three bouts and did well in a losing non-title bout with Tony Zale, now the champion. In 1941 he joined the Navy and for two years he served on the cruiser USS *Columbus* in the Solomon Islands. He trained for a comeback at the end of the war but was roughly handled by sparring partners and scotched the idea, taking out a referee's licence instead. But the lure of fighting was too great and in 1946 he came back under his fifth manager, Dolph Thomas. He won 13 of 15 fights in California but a planned match against Rocky Graziano fell through and he retired for good in 1948.

Apostoli became one of the best-known referees in the game. Twice-married, he worked as a successful West Coast advertising executive and kept in great shape. In 1965 the people of San Francisco gave him a testimonial dinner. With tears in his eyes, Fred told the large crowd, 'Your orphan boy has found home.' It came as a shock when he died of a heart attack on 29 November 1973. He was only 59.

Caring managers kept their boxers away from Ceferino Garcia. There was an aura of menace about the muscular Filipino with coffee skin and Oriental features, and his left hook was deadly. He was a welterweight for most of his career, one of the 147lb division's most dangerous men. It was only towards the end of his boxing life that he moved up a weight; he quickly became world champion. He features among the all-time kayo artists, with 73 quick wins to his credit.

The record books say he was born on 26 August 1910 in Manila, the capital of the Philippines. In fact he was probably born four years earlier and lied about his age when he moved to the United States. He had dozens of unrecorded fights in his home country before emigrating to California at the beginning of the 1930s. Ray Arcel, who sometimes trained him, called Garcia 'an excellent, excellent boxer'. *Boxing News* called him 'a tough, pugnacious fellow, well hardened to the business of fighting'. He was a tremendous hitter, particularly with his left hook, and he is credited with inventing the 'bolo' punch, a wound-up uppercut. (The term 'bolo' means, variously, a long Philippine knife for cutting sugar cane and a form of weighted lasso used by South American Indians.)

He was overmatched early in his American campaign, being knocked out once by Tommy Herman and twice by Freddie Steele and dropping several other decisions. But in February 1933 he beat Johnny Romero for the California welterweight title. By 1934 he was in the groove, scoring a string of knockouts over good-class opponents. A year later he fought well in losing two non-title decisions to the excellent world welterweight champion Barney Ross. Garcia called him the toughest man he ever boxed.

Garcia was in his prime between 1936 and 1940, losing only three of 41 bouts. He won well over half inside the distance. Only the very best beat him: Glen Lee, Barney Ross and Henry Armstrong. The Ross bout, their third, was Garcia's first title shot. They met in September 1937 in New York with Ross's welter crown at stake. The champion broke his thumb in training two days before but refused a postponement and won a bruising tussle on points.

Eight knockouts and a revenge points win over Glen Lee were rewarded with another shot at the title, which had passed from Ross to Henry Armstrong. It was Garcia's bad luck to challenge two such brilliant fighters. Armstrong was virtually unbeatable at this time and won the decision in November 1938. Garcia moved up to middleweight and won nine more fights, which included two defeats of up-and-coming Lloyd Marshall. Twelve years of struggle paid off in October 1939 when his hooks exploded on Fred Apostoli's chin to take the world title (see page 96). He defended it against Glen Lee before an adoring crowd in Manila in December.

Garcia's next contest was a return against Henry Armstrong, of which boxing writer Bert Sugar observed: 'Even though Armstrong won handily, the decision came down a draw, one of boxing's little prearrangements that weigh more heavily than any opponent.' Armstrong said he was offered $15,000 by the mobster Bugsy Siegel to take a dive in the fourth round, the money to be delivered at the Main Street Gym. He refused. In 1982 Armstrong told Jack Fiske of the *San Francisco Chronicle* that he won seven out of ten rounds. When the fight was over, referee George Blake held both of his hands in the air, signifying a draw, then ducked between the ropes, leaving the ring and 20,000 at the stadium in Hollywood without an explanation. Blake 'knew that if he gave me a fight, he wouldn't get out of the ring alive,' said Armstrong. 'I felt it was a plain robbery. Only those who saw the referee hold up both hands realized it was a draw. Otherwise, there was no announcement.'

The Filipino lost in his next defence, to Ken Overlin, in New York on 23 May 1940. He boxed a few times more, was inactive for two-and-a-half years, then returned to the ring in 1944. He finally quit after losing on points to Wild Bill McDowell. Garcia was named to Governor Earl Warren's California Sports Commission in 1950 and to the Eisenhower–Nixon Sports Commission in 1951. In 1980, at the age of 70 (or 74), he went to the Philippines and returned with a bride! He died of lung cancer on 1 January 1981 in San Diego hospital and was buried, fittingly, in North Hollywood's Valhalla Memorial Park.

★ ★ ★

Ken Overlin asserted his independence at birth, arriving prematurely and without the aid of a doctor. There were never any strings on Overlin. He spent his life on the move, first as a sailor, then as journeyman pugilist. Publicist Harry Markson called him 'the last of the great carpetbaggers'. Overlin himself was very frank. He said of boxing, 'It is a stinking racket but I like it.'

Of Irish–American descent, Kenneth Edwin Overlin was born on 15 August 1910 in Decatur, Illinois. He wasn't much of a scrapper as a boy, preferring basketball and football. After leaving school he worked as a bellhop but was fired and signed on for the US Navy. He had never had a street fight in his life and was not interested in boxing.

On the USS *Tennessee* of the Pacific Fleet, he played in the football team for Jake Shugrue, who was also the boxing coach. Shugrue persuaded him to box Paul Delaney, a professional, at Crystal Pool, Seattle, one night in 1927. Overlin won in a free-swinging brawl. He fought Delaney again the next week, won again, and got a taste for boxing. Soon he would compete wherever his ship was in port, up and down the West Coast from Tacoma to San Diego. Though the bouts do not show up on any records, he is also said to have boxed in Australia, the South Sea Islands, South America and Europe — indeed wherever his ship tied up.

Boxing became his career, but he still had to serve out his time in the navy. He transferred to the Atlantic Fleet and joined the USS *Idaho* at Newport News, Virginia. Boxing was illegal in this state at the time, but bootleg bouts were held in various towns. Before one early bout with Spike Webb of Florida, Overlin was married in the ring to Madeline Smith of Portsmouth, Virginia. The groom wore boxing trunks and ring shoes and Webb was best man. Promoters liked Overlin: he sold tickets to all his shipmates and would always bring in a good crowd. He decided he needed a manager and engaged Chris Dundee, a young ex-newsboy with a stable of fighters in Norfolk, Virginia. Dundee eventually helped him get a discharge.

After leaving the navy he became a journeyman, often travelling alone. His first name opponent was Vince Dundee, to whom he lost in August 1932. He became a favourite among the fans in Virginia; though he had no punch to speak of, he was shifty and ringwise and gave value for money. Between January 1933 and October 1936, Overlin boxed 60 times, losing just twice — to contenders Paul Pirrone and Jimmy Smith. He beat men like Al Diamond, Anson Green, Al Quaill and Oscar Rankins, all good fighters.

His good run was ended by losses to Ted Yarosz and Kid Tunero at the end of 1936, but he bounced back to beat Fred Apostoli and secured a title bout with Freedie Steele in Seattle. The bout was postponed twice when Overlin went down with jaundice. He had still not recovered when the contest went ahead in September 1937, and he was stopped for the first and only time in his career in four rounds.

Overlin continued to fight out of a suitcase, travelling from coast to coast and also fitting in a brief trip to Australia, where he failed to win in three bouts. He stayed in the good-but-not-great contender mould for several more years until a bout with Al Wardlow in August 1939. Wardlow had won 24 straight but Overlin floored him three times in the first three rounds and gave him a boxing lesson for the rest of the contest. Mike Jacobs was at ringside and was so impressed that he contacted Chris Dundee and signed Overlin to fight Garcia for the title.

The bout was postponed three times before they finally got together on 23 May 1940 in New York. Overlin, who went to training camp for the first time in his life, won on points after 15 rounds. He never had any inflated ideas about his own worth, however: 'We are just a lot of bums alongside Harry Greb and the other old timers. I think Harry could lick me and Garcia in the same ring the same night with no rest between.'

Overlin retained his title twice, both times against Steve Belloise, and fought 13 non-title bouts. He most wanted a unification bout with rival champion Tony Zale, but Sam Pian, Zale's manager, was a mortal enemy of Mike Jacobs and wouldn't let one of his boxers fight for him. Otherwise, life was pretty enjoyable. Once described as 'a good talker, kind of a wise guy', Overlin was a snappy dresser and was reputed to have 500 ties and 45 suits.

He lost his title to Billy Soose, who had beaten him once before, on 9 May 1941. It was the first fight with large-screen theatre television, broadcast from Madison Square Garden to 1,400 fans in the nearby New Yorker Theatre. Soose, who won on points, admitted, 'It was a lousy fight. Two boxers don't make a good fight. He would jab and I would jab, and then we'd hold.' Overlin's camp questioned the credibility of the judges and wanted the commission to investigate. But the decision stood.

He was still good enough to beat future heavyweight king Ezzard Charles in his next bout and took a few more decent scalps before retiring in 1944. In all he won 128 of 149 bouts, just 23 inside the distance. He re-married in 1941 (he had divorced his first wife in 1938) and settled in Norfolk, where he became sports director of the radio station WCAV and hosted a nightly sports programme. He also tended bar in various cities, including Reno, Nevada, where in 1962 he needed emergency surgery for head injuries after he was slugged by a customer's gun butt. He died in Reno on 24 July 1969.

They said no college kid could ever be a boxing champion. Billy Soose proved them wrong. Born on 2 August 1915, the son of a Hungarian steel worker in Farrell, Pennsylvania, he was so keen on fighting that he was once thrown out of a gym because he was too young to box. He made his amateur debut at 15, weighing 98lb, and became a Golden Gloves champion. Billy continued boxing at Penn State College under the guidance of old-timer Leo Houck. Some say he became the finest ever college fighter, winning all his 14 freshman and varsity matches by knockout. He decided to leave his studies and turn professional when a new rule was introduced banning all former Golden Gloves winners from inter-collegiate fighting.

Paul Moss, a local man who worked in radio and publicity in Hollywood, was asked to manage Soose by some Farrell businessmen who were backing the boxer to turn pro. Moss wired Soose the fare to California and pulled a useful publicity stunt by getting film star Dick Powell to say he was going to manage Soose. Moss himself was not the typical handler. Bob Considine wrote: 'Soose's relationship with his manager, Paul Moss, has created downright alarm in the beak-breaking business. It is revolutionary in that there is no master-servant aspect to it. Moss, a rugged-looking, quick-witted hometowns-man of Soose's, rarely goes into Soose's corner any more. Makes Moss nervous. . . . He can't look at Soose getting hit without a surge of sympathetic reaction.'

Soose, who was over 6ft tall, won his debut against Johnny Dean in the semi-final bout on the Henry Armstrong–Baby Arizmendi bill in March 1938. His qualities, according to Considine, were 'a clean, crackling right hand punch, a nagging, hooking left and some of the most classic footwork this side of a Currier and Ives print'. But he was only making $150 a fight and went into the red when he had to have his tonsils out. Then came an offer of $1,000 to fight experienced Al Quaill. Soose injured his right in the first but won with his educated left jab.

Moss got him a job in a steel plant in the hope of strengthening his right hand, then sent him to New York to work with Ray Arcel. He also wrote to Mike Jacobs: 'It is not my intent to bore you with words about this boy's fighting ability. Such a description would have to be secondhand if it were to carry any weight, since my experience in the boxing game is limited to what I have gathered around the country during the last six months, the sum total of which has convinced me that I know little or nothing. So I must rely on boxing men like Harry Keck, Ray Arcel, Nate Lewis, and I trust that they are at least partly correct when they say he is the most outstanding fighting prospect in the ring today.'

His first bout under Arcel was against the great Charley Burley. Moss approached Arcel in New York's Stillman's Gym and said, 'I made a match in Pittsburgh, and I'm not sleeping nights because everybody tells me that my fighter will get knocked out.' Soose, however, boxed skilfully and lost a close points decision. Afterwards, Arcel saw Soose crying in the dressing room and said, 'What are you crying about? I'm the happiest guy in the world. You went ten rounds with the greatest fighter living today.'

In his 13th bout Soose avenged his only other defeat, to Johnny Duca. But he injured his hand again. It required an operation and he was out of the ring for seven months. He came back in September 1939 to beat Joe Fedz in one round, then lost on points to the excellent Georgie Abrams. Soose ended what had been a frustrating year by beating five more opponents, including Paul Pirrone and Jimmy Jones.

The former college boy lost just once in 12 bouts in 1940, to Abrams, his nemesis. What made it a special year was that he beat both reigning champions, Ken Overlin and Tony Zale, in a month. He fought Overlin in an over-weight match in Scranton, Pennsylvania. The champion was a 3-1 favourite but at the beginning Soose sank a heavy right into his stomach and won from then on, according to the two judges (the referee gave it to Overlin). Moss then got him a bout with Zale, again over the weight. Zale hit him with everything in the first two rounds but he survived and to win the remaining eight.

Three more wins in 1941 earned Soose a crack at Overlin's title. He outboxed the boxer to win over 15 rounds on 9 May in New York. He later recalled: 'When I won the title I was the happiest guy in the world. But the next day I cried like a baby. I had nothing left to win. I didn't want to win any more titles.' He never defended his mantle. After three non-title bouts, including a third loss to Abrams, he relinquished it in November 1941 and became the number one light-heavyweight contender. He boxed twice more but his motivation had gone and he retired after losing to Jimmy Bivins in January 1942.

Soose later managed 400 acres of his own lakeside property at Lake Wallenpaupack, Pennsylvania, and opened a restaurant, hotel and marina. He sold most of the land in the late 1980s for $2.5 million. He nowadays winters at his second home in Florida.

7

The Rotten Apple

THE New York State Athletic Commission was a law unto itself in the 1930s. It ran boxing by diktat. New York was the world's premier fight city, with the best boxers and the biggest bouts. Its sporting rulers had power out of all proportion to their geographic area of control. Their worst trait was xenophobia. No European boxer was allowed to fight for the New York version of the world title in the 1930s, a time when Europe produced some of its finest middleweights. Men like Marcel Thil, Len Harvey, Jock McAvoy and Eric Seelig were frozen out.

Another power source operated on a different level. Hoodlums reached for the heart of the sport. With the repeal of Prohibition, the nature of New York's gangland changed. Mobsters who had made fortunes from illicit booze were looking for new rackets to organize and exploit. Where once the likes of Owney Madden bought parts of boxers' contracts and acted as sleeping partners, now they simply muscled in. Many licence-holding managers were no more than front men for crooks. If a manager didn't play ball, his boxers missed out on the important bouts. Or worse.

The most insidious of this new breed of villain was Frankie Carbo, *aka* 'Mr Gray'. A career gangster, he was implicated in dozens of crimes and arrested 17 times for offences ranging from vagrancy to murder. At 20 he admitted the manslaughter of a cab driver and was sent to Sing Sing prison. He was later indicted for shooting a member of the infamous Brooklyn killing crew Murder Incorporated. The prosecution's case collapsed when its chief witness, Abe 'Kid Twist' Reles, 'fell' out of a window while under police protection. Carbo was particularly interested in boxing; in time, his tentacles spread everywhere, partly through his control of America's leading promoter, Mike Jacobs, head of the Twentieth Century Sporting Club, and partly through his contacts with other powerful hoods such as Philadelphia's Blinky Palermo. Boxers who rejected his orders were frozen out of title fights. Bouts were rigged. Officials were bribed. Such was Carbo's grip on boxing, it took 30 years to curtail his activities.

The rest of the world recognized Marcel Thil as champion. New York had to be different. Its sporting commission, in disarray over the resignation of chairman James Farley (to become Governor Franklin Roosevelt's presidential campaign manager), sanctioned an elimination tournament of its own to find a successor to Mickey Walker. It nominated Chick Devlin, Frank Battaglia, Paul Pirrone and Ben Jeby. Boxers of the calibre of Dave Shade, Vince Dundee, Gorilla Jones and, of course, anyone from Europe, were omitted. Jeby eviscerated Pirrone in six rounds, flooring him six times. Battaglia, a Canadian, appeared to have beaten Devlin, but received only a draw. In a decider, Jeby outpointed Devlin over 15 rounds for the New York version of the world title on 21 November 1932.

Jeby was a native New Yorker, born on 27 December 1909 to poor Polish–Jewish immigrants in a fourth-floor railroad flat. His real name was Benjamin Morris Jebaltowski. In his teens he worked as a plumber's mate for $15 a week and boxed in 'watch' fights (ostensibly amateur bouts where the winner received a watch, which he would then sell back to the organizers for a few dollars). He was only 5ft 8in tall and lacked a finishing punch but compensated for that with a crowding, aggressive style. *Boxing Illustrated* called him 'a tough-bodied youth with a hook-nose that made his face look like the business end of a crowbar'.

Jeby turned pro at 18 under Hymie Caplin, the doyen of Jewish managers, and made steady but unspectacular progress as a prelim boy at venues like Ridgewood Grove and Broadway Arena. In 1930 he dropped a decision to Vince Dundee, but beat his brother Joe. His best result was a close points win over Len Harvey in 1931. Generally, however, he lost the big ones. He was outpointed by Dundee again and by Young Terry, and drew and lost against Dave Shade. He was left out of the NBA's championship tournament (see page 90) and in March 1932 was bombed out of the frame altogether by Battaglia, a trip-hammer hitter, in 80 seconds in Chicago.

Jeby took four months off to assess his future. He returned to the ring with four confidence-boosting wins, but he was still lucky to qualify for the NYSAC tournament. Being a New Yorker who rarely fought outside the city helped. There was nothing second-rate about his victory over Pirrone, however, nor his subsequent decision over Devlin. He then defended against Battaglia at Madison Square Garden in January 1933. Only 6,000 fans turned out to see Jeby plod forward and suck the resolve from the Canadian. The referee stopped it in round 12. After beating Pirrone in a non-title affair, Jeby drew with Vince Dundee over 15 rounds in March. In April came the peculiar no-contest with NBA champ Gorilla Jones (see page 91), and in July he turned the tables on another man who had beaten him, taking a 15-rounds points decision off Young Terry with the title at stake.

Jeby's reign ended on 9 August 1933, when he was knocked out in seven rounds by Lou Brouillard. 'Lou Brouillard was the best of the lot,' said Jeby. 'He was rough and tough, a good boxer and terrific puncher. His southpaw style was hard to figure out.' Jeby boxed on, but losses to Terry, Dundee, Teddy Yarosz and others ruled him out of contention. He retired in 1936, returning to the plumbing trade, and was active in union circles and local politics. His wife Evelyn was a former chorus girl. Later he worked for the New York Inspector General's office as a 'shoofly', investigating corruption. He brought to the job the same dogged determination which characterized his ring persona. Shortly before retiring, he was offered a civic job helping to clean up the Times Square area, but turned it down to devote his life to boxing. He hoped to recruit a stable of fighters and was a regular visitor at Bobby Gleason's gym.

Fighting Lucien Pierre 'Lou' Brouillard was like tangling with an angry fireplug. Short — around 5ft 6in — and squat, with bull shoulders, thick arms and no neck, Brouillard's idea of the noble art was to close in and hurl leather. One writer called him 'two parts stampeding buffalo, one part maniac'. Nominally a southpaw, he could bang equally painfully with either mitt. Like most abnormally aggressive boxers, he was pleasant and friendly outside the ring, with baby-blue eyes and a pug-nosed face vaguely reminiscent of Jimmy Cagney. He had a taste for camel-hair coats, Cuban cigars and German beer.

Brouillard was of French–Canadian extraction, one of nine children, and was born on 23 May 1911 in the village of St Eugene, outside Quebec. The family moved to New Hampshire when Lou was seven. The area was covered in soot from the chimneys of the nearby Manchester mills. He once said, 'We had lace curtains and every day the soot dirtied them. And every night my mother would wash and iron them.' He quit school at 15 and inevitably worked at the local mill, training at nights. He won 37 of 39 amateur contests and was called 'Larrupin' Lou' for his no-holds-barred style. He trained hard: 'I was such a stickler for training that one night while out with my girlfriend I had an ice cream. Fearful of putting on weight, I ran all the way home.'

Brouillard turned professional in 1928 under manager Maurice LeMoine and fought 64 times in his first three years, winning 60. In 1931 he broke into the welterweight ratings by outscoring Canada Lee and Baby Joe Gans and stopping Paul Pirrone and Al Mello. In July he beat the welter champion, Young Jack Thompson, in a non-title bout in Boston. Thompson, a boxer so slick it was said he could remove his socks without taking off his shoes, gave him a shot at the title in October. Brouillard came out swinging and dropped Thompson twice on the way to a points win. He was just 20.

He did not hold the title for long. In December he took some dreadful low blows before Paul Pirrone was thrown out of their non-title bout for fouling. Foolishly, he was back in the ring five days later for a tough ten-round draw with Baby Joe Gans. He hadn't recovered from either contest when, in January 1932, he met Jackie Fields. Fields recalled: 'Al Lacey, who was my friend, my trainer, told me not to worry about the left hand. Watch the right hand. In about the fourth or fifth round he hit me with that left hand, I thought the building fell on me.' Fields recovered, knocked Brouillard down in the eighth, and took his title on points.

Brouillard was finding welterweight hard to make. Before leaving the class, he scored his best win to date, outpointing the great Jimmy McLarnin and putting him in hospital for three days. He also changed managers to the well-connected Johnny Buckley, who handled heavyweight champ Jack Sharkey. Initially, he dropped several decisions as a middleweight, but in May 1933 he beat Sammy Slaughter and in July licked Mickey Walker before 14,000 fans in Boston Garden. 'I could've won by a bigger margin if I had not kept thinking he was holding back and would cut loose at any minute,' said Brouillard.

In August he challenged Jeby for the New York title. It was a dour struggle. Brouillard softened him up with a body attack before connecting with a right in the seventh to put him out for the count, only the second man ever to do so. He splashed out on a Massachusetts restaurant with a sign outside: 'Inside this place you eat it and like it.' The NBA switched its recognition to him after its own champion, Gorilla Jones, was suspended.

Again, he found it easier to win the title than to keep it. On 30 October he lost to Vince Dundee in 15 dull rounds, Dundee being smart enough not to trade blows with him. So Brouillard was a double ex-champion at 22. For the next two years he boxed at the highest level without getting another title shot. He twice beat Bob Olin, a future light-heavyweight champion, took decisions from Al Gainer, Young Corbett III and Swede Berglund, and beat the much-avoided Oscar Rankins inside the distance. In November 1935 he went to Paris to meet the real champion, Marcel Thil. He was outpointed in a non-title fight, but victory over the Belgian champion Gustave Roth secured him a challenge for the title. He lost on a disputed foul, a result repeated 13 months later.

He should have retired, but he carried on, and even then lost only to men of the first rank. He was stopped for the only time in his career by Tiger Jack Fox, one of the all-time great knockout artists, and was outpointed by top light-heavyweights such as Gus Lesnevich, Anton Christofordis and Lloyd Marshall. He finally bowed out in January 1940 after a loss to Henry Chmielewski. After Pearl Harbor at the end of 1941, he joined the army as PT instructor, then worked at a shipyard. An injury forced him to retire. His wife Minnie, the daughter of gym owner Joe Beston, raised and sold golden retrievers at their home in Hanover, 30 miles from Boston. They had six children and a small army of grandchildren. Brouillard died on 14 September 1984 after a long battle against Alzheimer's Disease.

Boxers like Vince Dundee no longer exist. He fought 120 times before getting a title shot: ten thankless years of pain and bruises in smoky clubs and draughty arenas. His family — real name Lazarro — were Italian but emigrated from Rome to Baltimore before Vincent arrived on 22 October 1907. He was the youngest of five sons who all liked to fight. At the age of 15 Vince followed his brother Joe into professional boxing under manager Max Waxman. They were to become the first brothers to win world titles, Joe at welterweight, Vince at middleweight.

Dundee learned his trade in four and six-rounders in Baltimore. A light-hitter, he was a steely character who knew every trick in the book and a few not in any book. He knew all the angles and was very hard to tag cleanly. He went unbeaten in his first 40 contests before dropping a decision to Andy DiVodi in New York. Dundee laboured on, boxing about once a month, winning most but dropping the odd decision. By 1930 he still hadn't broken into the top echelon. Jackie Fields had outpointed him four times. He did halt the winning streak of Ben Jeby, but then lost to My Sullivan.

The turning point for Dundee can be traced to his two 12-rounders in New York early in 1931 against Len Harvey. The British champion was one of the best technicians in the game. He was fresh from victory over Dave Shade, securing his status as the number one contender to Mickey Walker, still the nominal champion, and had been promised a world title clash. Harvey sailed to New York to showcase his talents and Dundee was selected as his first opponent at Madison Square Garden. All went to plan in the first round. Harvey uncorked a beautiful left hook to send Dundee to the boards for 'nine', then floored him again immediately for the same count.

Dundee now showed his mettle. He survived and rough-housed his way through the next few rounds, wrestling and mauling to avoid Harvey's cleaner long-range shots. After 12 rounds Harvey's corner thought he had won comfortably and were shocked, therefore, to see the unanimous decision go in favour of Dundee. The crowd booed and hurled debris into the ring. Gilbert Odd, in his biography of Harvey, wrote: 'There was no doubt in the minds of Harvey's companions that they had been well and truly taken for a ride by the gangster element that seemed to have New York boxing in its grip at that time. By making Len a strong favourite the bookmakers had cleaned up nicely with the adverse verdict.'

Five weeks later, they fought again. Harvey was favourite once more, but suspiciously large amounts were bet on Dundee in the hours before the start. This time, the visitor intended leaving nothing to chance. 'Harvey hit him with everything but the ringposts,' wrote Odd. Dundee ground his way back into the contest in the later rounds, but was punched across the ring in the last. Yet when the decision was announced, the referee and one judge had voted for him, with only one official going for Harvey. The booing was prolonged and police entered the ring to prevent a crowd invasion. That night, Dundee was taken to hospital by ambulance and remained there for several days.

Despite the punishment, Dundee was now a leading contender. He beat Jeby in June, but without the benefit of home advantage dropped a decision to Thil in Paris and could only draw with Jack Hood in London. Returning to the States, he then compiled 22 wins on the trot, his victims including Solly Krieger, Young Terry and Ken Overlin. His first tilt at the title was a draw with Jeby, now the New York champ. They could have passed for twins, sharing the same hunch-shouldered, broken-nosed, stolid aspect.

In late summer 1933, Dundee seemed to lose any chance of a further title fight by dropping two decisions to the division's rising star, Teddy Yarosz. But, boxing being what it is, he was Lou Brouillard's next challenger and took the crown off him after 15 rounds in Boston. He stayed there for his first defence against local favourite Andy Callahan, known as the 'Irish Hand Grenade'. Before a sell-out crowd the 'Grenade' detonated three big punches on Dundee's jaw in the first round and dumped him on the floor. The champion got up and slipped and rolled his way out of trouble. For the next few rounds he called on his vast experience, staying close to reduce his opponent's punching space. In the 12th he dropped the challenger for 'nine', then pulled away in the last three rounds to take the decision.

He beat Al Diamond on points in his second defence, in Paterson, New Jersey, in May 1934. But in September his title was pinched by the quick-hitting Teddy Yarosz, who won a 15-round decision in Pittsburgh. Ten months later, Dundee was stopped for the first and only time of his career. Freddie Steele floored him eleven times before the referee stopped the fight in round three. Despite three cracks in his jaw he was on his feet at the end.

Dundee staged a six-fight comeback in 1937 but, after dropping decisions to Billy Conn and Honeyboy Jones, he hung up his gloves for good. Not long after he survived a collision with a fast-moving passenger train that hurled his car 300 feet. Soon after, he was stricken with multiple sclerosis, eventually becoming a helpless cripple. Boxing mourned his death in Philadelphia on 27 July 1949. He was still only 41.

Had Teddy Yarosz possessed a punch to match his boxing skills he would have been unbeatable. In his 13-year career, encompassing 127 fights, he won only 16 inside the distance. Yet such was his skill that he cut a swathe through the welterweight and middleweight ranks. A fast-hitting, neat-boxing mechanic, he won the New York–NBA world title and at his pinnacle had lost just two of 86 fights. A crippling leg injury ended his reign and he was never the same force again.

Yarosz was born to a Polish–American family in Monaca, near Pittsburgh, Pennsylvania, on 24 June 1910. His brother Tommy became a top-ranked light-heavy. Yarosz, a tallish, clean-cut youth, turned pro as a welterweight. He was managed by Ray Foutts, an Ohio promoter. In four years he racked up an unbeaten sequence of 58 wins and a draw to become one of the most exciting prospects in boxing. People first took notice when he licked Bucky Lawless in July 1931; Lawless had twice beaten world welter champion Young Jack Thompson. In his 49th fight Yarosz beat left-hooker Jimmy Belmont to decide the best welter in the Pittsburgh area.

Eddie 'Kid' Wolfe handed him his first defeat in January 1933. (They fought four times in all, winning one apiece with two draws.) Yarosz bounced back with wins over former welterweight champion Tommy Freeman, former middleweight challenger Sammy Slaughter, Paul Pirrone and, as we have seen, Vince Dundee (twice). Young Terry beat him on points but again he rebounded, beating the highly-rated Jimmy Smith, Ben Jeby and former world champion Pete Latzo among others. Expert tuition from Ray Arcel refined his sharp-shooting style. Yarosz was a growing boy and often struggled to reduce weight. In July 1934 he collapsed at the end of a winning bout against Tait Littman. Weight-making was blamed.

His chance at the title came on 11 September 1934 against Vince Dundee. Yarosz had hometown advantage. At the end of 15 rounds he again collapsed and had to be carried to the dressing room. But the referee and a judge gave him the fight, though most spectators thought Dundee had done enough. According to *The Ring*, Dundee 'stood around bewildered by what he considered a bad decision and the sight of his conqueror being carried out practically dead to the world'.

The new champion wisely rejected an offer to fight Jock McAvoy in England, choosing instead to pick up easy purses in non-title fights. On New Year's Day 1935 he took on an unheralded trier called Eddie 'Babe' Risko in Scranton, Pennsylvania. Yarosz was at his peak and was supremely confident. In the upset of the year, he was dropped in the first round and tore a cartilage in his right leg. He never recovered. Risko had him down six times before the referee called a halt in round seven. The champion needed a leg operation before he could return to the ring.

They were re-matched and met for the title on 19 September in Pittsburgh. Risko had lost three times since their previous bout and Yarosz was a clear favourite, but just before the fight his leg went again. He bravely hobbled into the ring but was dropped for 'nine' in rounds six and seven and lost the decision. Yarosz needed another operation and his leg was put in irons to heal.

After a great deal of pain and physiotherapy, Yarosz launched a comeback. He looked as good as new in beating seven top middleweights in a row, including Risko, Ken Overlin and Lou Brouillard. But his title hopes faded when he lost twice to Pittsburgh's latest discovery, Billy Conn. Yarosz had now become a high-quality 'opponent', good enough to test, and sometimes beat, some excellent boxers, but never winning often enough to earn another title shot. Wins over Conn in a return, Ken Overlin, Archie Moore, Jimmy Reeves and Lloyd Marshall were cancelled out by losses to Carmen Barth, Georgie Abrams, Jimmy Bivins, Ezzard Charles and others. After losing a decision to Joe Muscatoe in February 1942, he retired. He died in his home town on 29 March 1974, after a long illness.

★   ★   ★

Eddie Risko's world title pretensions exploded in less than three minutes on a freezing December night in 1935. The champion who had come from nowhere was blasted into oblivion by a man unknown in American boxing circles. Risko's title wasn't at stake that night. But defeat revealed what many already knew: he was one of the worst boxers ever to hold a version of the middleweight crown.

He was born Henry Pylkowski, of Polish–Lithuanian extraction, in Syracuse, New York state on 14 July 1911. He grew into a big, handsome, powerful fellow. Work in the Syracuse coalmines gave him the body of an Adonis. He joined the US Navy and won the middleweight championship of the Atlantic Fleet in 1931 and 1933, boxing in seaports all over the world. He originally turned pro under the name Henry Pulaski, which he changed to Eddie Risko after a couple of years. He had little flair and was one-paced. In January 1934 he was knocked out by Swede Berglund in four rounds. The rest of the year went well and included wins over a fading Bucky Lawless, but there was little to suggest title potential. Indeed, Risko had boxed just two ten-rounders in his life when in January 1935 he met Ted Yarosz in a non-title fight. Most of his contests had been six-rounders.

His sensational defeat of Yarosz catapulted him to recognition. He was brought to New York three weeks later to meet Vince Dundee. The vastly experienced Dundee appeared to have won easily at the end of ten rounds; to the crowd's amazement, one judge and the referee awarded the bout to Risko. John Phelan, chairman of the NYSAC, was at ringside and immediately went into a huddle with fellow commissioner Bill Brown and the officials. Fifteen minutes later, the decision was reversed. Phelan said judge Sidney Scharlin had Dundee ahead on rounds but for some reason had marked Risko as winner on the back of his card. Brown left hastily, saying he was 'afraid to look people in the face'.

New Yorkers were unimpressed with the visitor. The *Times* said, 'Risko is nothing but a strong, willing fighter. He knows little or nothing of the rudiments of boxing. He winds up and thrusts his blows like a seaman battling on the after-deck of a man-o'-war in fleet competitions.' Ensuing wins over Paul Pirrone, Sammy Slaughter and Frank Battaglia suggested that perhaps the Yarosz result was no fluke, but losses to Jimmy Belmont and Pirrone in a return kept Risko's talent in perspective. Nonetheless, he secured a title fight and won from Yarosz. Around this time the hoodlum Frankie Carbo moved in to act as 'adviser' to his manager, Gabe Genovese. Risko next won three non-title bouts, earning money without risking his title, though ominously Frank Battaglia had him on the floor.

Five days before Christmas Risko took on Jock McAvoy of Rochdale, England. Risko's handlers insisted that McAvoy weigh above the limit, to protect the title. It was a mistake, allowing McAvoy to come in at 12 stone, seven pounds heavier than Risko. Indeed the whole venture was a blunder. McAvoy was not the stereotypical British boxer. He was a human wrecking ball who was to stop or knock out an incredible 92 opponents in his career. As they waited to start, the 'Rochdale Thunderbolt' stood gnawing his glove, an ominous habit. At the bell, he simply walked across the ring and swept Risko off his feet with a crushing right. The champion jumped up too quickly and was mugged without mercy. He went down a total of six times before the referee counted him out after two minutes and 48 seconds of the first round.

Justice demanded a title fight for McAvoy. But the shadowland of Frankie Carbo offered no such possibility. Carbo would have lost his hold on the championship if it had gone abroad. In February 1936 Risko returned to the ring with a successful points defence against Tony Fisher. Then he lost two of his next three bouts. On 11 July 1936, Freddie Steele took his title on points in Seattle.

Risko was subsequently beaten by Teddy Yarosz. He redeemed himself with a win over the over-praised kayo artist Harry Balsamo and a couple more wins brought him a rematch with Steele. Again, he lasted the distance but lost the decision. It was the end of the line for Risko. He won only one of his last 13 bouts and was stopped eight times. In one 19-day period alone he lost three times inside the distance, something which would not be allowed today, as contestants are forbidden from boxing for a certain period after a knockout defeat. His conquerors included Al Hostak, Billy Soose and Lloyd Marshall, who put him into retirement in 1939. He died on 7 March 1957 in Syracuse.

Freddie Steele was perhaps the best American middleweight of the 1930s. A gutsy and talented Irish–American, he overcame appalling luck to win the title. Steele was his stepfather's name; his real father walked out three months after Freddie was born on 18 December 1912 in Seattle. They had no contact until years later when Steele received a congratulatory post-fight telegram from him. The boy's interest in boxing began when at the age of six he watched Tod Morgan, a well-known boxer of the time, in training. His family settled in Tacoma when he was 13 and Steele became a good high school athlete. After a brief spell as an amateur boxer, his uncle took him to Dave Miller, who became his manager.

Steele started as a professional welterweight at the age of 15. He grew to be 5ft 10½in, with a 73-inch reach, which gave him substantial physical advantages over most of his opponents. He won fight after fight to become the best at his weight in Washington state. Then, late in 1931, he developed serious kidney problems. Doctors told him he would never fight again, but he recovered during a five-month break from boxing. By the age of 19 he had dropped just one decision, to Tony Portillo, in 60 fights. His best results had been two impressive knockouts of Ceferino Garcia, the volatile Filipino.

Disaster struck in January 1933 when Leonard Bennett broke Steele's jaw. He fought on to win a six-round decision, then fainted from the pain. Just when his jaw had healed, his car skidded into an apartment house and burst into flames. Steele was knocked unconscious and would have died but for neighbours who dragged him from the burning wreck. Later that year he was stopped in the first round by Nash Garrison. He shrugged off these calamities to go 44 bouts without defeat, beating the best boxers in the US and winning the New York–NBA title.

In 1935 he crashed the rankings by stopping Fred Apostoli, breaking Vince Dundee's jaw (becoming the only man ever to stop him) and outpointing former champion Gorilla Jones. A year later he secured a title shot by beating Eddie Risko in a non-title match. They fought with the crown at stake in Seattle in July 1936 and Steele won on points. He followed it with six non-title wins, including a brilliant two-round defeat of Gus Lesnevich. Carbo moved in on Steele after he won the title.

His first defence was against Gorilla Jones in Milwaukee in January 1937. Steele was stunned in round seven by a right to the jaw and replied by dropping Jones with his own perfectly timed right cross. This was the only high spot of the fight, which Steele won on points. He made four more successful defences, against Risko, Frank

Battaglia, Ken Overlin and Carmen Barth. Harold Conrad of the *Brooklyn Eagle* called him 'one of the modern school of pugilism, a clean-cut, well-spoken lad, with a surprising sense of humour for a guy who can be so serious in the ring'.

Boxing fans had been waiting a long time for the two best middleweights in the world to fight. It finally happened in January 1938 when Steele met Fred Apostoli in a non-title fight. Apostoli had beaten Marcel Thil the previous year. The contest was even until round seven, when a low blow knocked the fight out of the Seattle man. A New York law forbade the awarding of fights on a foul and Steele was given 18 seconds to recover. It wasn't enough. He was shipping punishment and bleeding, though still on his feet, when the bout was stopped in the ninth. New York ordered Steele to put his title on the line in a rematch with Apostoli. He refused and was stripped of his title by the NYSAC in February. Perversely, he retained the recognition of the NBA.

Steele beat Solly Krieger in a non-title fight, then met Al Hostak in a defence. All those fights finally caught up with him: he was wasted in one round. He retired for three years, was knocked out in a comeback bout in 1941 by Jimmy Casino, and retired for good. His record showed 139 contests, of which he won 124 and lost just six. Steele became a moderately successful movie actor, appearing with the likes of Robert Mitchum and George Raft. He died on 23 August 1984 in Aberdeen, Washington state.

Al Hostak was built like a pipe cleaner. With corn-blond hair, blue eyes and skinny arms, he looked like the kind of guy who got sand kicked in his face on the beach. But he was one of the hardest-hitting of all middleweights. Scribes often compared him to Stanley Ketchel, though he lacked the 'Assassin's' inner fury. Hostak would stalk like a mantis, his hands held high, looking to connect with electric punches at blinding speed. He was particularly dangerous in the early rounds, taking out opponents before they knew what had hit them.

Hostak was born in Minneapolis on 7 January 1916, the son of a Czechoslovakian glass worker. The family later settled in the Seattle suburb of Georgetown. His father bought him some boxing shoes and he started training at old-timer Eddie Marino's gym in Seattle. He was not a particularly good young athlete but showed promise as a boxer.

Hostak is credited with winning 24 amateur fights, 17 by kayo. His first pro bout was in 1934, apparently against an opponent calling himself the Tukwila Woodchopper. Hostak hacked him down in two. He fought in Seattle without defeat for almost five years. A five-round knockout of Mike Bazzone in 1936 started him on a run of 17 straight wins inside the distance. His victims included Young Terry, Eddie 'Babe' Risko and Swede Berglund.

On 26 July 1938 promoter Nate Druxman matched him with champion Freddie Steele for the title. Hostak had long had to play second fiddle to Steele in their home town. Jack Dempsey was brought in as referee and 30,000 fans packed into a local ball park. In a scorching display, Hostak dropped Steele four times and knocked him out in just 1min 42sec.

After winning a non-title bout, Hostak put his title on the line in November against Solly Krieger. Before another big Seattle crowd, Hostak was boxing well until he hit Krieger on the head with a left. The impact broke three bones in his hand. Shortly afterwards, he broke a blood vessel in his right hand. Krieger won on points.

Solly Krieger has been described as 'the last world champion of the Jewish Golden Age', that spell during the 1920s and '30s when New York's Jewish community produced some of the world's best boxers. He was born on 28 March 1909 in Williamsburg, Brooklyn. His father was an immigrant tailor from Poland. Solly was an excellent high school athlete, a member of his school's baseball, football, soccer and basketball teams. He also loved boxing, but his father did not. To disguise his activities, Solly used the name Danny Auerbach for his first amateur bouts at 15.

He won a sub-novice Golden Gloves title in 1928 with seven victories, and repeated his success in an inter-city tournament in Chicago. He also worked as an errand boy in a silk house after leaving school. Krieger turned pro late in 1928 with Hymie Caplin, mentor of ghetto wizards Sid Terris, Ruby Goldstein and Al Singer. He fought prelims for a couple of years before moving up to main events. He showed power in flooring Hans Mueller ten times in eight rounds, but then was kayoed for the first time by the vastly more experienced Vince Dundee in October 1931.

Krieger boxed without particular distinction until 1934, when he became plagued by elbow trouble. Early in his career he had been a clever boxer with a good punch, relying on movement and skill. However, after injuring his left elbow in a handball game he developed bursitis, which required surgery. He never regained full extension of the arm. With his jabbing ability reduced, he developed into a weaving aggressor with a potent left hook. He said, 'I started walking in on my opponents, but I countered. People used to think I was taking a beating but I could weave while standing still. That operation was the turning point of my life.'

For the next two years he won regularly, featuring in some thrilling bouts. His points win in 1936 over Oscar Rankins, a red-headed black fighter, was one of the best bouts ever seen in Pittsburgh. Krieger was on the verge of collapse early on but had Rankins on the floor at the final bell. He also had good wins over Frank Battaglia and Harry Balsamo.

In 1937, he dropped several decisions and was stopped by Fred Apostoli with a cut eye. He put himself back in contention with a great upset over Billy Conn in Pittsburgh. Conn observed: 'Krieger, he fixed me up the first time. He beat me. I had won about 38 fights in a row. I was a little out of shape and I got a great lesson from Mr Krieger. I was never out of shape afterwards. That was a bad man to take it easy with, Krieger. He gave me a lesson, boy! He just banged me all over the place. He was a real good hitter and he could take it. You couldn't hurt him. I got even with him a couple of times.'

A run of knockouts, briefly interrupted by a couple of points wins, brought Krieger his shot at Al Hostak. The challenger was staggered several times by short rights but settled into his rhythmic pressure and gave the champion a systematic hiding to the ribs. Hostak stood no chance after damaging his hands in mid-bout. Krieger closed both his eyes and knocked him down for 'two' with a left hook in the 14th round. Yet he won only on a majority decision, one judge calling it a draw.

Krieger had seven non-title bouts, losing two to Billy Conn, before he gave Hostak a return on 27 June 1939. The Seattle man's hands were healed and he was back to his best. He put Krieger down for 'nine' in the third and then for 'seven', when he was saved by the bell.

Right hands sent him down twice more in the fourth and referee Jim Braddock stopped it. Krieger then moved up to light-heavy, where his blows didn't carry the same force. He retired in 1941 after losing to Lee Savold.

Krieger was a rather reserved person but had dabbled in politics while boxing, once standing unsuccessfully for councilman. During his career he blew most of his earnings on the horses. On retirement he opened a tavern in Brooklyn, which flopped. He moved down to Miami Beach and worked for Pumpernick's restaurant, becoming its most famous parking attendant. He died in Las Vegas in 1965.

Hostak was the champion again. And he was punching harder than ever. In his first defence, he demolished Germany's Eric Seelig in 81 seconds. It needed an iron man to beat him. Such a man was Tony Zale. He outpointed Hostak in a non-title bout, then flattened him in two championship fights (see page 122). The Seattle slugger then dropped a couple of decisions and was inactive for over a year. He came back to stop hard men Glen Lee and Anton Raadik and was active on and off until 1949. He owned a gas station bought while he was champion and later became deputy sheriff of King County.

8

Rocky and the Steel Man

TONY ZALE was two years old when his life changed forever. His father died, struck by a car while cycling from a drug store with medicine for his son. Young Tony was traumatized. For months after, whenever he saw a man on a bicycle, he would toddle to his mother, calling out, 'Daddy's coming.' He later told the Los Angeles *Herald Examiner*, 'I developed a shyness, terribly. I couldn't face people. My mother would take me to visit people and I'd hide. Boxing helped me out of that, not completely, of course. If you're backward, if you're leery, if you are ashamed, you can't proceed. When I'm in the ring I'm free.' Only in a boxing ring could he express himself.

Zale was born on 29 May 1913 in the slums of Gary, an Indiana steel town. His family were Polish–American Catholics and he was christened Anthony Florian Zaleski. The death of his steelworker father left Mrs Zaleski to raise five sons and two daughters. With no money coming in, the children worked as soon as they were able. And that meant the steel mills. 'It seems like I worked in the steel mills ever since I was weaned,' said Zale, 'and it was backbreaking work. But my mother would have broken my *neck* if I'd ever stolen anything from anybody. Our home was hungry, but it was a proud home. We all brought back whatever money we earned to keep it going.'

He detested the mills: 'I hated getting up at six in the morning and breathing the burnt air, catching the hot rivets that could burn a hole right through you if you missed. I wanted out. So when I went to the gym one Saturday to watch my older brother box, the sweat around the punching bags and in the ring smelled like Chanel Number Five to me. I knew then that the ring ropes, the canvas and the punching bags were the way out.'

His brother John took him to a local fight club where one of the men, on seeing his physique, said, 'You look like you're made out of steel.' The nickname 'Man of Steel' stuck throughout his life. Zale started boxing as amateur at age 15. Zale found he forgot his shyness in the ring. He willingly took the beatings and became a regular at Johnny Coulon's club on Chicago's South Side.

The small halls hummed with activity, with six shows a week. Zale was not endowed with great natural talent. His style was predictable and he had trouble with smart movers. But he was patient and determined and slowly improved. He had a raw-boned, intimidating appearance. One magazine described him thus: 'The flesh on his face was parchment stretched tightly across his cheekbones. His hair, thin and mouse-blond, seemed always damp and snug on his head like a skullcap. But his body was chiseled, it seemed, out of some substance that normal men never own.' He strutted rather than walked, with his head and shoulders back and his chest pushed out.

In 1931 he won the lightweight title in the Indiana Golden Gloves. A year later he lost in the welterweight finals of the Chicago Golden Gloves. And in 1934 he made it to the national finals in Madison Square Garden, New York. His opponent, Melio Bettina, who went on to take the light-heavyweight world title, won on points. Zale's body-punching skill, his greatest asset, began here. Bettina hammered him around the kidneys and Zale saw the importance of defending his sides with his elbows and of delivering the same blows himself. Billy Soose once said that when 'Zale hits you in the belly it's like someone stuck a hot poker in you and left it there'. He finished with an amateur record of 87 wins and eight defeats.

He turned pro in 1934, two weeks after his 21st birthday, and fought once a week. He won his first nine contests, but then lost eight of his next 20, including a knockout by Johnny Phagan. His managers were impatient with his lack of success and the money dried up. Zale, for the only time in his life, lost heart. He quit and went back to the mills. Zale later called it 'the worst beating I ever took'. With the exception of a draw in 1936, he was out of the ring for two years.

He returned in July 1937, guided by Sam Pian and Art Winch, handlers of the great welterweight Barney Ross. This time he gave it everything. He scored four wins, lost to the talented Nate Bolden, beat him in a rematch, and rounded off the year with another win. In 1938 he won twice more, then he faced a setback that would have crushed a lesser man. Jimmy Clark caught him cold in the first with a fast right and Zale was knocked out. In the dressing room he remembered nothing of the fight. His brother told him what had happened, and Zale spent the next few weeks in the gym working out how to block right crosses. In a rematch, he slaughtered Clark in eight rounds, and later knocked him out again in less than six minutes.

In 1938 Zale began the run that would take him to the title, winning seven fights in a row, six inside the distance. He was matched with Al Hostak, the NBA middleweight champion, in a non-title bout in Chicago in January 1939. Hostak had been flattening everybody, and he dropped Zale early on, but the 'Steel Man' came back to win. Later he admitted he couldn't remember anything of the early rounds.

Zale kept winning and Hostak was forced to grant him a title challenge. It took place in Seattle on 19 July 1940. Zale won in 13 brutal rounds. He recalled, 'Al was a courageous, fast puncher whose only weakness — if he had one — was his mid-section. It took me six rounds to get one good right smash below his ribs, but he fell apart after that. I figure it took me ten years to throw that one punch.' For the bashful Zale, there was no big celebration. He returned quietly to Gary.

A month later he surprisingly lost a non-title bout with Billy Soose. In November Zale outscored former champion Fred Apostoli in another non-title affair, and in January 1941 he stopped Tony Martin and outpointed Steve Mamakos. Mamakos put up a good fight, and was granted a chance at the title in Chicago on 21 February. Zale won in round 14. On 28 May in Chicago, Al Hostak tried to regain his title, but Zale let the punches go and simply blew him away inside two rounds.

Billy Soose gave up his claims (see previous chapter) to the world title, and on 18 November Zale was matched with Georgie Abrams to unify the different strands of the championship. Abrams was an unlucky middleweight. He had all-round talent and was at least as good as many of the 'champions' of the previous decade, but he never got the breaks. He beat Soose three times, after the last of which he was recognized as champion by the American Federation of Boxing, a minor midwest organization. It was the nearest he came to being a champ. Zale won on points after what *The Ring* called '15 rounds of blazing warfare that equalled anything in ferocity that historic middleweight battles down through the annals can offer'. Abrams floored the 'Man of Steel' for 'nine' in the first round, but in the second took a thumb in the eye. In the third he was butted and cut over his other eye, yet he staggered Zale in the eighth with a chopping left hook. Zale pulled out everything to win the decision. Abrams nearly lost his eye.

In February 1942 Zale lost a disputed decision in a non-title fight with the great light-heavyweight Billy Conn. It was his last bout for almost five years. Zale, a great patriot, joined the Navy and was stationed in Puerto Rico. Trainer Ray Arcel said, 'He was in the Coast Guard for four years. He was down in Puerto Pico. And he was a devout Catholic. He would never go out when they had a night off. He'd go in the gym and spar.' There was no question of the authorities taking away his title while the war was on. Zale came back in 1946 with a string of non-title kayos. But while he had been away, a new contender had risen through the ranks. The 'Steel Man' was about to meet the 'Rock'.

If Tony Zale's childhood was hard, Rocky Graziano's was anarchic. His real name was Rocco Barbella and he was born on 1 January 1922 in a decaying tenement in New York's lower East Side. He was Nick and Ida Barbella's fifth baby, but only the second to live more than a few months. Twin sisters born later died of pneumonia when there was no money to buy coal for the stove. The Barbellas were of Neapolitan descent; Nick was a former boxer, sometime dock worker and petty criminal. He gave Rocco his first taste of boxing, making him fight his older brother Joey in their flat to entertain his friends. Rocco hated it.

They moved to Brooklyn, where Rocco ran wild from the age of five. Hyperactive and a persistent truant, he would wait outside the schoolyard to mug other boys. 'I wandered all over the city, stealing what I could find to eat, sleeping when I got tired, wherever I was. I only come [sic] home when I got too lonesome and wanted to talk to somebody.'

His criminal education began in earnest when he returned to the East Side to live with his grandparents. He stole from trucks at stoplights, raided candy machines in subway stations, and sneak-thieved from cars. At 11 he was sent to the Catholic Protectory for stealing a bike. He emerged worse than before. Nicknamed Rocky

Bob, he led a mob of thieves and punks — 'Rocky Bob's mob was the class of the East Side' — in raids against rival cliques of Jews, Irish and Italians in dance halls and social clubs. By the age of 17, after three spells in the Protectory, he was the quintessential East Side hoodlum: good-looking in a tough way, hair slicked back, peg suit, pork pie hat and pointed shoes.

Further trouble led to the New York State Vocational School, the grim Tombs prison and the city reformatory. Barbella saw all authority as a challenge and frequently fought with the guards. Paroled, he filled in when a friend dropped out of an amateur boxing tournament. His natural punching power and street savvy took him all the way to the Metropolitan AAU welterweight title. A neighbourhood shark called Lupo the Wolf then fixed him up in watch fights. Graziano's philosophy was simple: 'I just come out to kill the bastard opposing me. If he hit me, I got like a wild animal . . . Sometimes the referee warned me about dirty fighting. What the hell do I care about dirty fighting?' While Rocky Bob cleaned up in the ring, his mob picked pockets and snatched purses in the crowd.

In 1940 he had his first professional bout for manager Eddie Coco under the name Robert Barber, knocking out 'this coloured guy' in the first round. His second opponent went in three. But in 1941 he was back in prison for violating parole and landed in Rikers Island penitentiary after a riot. Released in 1942, he was inducted into the US Army and sent to Fort Dix, New Jersey, for basic training. On his first morning he flattened a corporal for shouting at him. Hauled before the captain, he decked him as well and went on the run.

Short of money, Barbella went with his friend Terry Young, a pro boxer, to see manager Irving Cohen at the famous Stillman's Gym. Graziano later said he flattened a sparmate and Cohen begged him to sign. Others say Graziano was outboxed but that Cohen was impressed by his guts, and took him on. He started fighting under the name Tommy Rocky Graziano, taking the first name and surname from two friends to hide his identity from the military police. His first fight, in March 1942, was against Curtis Hightower at the Fort Hamilton Arena, Brooklyn, in front of 2,000 soldiers. No one recognized him, and he won in round two. Seven fights later he was caught by the police.

Private Rocco Barbella was court-martialled, dishonourably

discharged, and sentenced to one year in a military jail. There he joined the boxing team and for the first time realized the futility of his life. He was freed in the spring of 1943, still only 21, in the best shape of his life and with a changed outlook. By the end of the year he had fought 18 times, winning ten inside the distance, five on points, drawing once and losing twice. He was still wild, but his power was breathtaking. One victim, George Stevens, remarked, 'Man, that boy's got mayhem in his hands.' He graduated to eight-rounders, and got married, to Norma Unger.

In 1944 Graziano lost just once in 17 bouts. He was the hero of the small clubs in and around New York. Then, in November, came the big time: a main event at Madison Square Garden against Harold Green, a cagey pro. Green outsmarted him, dodging his rushes, tying him up and catching him with left hooks. They met again in December. Green outboxed his opponent until the tenth and last round, when Graziano launched a last-ditch assault. Green was floored with an overhand right, but the bell rang as the referee reached 'six'. Green got the decision.

Graziano's career had hit a dead end. Critics wrote him off as a flash in the pan. He was put up as cannon fodder for Billy Arnold, one of the best young prospects in the game, a 19-year-old Philadelphian with 32 wins in 33 fights, 28 inside the distance. Arnold, spoken of as a pocket Joe Louis, was controlled by Blinky Palermo and was a huge favourite, the price going as high as 11 to 1 on. The fight was set for eight rounds, and 14,000 people piled into Madison Square Garden on 9 March 1945.

Graziano started fast, unloading bombs, and took the first round. But in the second he was caught with some classic combinations, and started to flounder. The third round turned out to be a pivotal moment in fistic history. Arnold appeared to be in control when he walked into a shocking right. Another knocked him through the ropes onto the ring apron. Arnold hauled himself up, but another overhand missile sent him back again. He was on his feet at 'six', but was put down again face first for a count of 'seven'. After a final Graziano assault, the referee rescued Arnold. The 'Rock' was now a star.

That explosive performance changed everything. Graziano was big-time box office. In May he faced Al 'Bummy' Davis in New York. Davis, from the Jewish ghetto of Brownsville, had a similar background to Graziano and was a notoriously dirty fighter. They put on riotous melée, both hitting the canvas before Davis went down for good in the fourth. Six months later Davis died in a hail of bullets when he attacked four gunmen with his fists during a bar stick-up.

In June Graziano met the world welterweight champion, Freddie 'Red' Cochrane, at Madison Square Garden. The fight underlined both his faults and his strengths. Cochrane, aged 30, was a vastly experienced but vulnerable fighter, having lost 32 of his 112 fights. He was on a run of five straight inside-the-distance wins. For nine rounds he outboxed his artless young rival. In the tenth and last session, Graziano mounted one of his kamikaze swoops. It was enough to blast Cochrane to defeat. Two months later they met again in what was a carbon copy of the previous bout, with Cochrane building up a big lead before Graziano cut loose to win in the final round. Both bouts drew more than $100,000 at the gate.

Graziano's heart-stopping wins brought him a rematch in September with Harold Green, now unbeaten in 22 fights. Green won the first two rounds, but in the third he took a right and went down. Nat Fleischer, in *The Ring*, wrote, 'At eight he reached a sitting posture but couldn't rise, and as he sat, with the tears coming down his cheeks, it was apparent he would be counted out.' As the count was completed, Green sprang up and charged Graziano. His cornerman, Charles Duke, followed, throwing punches. Green was subsequently suspended and fined $1,000 for inciting a riot and Duke had his licence revoked. Forty-five years later, in an interview with *The Ring*, Green claimed the fight was fixed. He said that he was told to 'lay down' in the eighth round by Duke, who was alleged to have underworld ties. Green said he 'went' in the third instead because he didn't have the heart to continue and his subsequent reaction was one of shame and anger. He said he agreed to the fix because he thought it would help him get a title shot.

Whatever the truth, Graziano was now the biggest draw in boxing outside Joe Louis, and a leading contender for Zale's crown. His next opponent, George 'Sonny' Horne, was outpointed in January 1946, and in March came a bout with Marty Servo, who had just won the welterweight title. Graziano was a slight favourite, but just before fight-time there was a dramatic switch in the betting odds, making Servo a 10–1 favourite and creating rumours of a fix. The fight was almost cancelled, but Graziano insisted on going ahead. He butchered Servo inside two rounds, breaking his nose so badly that he was forced to retire. Graziano now had eight wins on the trot, seven inside distance. Tony Zale was back from the Navy and was also in sizzling form. The stage was set for the first middleweight title fight since 1941. Graziano, at 24, was a seven-to-two favourite over the 32-year-old champion.

★   ★   ★

None of the 40,000 fans who filed through the Yankee Stadium turnstiles on the evening of 27 September 1946, paying a total of $342,497, could have anticipated what they were about to see. There have been few, if any, fights like it in the whole of boxing. It was more akin to ancient gladiatorial combat than anything seen in the 20th century.

Graziano attacked like gangbusters from the first bell. Zale willingly met him and they collided in mid-ring. The champion kept Graziano away with jabs, then cracked a short left hook to the jaw. Rocky went down. He rose at 'four', but was caught by a mix of head and body blows. Graziano covered up until his head cleared, then surprised Zale with a wild attack. A huge right staggered the champion. Three more followed in quick succession and Zale was on the verge of going down himself when the bell rang. It had been a sensational first round.

Zale showed caution in the second but there was no holding Graziano. He stormed in and made the champion give ground under a fierce fusillade. Zale tried to fight back, but the 'Rock' punched through his defences and bloodied his mouth and nose. A scything right sent Zale crashing to the canvas, his bloody mouth agape, his right hand grabbing at the bottom rope. Referee Ruby Goldstein jumped in to stop Graziano slugging his foe on the floor and by the time he had persuaded him to go to a neutral corner, there was only time to count to 'three' before the bell rang. The ballpark was in an uproar.

The third round was brutal. Graziano punched his groggy rival from pillar to post, brushing aside his attempts to retaliate. He landed wicked left hooks and right crosses to the face and his hooks left blotches on the 'Steel Man's' torso. But Zale, using all his experience, managed somehow to avoid the pay-off blow, keeping the angles tight and denying Graziano room. 'I hit him and hit him and he staggers,' recalled Graziano, 'but every time I haul back for the killer, he has got me standing off balance.' The champion was still on his feet at the bell.

Unbelievably, Zale came out fresh for the fourth. He began to sink his fists into Rocky's ribs, and now it was the challenger who backed off first from the exchanges. Graziano tried a favourite move, leaning on his back foot to draw his opponent in for the right hand, but Zale was on him too quickly, pounding his belly and kidneys. Graziano was relieved to hear the bell.

For the first minute of the fifth round, Zale kept up his body attack. Graziano was biding his time. As Zale came in for another assault, the 'Rock' was ready. He struck with a quick one-two, then launched into an orgy of punching. Rights and lefts, swings, hooks, crosses and uppercuts rained in on Zale as the crowd went crazy. His head was punched from side to side and his knees bent as Graziano caught him in a blistering crossfire. But the 'Man of Steel' refused to buckle. He was saved again by the gong. His cornerman tried everything to revive him, but it was a weary champion who answered the bell for the sixth. Graziano roared in again. This was it. The world title was in his grasp.

The next thing he knew, he was sitting on the floor. A pile-driving shot to the solar plexus had knocked all the wind out of him. He rose, but his feet seemed rooted to the spot as Zale wound up a left hook and bounced it off his chin. Graziano fell heavily on his seat, his legs paralyzed. He grabbed the ropes to pull himself up, but his lower body wouldn't obey. Finally, he was up, but it was too late. Goldstein had counted him out. Graziano threw himself at Zale but was restrained by his trainers, while the champion, exhausted, was supported in his own corner.

According to Red Smith, Zale looked the loser. In his dressing room, he 'stood facing the press with [Art] Winch behind him, supporting him with both hands under the armpits. Tony kept trying to say something but his words were indistinguishable. Every few seconds he would sag toward the floor and Winch would straighten him up. At long last Tony got four words out. "Clean living did it," he mumbled.' The pay cheque was some compensation. Each fighter got 30 per cent ($78,892) of the gate, under a curious agreement that actually guaranteed Zale more if he lost.

Both boxers took a well-earned rest. But Graziano was soon in trouble again. In December he was due to meet perennial loser Reuben Shank. Graziano was the prohibitive favourite, but outside New York large sums were bet on Shank, a possible indication that a fix was on. With three days to go to the fight, Graziano wrenched his back in training and had to pull out. A new district attorney, Frank Hogan, was crusading against boxing, and on 26 January Graziano was hauled in and questioned. The DA's line was that Graziano had been offered money to throw the fight, had refused, and had then pulled out to avoid crossing the crooks.

The boxer was called to testify before a grand jury. He said he had been offered a bribe to throw the fight, but maintained that such offers, real and phoney, were commonplace in gyms and he simply ignored them. However, the NYSAC, now chaired by Colonel Eddie Eagan, was under fire from Hogan to act. On 7 February it concluded that Graziano's failure to report the 'bribe' and to name whoever made it violated the commission's rules. His licence was revoked *sine die*. No evidence exists that Graziano ever threw a fight. Boxing needed cleaning up, and Graziano was an easy target — a high-profile scapegoat with a criminal past. The return fight with Zale scheduled for March was called off.

A valid criticism of Zale is that he denied many top contenders a title fight. While Graziano was suspended, boxers like Marcel Cerdan, Charley Burley and Jake LaMotta were ignored. When Zale did get down to business, it was in non-title bouts against modest opposition. He won five such bouts inside the distance in 1947.

The return with Graziano was finally made for Chicago Stadium on 16 July 1947. More than 18,000 fans paid $422,009 to see it. Zale got $140,682, Graziano $70,341. It was a chilling sequel. Graziano wrote: 'This was no boxing match. It was a war and if there wasn't a referee, one of the two of us would have wound up dead. Today I still can't look at the pictures of that Chicago Stadium fight without it hurts me and I get nightmares that I am back in the ring on that hot July night and I am looking out through a red film of blood.'

The Associated Press blow-by-blow wire account described the first round thus:

Graziano landed a hard left hook to the chin and staggered Zale with a smashing overhand right. Zale held after being tagged with another right. Zale crossed a ripping right to the chin. Zale drove a left to the face. Zale drove Graziano into the ropes with a vicious right. Zale drove both hands to the body and took a hard right to the face in return. A hook drew a red mark on Graziano's eye. They exchanged short rights to the head. Zale fired left and right to the face and took a hard right in return. Zale drove Graziano into the ropes. Each landed a left on the chin. Zale dug his right to the body and shook him with a left. They were fending at the bell.

They were just getting started. Zale rushed out for the second and immediately shook his rival with a right. They blasted away in mid-ring. Graziano's left eyebrow was cut, but he rocked Zale back on his heels with a right haymaker. Zale switched to the body and they were swopping hooks at the bell. The fight so far was even, but Graziano's right eye was shutting already and his left was bleeding. Whitey Bimstein used carpenter's wax, a dangerous substance, to staunch the blood.

Zale stuck two jabs in Graziano's face at the beginning of the third, then caught him with a left-right to the body. As Graziano's hands came down, a short right dropped him on the deck, with blood spurting from his right eye. He was up before the referee could count but ran straight into more trouble. Zale was now mixing his punches beautifully, digging his right deep into Graziano's middle, then jabbing to find the range before pinpointing Graziano's damaged eye. Rocky's head began to spin and he covered up on the ropes as Zale whaled away. Desperately he hit back with a flailing uppercut but his resistance was swept away on a tide of leather. He was taking a beating to the body as the round ended.

Referee Johnny Behr called over the commission doctor, John Drammis, to examine Graziano's right eye. It was shut solid, a swollen lump of flesh. Bimstein pleaded that he be allowed to continue and the doctor agreed. The referee said he'd allow the challenger one more round. According to ring legend, Bimstein or another Graziano cornerman, Frank Percoco, used a coin to split the swelling, releasing the blood inside.

Graziano was now fighting on instinct; Zale was also near exhaustion. The pace slowed as the champion stuck to his tactic of jabbing mixed with a body attack. Zale's fatigue showed as he missed with a right and spun around almost to his knees. Graziano was still pitching right hands, but could hardly see for the blood in his eyes.

They were trading punches at the bell.

The fifth saw one of the most dramatic comebacks in the history of the sport. Graziano wrote: 'Then I got a second wind . . . and I sucked it deep in my lungs and I felt new strength tingle down my arms and legs and I yelled that I was going to kill that stinking rat bastard and I tore into him and never stopped. I hit him until both my fists go numb. I hit him until he can't hit back no more, he can't hold his hands up. He sways over and I grab his throat and straighten him back up and hit him again.' Graziano threw punches in a wild, blind rage. Again and again he crashed jolting rights against Zale's jaw, hurled hooks to the ribs, and the champion wilted under the torrent. A left hook sent him staggering as the stadium erupted. The bell rang.

Graziano's homicidal assault continued in the sixth until even the 'Steel Man' could take no more. Zale wilted as the punches crunched on his jaw. He reeled across the ring and Graziano chased him. A massive right sent him into a corner, another kept him there, and a third put him over the middle rope, where he hung, doubled up on his stomach. Behr jumped between them to stop the slaughter and Graziano was the new middleweight champion. As well-wishers poured between the ropes, a radio reporter shoved a microphone in front of Graziano. 'Hey, Ma, your bad boy done it!' he shouted.

The new champion's happiest moment was his return to the East Side. Crowds turned out in their thousands to watch his motorcade. Even a second ban, in Illinois, following the revelation of his army desertion, could not dampen the celebrations. The champ was in demand. Comedian Lou Costello reportedly offered Graziano $200,000 to defend against Jake LaMotta in Los Angeles. But he was committed to a return with Zale and what would have been a fascinating encounter never materialized.

Zale, meanwhile, went quietly away to gather himself. He refused to believe Graziano was the better man and insisted the referee had stepped in too soon. Six months later, he served notice of intent in his first comeback bout, belting poor Al Turner through the ropes and out of the ring in the fifth round. Two more opponents were dismissed in short order. He was ready.

Graziano warmed up for their rubber match with a ten-round

decision over Sonny Horne in Washington, for which he was paid just one dollar; the rest went for children with infantile paralysis. Three days later, he and Zale signed to resume hostilities. The bout was originally slated for Miami, then Atlantic City. It finally landed in the Ruppert Stadium in Newark, New Jersey, on 10 June before 21,497. There were seven rows of pressmen. The fight was postponed one day for rain. They didn't weigh in again and there is little doubt that Zale, at least, was over the weight limit.

Zale was now 35 but in great condition. Graziano, despite a $120,000 guarantee and being 12–5 favourite, seemed sluggish and unmotivated. Zale took charge from the opening bell and his first body shot drew a groan from the champion. Zale kept his boxing tight, sliding inside Graziano's swings to land his own, shorter punches. Halfway through the round, he unleashed a double left hook, and Graziano went over. He rose without a count but was clearly hurt and was pinned on the ropes until the bell.

The second round was quieter, Graziano coming back into the fight while Zale bided his time and looked for openings. He already had the champion's face marked and was blocking most of his blows. In the third, Zale struck, catching Graziano with a beautiful left hook that sent him floundering against the ropes. A series of punches, capped by a combination right to the body and left hook to the chin, dropped Graziano heavily. He was up at 'four', clutching onto the ropes to steady himself, but was clearly out on his feet. Zale teed off with a duplicate right-left combination to the chin and Graziano went down as if shot. He was counted out, spreadeagled on the canvas. It was all over after 68 seconds of the third. Graziano was taken to hospital for checks. Bimstein told the press, 'I can't understand what got into him. He seemed petrified when he entered the ring.'

It was Zale's last great performance. After 87 professional bouts, the 'Man of Steel' was going rusty. He was committed to a defence against Marcel Cerdan of France; they met in Jersey City on 21 September. Courage and ringcraft took Zale into the 12th round, but he finally crumpled under Cerdan's blows and his corner pulled him out before the 13th. Zale retired from the ring and married again. He worked for many years as a boxing coach for the Catholic Youth

Organization in Chicago and became head boxing coach for the Chicago Park District, visiting gyms across the city to monitor young boxers. According to the LA *Herald Examiner*, 'What endures for Zale is the notion of what a fighter's life should be — excess only in work, adherence to regimen, sacrifice, stoicism.'

Graziano stayed out of the ring for over a year before deciding to fight on. His New York licence was restored in May 1947 and after two brisk knockouts in the summer he returned to the Big Apple for the first time in three years. His opponent was the up-and-coming Charley Fusari. Before a huge crowd at the Polo Grounds, Graziano was run ragged for nine rounds. In the tenth he suddenly clicked into a blind fury. He swamped Fusari, pinned him on the ropes, grabbed his neck with his left glove to hold him down and punched with his right. With 56 seconds to go, the referee had to jump between them to stop Fusari from being killed.

With his popularity greater than ever, Graziano fought on, compiling an impressive run against rising youngsters and over-the-hill veterans, including a three-fight series with Tony Janiro that resulted in a draw, points win and another of those last ditch kayos, the fight being stopped with 14 seconds to go. In all he reeled off 20 wins and a draw in 21 fights, and in April 1952 he was matched with the new middleweight champion, Sugar Ray Robinson, in Chicago. The old fire flickered briefly when he scored a flash knockdown, but then he was gone, flattened in round three. In his last bout, on national television, he was easily outpointed by Chuck Davey.

The 'Rock' found a successful second career in showbiz after a chance meeting with actor Marlon Brando. He made a fortune out of a successful sitcom and commercials, from cereals to dog food, becoming one of the best-known faces in America. He was a sought-after speaker and collaborated in two successful books. A film was made about his life, starring Paul Newman and called *Somebody Up There Likes Me*. He could hardly believe his own success: 'Half the time I don't know what I'm doin'. But I'm doin' great.' He died a much-loved figure in 1990.

9

Tears and Tough Guys

IT TOOK a Frenchman to bring romance to boxing. Marcel Cerdan caught the mood of post-war France. Born within sound of the Foreign Legion bugle, he was as rugged as a commando, with broad shoulders, crinkly black hair and a gold-toothed smile. He served with the Free French forces and as a boxer became the idol of his country. His love affair with Edith Piaf, the great French singer, has been immortalized on film and in print. Indeed, Cerdan was worshipped by his fans. 'He was the only fighter who attracted crowds to follow him at a distance, without actually exchanging words,' wrote Reg Gutteridge. 'They bantered with Muhammad Ali and fought to touch him; but people seemed in awe of Cerdan.'

He was born in Sidi-bel-Abbes, Algeria, fortress-home of the French Foreign Legion, on 22 July 1916. It was a cultural *mélange*, described by P. C. Wren in his fictional adventure *Beau Geste*:

Entering the town itself, through a great gate in the huge ramparts, we were in a curiously hybrid Oriental–European atmosphere in which moved stately Arabs, smart French ladies, omnibuses, camels, half-naked negroes, dapper officers, crowds of poor Jewish-looking working-folk, soldiers by the hundred, negroes, grisettes, black newspaper boys selling the *Echo d'Oran*, pig-tailed European girls, Spaniards, Frenchmen, Algerian Jews, Levantines, men and women straight from the Bible, and others straight from the Boulevards, Arab policemen, Spahis, Turcos, Zouaves, and Chasseurs d'Afrique.

Cerdan's father, a Frenchman with a Spanish wife, had no money and a variety of jobs. In 1922 they moved to the equally exotic Moroccan town of Casablanca where he found work as a butcher. He made all four sons box. The youngest, Armand, was evidently the most promising but gave up sport following a football accident. Marcel also loved soccer but from the age of eight was pushed into boxing, training in a makeshift gym above the garage of his father's Parisian friend Lucien Roupp. He quit school at 11. He became a good amateur boxer, though on one occasion he was almost too scared to fight when confronted by a campaign-hardened Légionnaire. 'You cannot know what it is,' he explained, 'unless you have been brought up with the sound of the bugle and the sight of the regiment marching out of the gate.' He won on points.

In November 1934 Cerdan turned pro with Roupp as his manager, outpointing a family friend, Marcel Bucchanieri, in his first bout in Meknes. For the next three years he cut his teeth on Arabs and Frenchmen, murderous men drawn from the Légion and the mean streets of Casablanca, Oran and Algiers. He beat them all. He also won five fights in Paris and in February 1938 took the French welterweight title from Omar Kouidri in Casablanca. Other classy victims included the Italian Cleo Locatelli and Gustave Humery. But in January 1939 his run of 41 straight wins was broken when, with an easy victory in sight, he was ruled out for a low blow against Harry Craster in London.

He came back to win the European welterweight title in June, beating Saverio Turiello in Milan. At this point in his career, he was strongly mooted as a challenger for Henry Armstrong, the fabulous world welterweight champion. It was potentially one of the dream match-ups in boxing history. 'Hammerin' Henry' was a perpetual-motion whirlwind who set a record of 18 welterweight defences. Cerdan, who trained with bantamweights for speed, was a well-armoured steamroller with a wallop in both fists. What would have been the fight of the decade was scotched, however, when war broke out in Europe. France was invaded and for 18 months Cerdan served with the French navy.

He resumed his career in 1941 after the German occupation of Casablanca, and eventually boxed in Nazi-occupied France, where a committee had replaced the French Boxing Federation. After an impressive run of knockouts he was ruled out for fouling Victor Buttin, only his second loss in 64 fights. In his next contest, Cerdan was summoned to defend his European title in Paris for the edification of German troops. He cut short their enjoyment by demolishing José Ferrer in one round, refused to attend a post-bout officers' party and fled the country on false papers. He expected to be arrested but was saved when Allied Forces liberated Casablanca.

Cerdan joined the Free French navy and entertained the advancing troops with boxing matches, first in Africa, then in Italy. In Rome he knocked out three victims in four rounds to win an Inter-Allied tournament. Word began to filter back to the States about the Frenchman who fought like a throwback to the days of Greb and Walker. Paris was liberated in August 1944 and Cerdan was back there boxing within seven months.

He was 29 when the war ended. Time was against him. But Cerdan, who had grown into a middleweight, continued to press for a world title fight. He won the French 160lb title and in July 1946 took on Holman Williams, one of the best boxers in the world. Like Cerdan, Williams was too good for his own good, a masterful boxer with an endless catalogue of moves. He was also black and struggled in vain against boxing prejudice. In his best performance to date, Cerdan won on points after ten rounds in Paris.

Lew Burston, an international boxing figure, oiled the wheels for Cerdan to showcase his talents in New York. Legend has it that the Frenchman injured his back on the boat across the Atlantic while saving a female companion from falling overboard. He was still fit enough to beat the excellent Georgie Abrams in a close fight in December. He then returned to Europe, winning the vacant continental title in February 1947 by beating Belgian champion Léon Fouquet. Cerdan, never keen on training, had to shed nearly a stone in two weeks to make the weight. He promptly took care of Fouquet in 126 seconds. Nine days later, he was back in London to drop Bert Gilroy eight times on the way to a fourth-round knockout.

Cerdan gave the States another try later that year. In New York he shattered Harold Green with a right to the jaw in round two. In Montreal, Canada, he broke two of Billy Walker's ribs and dropped him twice before the referee stopped it in the first. His next opponent was an Estonian, Anton Raadik, in Chicago. Cerdan battered him for nine rounds but ran into trouble in the tenth and was dropped three times. He was saved by the bell, and the crowd of 10,000 booed the decision in his favour. He again returned home, complaining that his

American sparring partners kept trying to knock him out.

Europe's middleweights were no match for Cerdan. He knocked out Italian champion Giovanni Manca in two rounds in defence of his European title and Jean Walzack in four for the French crown. Walzack was counted out on one knee after taking approximately 50 hooks in less than two minutes. Then it was back to the US to meet Texan Lavern Roach, voted Rookie of the Year for his 1947 form. He received an unsentimental lesson. Roach was dropped in the second but the referee engaged in an argument with the timekeeper about whether a punch or a trip was responsible. By the time he got round to counting, with Roach rising at 'nine', the fighter had actually been down for 24 seconds. It did him no good. He was floored six more times before the fight was stopped in the eighth round.

Perversely, defeat brought Cerdan a title fight. After a gruelling close-quarter slog with Lucien Krawsyck, a rugged Polish southpaw, Cerdan lost his European title to Cyrille Delannoit in May 1948. Though it was a dubious decision, and Cerdan regained his title two months later, it helped convince the Americans that the 32-year-old Frenchman was fading. They announced soon after that he would receive a shot against world champion Tony Zale.

'In Paris,' wrote the novelist Irwin Shaw, 'everything begins and ends at a cafe table.' Marcel Cerdan first met Edith Piaf at a table at the Club des Cinq. There was no instant attraction. She was tiny and far from pretty, and their romance took time to bloom. But she was the irresistible soul of proletarian Paris, her bitter-sweet songs capturing the essence of her war-weary country. Cerdan, who was married to a grocer's daughter, Marinette, began to see more and more of Piaf.

Their love affair became an open secret. Cerdan refused to divorce his wife for religious reasons, but it didn't stop his romance becoming spice for the gossip columns. At one New York press conference, Cerdan told the reporters, 'You are interested in only one thing, so let's not waste time. You want to know if I'm in love with Edith Piaf. Yes, I am. As for her being my mistress, if she's only that, it's because I'm married. If I was not married and did not have children I would make her my wife. Anyone here who has never cheated on his wife, raise his hand.' It is said that none of them did. On a couple of other occasions he was even more direct, punching journalists who had upset Piaf.

The singer was at ringside to watch her lover fight the great Tony Zale on 21 September 1948 in Jersey City. The 'Man of Steel' won only a single round, the fourth. He was outboxed and outhit four-to-one and only courage kept him going. At the bell to end the 11th round, after a sustained assault from the Frenchman, Zale slumped onto his knees, like a puppet with its strings cut. He couldn't even stand up for the 12th. Cerdan was crowned champion.

Wild celebrations broke out. *New York Times* columnist Arthur Daley wrote, 'French sportswriters vaulted into the ring to kiss Cerdan; photographers left their cameras. The French broadcaster leaped under the ropes *sans* his mike, remembered it and almost choked ringsiders in a tangle of wire. . . . Then came the locusts, many wearing berets. They stormed the aisles. The police fought valiantly. Never was one man kissed by so many. Son of a pig! It was amazing.'

Cerdan enjoyed his success. New York became a playground for him and Edith. Lucien Roupp was edged out and a few months later Cerdan paid him off. He was now guided by his brother Armand and Jo Longman, who handled his business interests. He won two non-title fights, beating Dick Turpin in London and Lucien Krawsyck before his family and friends in Casablanca. Krawsyck, who on a previous occasion had given him a hard fight, was dropped five times before his seconds threw in the towel.

Cerdan was drawn back to America to defend his title. His opponent was Jake LaMotta, a bull-like man who, like the champion, had boxed for years in the wilderness. Their contest was on 16 June 1949 in Detroit. After an early flurry, LaMotta wrestled Cerdan to the floor. The Frenchman pulled a tendon in his left shoulder and could barely lift the arm. LaMotta was no man to fight one-handed, but Cerdan fought on fairly level terms until the handicap became too great. His corner pulled out at the end of the ninth.

A rematch set for September was delayed when LaMotta injured his shoulder in training. It was re-scheduled for 2 December. 'This is the fight of my life,' said Cerdan. 'I will win it, or I will die.' On 27 October he boarded an Air France Constellation in Paris, bound for New York's LaGuardia Airport. It was diverted from fog-bound

Shannon Airport and headed south for a fuel stop in the Azores. As he descended, the captain suddenly lost radio contact with the control tower. The plane crashed into the top of the 2,600ft Mount Redondo on the island of São Miguel. None of the 11 crew or the 37 passengers survived. Cerdan was identified by his wristwatch.

Piaf screamed and collapsed when she heard the news. She was due to sing that night in the New York's Versailles night club. Persuaded to go ahead with the performance, she told her hushed audience, 'This evening I shall be singing for Marcel Cerdan.' She could manage only four songs, including the haunting *L'Hymne à l'amour*, before fainting.

Cerdan's body was taken back to Casablanca for burial. Forty taxis carried the flowers. There was later an emotional meeting between Piaf and Cerdan's wife Marinette, and they became friends. One of Cerdan's three sons, Marcel junior, went on to become a moderately successful boxer but could never live up to his father's reputation. Cerdan had one of the best records of any European boxer. He lost just four times in 115 fights, winning 66 inside the distance and 45 on points. Yet it could be that his career had been about to end. According to reporter Gerard Walter, a doctor had told Cerdan that if he continued to box he risked losing his eyesight. He was posthumously awarded the Legion of Honour.

Jake LaMotta was the toughest middleweight of all. 'He was like an animal,' said Robert de Niro, 'always going directly into a situation.' De Niro played LaMotta in the film *Raging Bull* as 'a man without any redeeming features at all'. Hard-hitting columnist Jimmy Cannon called him 'probably the most detested man of his generation'. LaMotta never squawked about his bad reputation. He showed little compassion for others and none for himself.

His background was similar to Rocky Graziano's. He was born on 10 July 1921 in Manhattan's Lower East Side, the son of an Italian father from Messina and an Italian–American mother. When he was a few years old, the family moved to the Bronx, where they lived in a succession of slum tenements. 'I was a bum and I lived like a bum in a bum neighbourhood,' said LaMotta. His father peddled food from a horse-drawn wagon. He was a brutal man who beat his wife and five children. One Christmas he gave them nothing but a lump of coal each; he said Santa Claus was punishing them for being bad. When young Jacob was bullied by older boys, his father thoughtfully gave him an ice-pick, with the words, 'Here, you son of a bitch, you don't run away from nobody no more.'

Jake became a child of the streets. Morose and unsmiling, he had dreadful rages. In his autobiography, he wrote, 'Everybody has a temper, but mine was set on a hair trigger — something would set me off, the temper would go and I just wouldn't give a good goddamn what happened — you could kill me, you could literally kill me, you could blow up the whole world and I wouldn't give a good goddamn, I'd kill you first. And what made it worse was that I had mastoiditis when I was eight, from the cold in the tenements, and one of my ears was bad. I would see a kid talking but I couldn't hear him, and half the time I'd get the idea he was kidding me and I'd belt him. That's also part of the reason I never got past the tenth grade in school, not that I'm making excuses, I was not exactly a scholar anyway.'

He started boxing when he was about eight, made by his father to fight other children for nickels and dimes in Bronx social clubs. His main occupation was crime. To a hard-core hooligan like LaMotta, joining the Mob was the pinnacle of ambition. He became an expert mugger and held up dice games at gunpoint. When he was 16 he battered a local bookie, Harry Gordon, with a lead pipe. For years LaMotta lived in the mistaken belief that Gordon had died in the incident. He was finally caught burgling a jewellery store and was sent to the State Reform School at Coxsackie, New York. He joined the boxing programme there and stuck with the sport on his release, competing successfully as an amateur and in semi-professional 'smokers'.

He turned pro in March 1941 under Mike Capriano, serving his time as a four- and six-round prelim boy. Almost from the start, he was up against fighters that others avoided. He also put on weight easily and faced a constant battle-of-the-bulge throughout his career. Still, he dodged no one. He won 14 and drew one of 15 contests before stepping up to his first ten-rounder against Jimmy Reeves, a light-heavyweight. Reeves clobbered him for several rounds but, to the amazement of the audience, LaMotta walked through the storm and flattened his tormentor in the final round. The bell went as the count reached 'nine' and Reeves got the decision, to the crowd's disgust. One writer said, 'Had the fight been held in an alley there isn't any doubt in my mind which man would have been the winner.'

Despite another loss to Reeves and a boxing lesson from Nate Bolden, LaMotta was beginning to attract good press notices. The papers dubbed him the 'Bronx Bull', a 'one-man gang' and 'Mr Five-by-Five'. He had a swarming style, coming at opponents from his low centre of gravity with short arm hooks. Lester Bromberg said his 'science, if any, was a form of cunning'. But it was his incredible durability that set him apart. Joey DeJohn, a noted puncher, once hit LaMotta with such a hard one-two that he started towards a neutral corner, expecting his opponent to fall. He felt a tap on his shoulder and turned to see LaMotta grinning at him. Rocky Graziano, who knew him from the streets, called him 'hammerhead'. Hundreds of street fights had also taught him about balance and the importance of staying on your feet.

LaMotta had a good but not spectacular record when in February 1943 he was matched with Ray Robinson of Detroit. Robinson had beaten him several months earlier and was expected to do so again; he was the shooting star of the welterweight division, a classy box-fighter unbeaten in 35 fights. It was the kind of challenge LaMotta relished. He swarmed all over 'Sugar Ray', knocking him through the ropes with a left hook for a nine-count in the eighth round and taking the decision at the end of ten hard sessions. It was Robinson's first defeat; he wouldn't lose again for eight years. Three weeks later, they fought again. This time Robinson got the decision, although LaMotta scored the only knockdown and claimed he'd been robbed. Defeat didn't affect his new rating as one of the top contenders for Tony Zale's title.

Over the next four years, the only people to beat LaMotta were Robinson (twice more), ex-welterweight kingpin Fritzie Zivic and Lloyd Marshall. He overcame people like Jimmy Reeves, Zivic (three times), George Kochan, Bert Lytell, Tommy Bell, Bob Satterfield, Holman Williams, Anton Raadik and Tony Janiro. But with Zale inactive because of the war, then tied up in his vendetta with Graziano, LaMotta couldn't get a title fight. He claimed he was kept on the sidelines because he wouldn't accept a Frankie Carbo plant as his manager. This was the reason, he said, why he rarely fought in New York. His brother Joey acted as his manager.

Outside the ring, LaMotta's life was barely under control. He was prone to fits of jealous fury, causing his first wife to leave after a year. He frequently hit his second wife, Vickie. There was a brawl with some gangsters in which his best friend, Pete Petrella, was shot in the arm. LaMotta also raped Petrella's girlfriend, something he admitted in his book published in 1970.

In the boxing ring, 1947 started well for LaMotta, with wins over Tommy Bell and Tony Janiro. Then a disputed loss to Cecil Hudson ended the 'Bull's' 13-bout unbeaten streak. His next opponent, in November, was Billy Fox, a black 22-year-old from Philadelphia with a strange record of 49 knockout wins and one loss. There were heavy rumours that the bout would be fixed. LaMotta won the first round, then seemed to stop trying. In the fourth round Fox was punching LaMotta at will — 'Fox had hit me about fifteen times with everything he had, which wasn't enough to dent a bowl of yoghurt' — when the referee stopped it. There was an investigation into the bout and a doctor testified that LaMotta had been suffering from a ruptured spleen. He was fined $1,000 for concealing an injury and banned for seven months.

The truth emerged in 1960. According to testimony LaMotta gave to a senatorial committee investigating boxing, his brother Joey was approached with a bribe to throw the fight from Blinky Palermo, Fox's manager, and 'Honest' John Daly, an associate of Frankie Carbo. LaMotta said he turned down the $100,000 offer but agreed to lose in return for a shot at the middleweight title.

LaMotta won all five bouts in 1948 but lost on points to Laurent Dauthuille in a bloody brawl in February 1949. There was more controversy in his next bout, when he outpointed Robert Villemain in New York. Judges Harold Barnes and Harry Ebbetts were subsequently suspended by NYSAC chairman Eddie Eagan. They had both voted for LaMotta, even though Villemain forced the fighting all the way and appeared to be well in front. Spectators jeered the verdict for more than five minutes. According to *Boxing News*, Eagen 'stated that while complete confidence remained with the two judges, in view of the international importance of the contest and the fact that their cards were contrary to the viewpoint of practically all who witnessed the bout, it was felt that some disciplinary action was necessary'.

LaMotta was unperturbed. He won two more bouts inside the distance and was finally rewarded, either for his boxing efforts or the

Fox fix, with a title bout. Still, he claimed he had to pay $20,000 for the privilege and his purse was only $19,000. Marcel Cerdan flew over to Detroit, where LaMotta had a big following, and they fought on 16 June. The Frenchman was wrestled to the floor in the first round for no count but injured his shoulder (see page 138). He retired on his stool at the end of the ninth.

Cerdan died before they could fight again. LaMotta won three of four non-title bouts and was set to meet his old reform-school buddy, Rocky Graziano. Sadly the 'Rock' broke his thumb in training. His place was taken by Tiberio Mitri of Italy, who was on a 52-bout unbeaten run. LaMotta bulled his way to a points win. His second defence, against Laurent Dauthuille, was a classic. The rugged Frenchman boxed to a huge points lead over the first 12 rounds. LaMotta got going in the 13th but was still miles behind when the last round started. He played 'possum', an old trick where he would pretend to be hurt to draw his opponent in. Dauthuille knew what the champion was doing but still went for a knockout. LaMotta staggered him with a left hook then unleashed a stream of punches to floor the challenger. He was counted out with 13 seconds left.

All those trips to the steam room were taking their toll. On 14 February 1951 a weight-weakened LaMotta took on Sugar Ray Robinson in Chicago. The fight was close and exciting for the first few rounds. By the fifth both were bleeding from the mouth. By the eighth Robinson had a slight edge on the scorecards and started catching LaMotta with combinations. Jake mounted a ferocious assault in the 11th, trapping Robinson on the ropes, but his energy soon abated. In the 13th he was battered mercilessly but refused to fall. The referee stopped it.

Moving up to light-heavy, LaMotta lost to Bob Murphy and Norman Hayes and drew with Eugene Hairston. Then he beat all three in rematches. In December 1952 he fought Danny Nardico, an ex-Marine. For the first and only time in his life, the 'Bronx Bull' was knocked down by a right hook in the seventh round. He got up and lasted to the bell, but was retired by his corner. After a brief, three-fight comeback in 1954, he retired for good.

Inevitably, retirement was a bumpy ride for LaMotta. He bought a nightclub in Miami Beach but landed in jail for aiding and abetting prostitution. On his release, he appeared in TV shows and plays and became a stand-up comic. His testimony before the Kefauver

committee in 1960 (see page 142) shook boxing to its roots. For a
while he was a pariah among the fraternity, but gradually the old
antipathy thawed. He found work as an after-dinner speaker and
stand-up comic and is now one of the enduring characters of the
game.

Cerdan and LaMotta weren't the only men who were avoided for
years by champions. The 1930s and 1940s saw several excellent black
fighters who never got a sniff of the title. Budd Schulberg called them
Murderers' Row. Foremost among these were Charley Burley, Lloyd
Marshall, Holman Williams and Archie Moore. Moore did win a
world title, at light-heavy, at an age when most boxers have retired.
The others got nowhere. As an indication of their ability, in March
1943, when Tony Zale was champion, the three top-rated contenders
were Moore, Burley and Williams. Jake LaMotta was fourth,
followed by two more black boxers, Jack Chase and Eddie Booker.

Burley was possibly the best of them all. Sugar Ray Robinson once
said he was 'too pretty to fight Charley Burley'. He was only half-
joking. Burley came from Pittsburgh and was a star amateur. He was
also a man of strong principles and apparently refused to go with the
US boxing team to Hitler's Berlin Olympics. He was highly ranked as
a welterweight when Henry Armstrong was champ, and often had to
give away weight just to get work. Archie Moore, whom he whipped,
said he was the best boxer he ever fought. Burley claimed he was once
offered a title bout but only if he threw a fight first. He refused and
never received another chance.

Lloyd Marshall, whose best weight was about 165lb, beat eight
men who at one time or another held a world title: Ken Overlin,
Babe Risko, Ted Yarosz, Lou Brouillard, Ezzard Charles, Jake
LaMotta, Joey Maxim and Freddie Mills. He was a deadly puncher.
By contrast, Holman Williams was a master boxer. Joe Louis called
him a 'perfect fighter' and trainer Eddie Futch asserted he was the
greatest of all. His skill can be gauged by the fact that he fought
Burley seven times, winning three, losing three and drawing one.

10

Sugar Ray

SUGAR Ray Robinson was boxing's class act. Accolades festooned him. Often called the best pound-for-pound boxer of all, the 'Sugarman' seemed to soar above the blood and pain of his primeval calling. He was a fistic dreamer, searching for the move, the punch, that no one had seen before. Like all great sportsmen, there was a tangible air of expectancy whenever he performed. He could turn a soft-shoe shuffle into a public execution in the flash of a fist. Robinson influenced a whole generation of boxers, including Muhammad Ali. In 1978 the Boxing Writers of America voted him the best boxer who ever lived. Reg Gutteridge, the much-travelled British boxing commentator, reckoned him to be 'as close to perfection as any boxer I have ever seen'. Politician Jesse Jackson called him 'an original art form'.

It was vanity which made him great. 'My ego makes me tick,' he said, 'In the ring it would sometimes tick like a timebomb.' Handsome and debonair, his hair marcelled in place, he was swift and sleek, graceful as a dancer. It was not the fighting that turned him on, he said, but 'performing for people, being on stage in the ring'. Offstage he was an incorrigible womanizer and blew cash like confetti. He also had an exaggerated reputation for greed. Peter Wilson, who covered his greatest fights, wrote, 'Robinson may be filled with conceit. He may be, as I have suggested, arrogant to the point of infuriation, but he knows his own worth and he does know his own mind.' For a boxer to know either was a cardinal sin in the eyes of promoters and managers, and Robinson was sometimes vilified for it.

He was born in Black Bottom — 'Black because we lived there, Bottom because that's where we were at' — Detroit, on 30 May 1920, the son of a displaced Georgia sharecropper who named him Walker Smith Jr. As a child, he didn't like to fight and would sometimes hide behind his older sisters for protection. He did admire the neighbourhood hero, however, a young amateur boxer named Joe Louis. Walker would sometimes carry his kitbag. His parents separated and his mother, a seamstress, took her son and two daughters to New York in 1932, first to Hell's Kitchen, then to Harlem. The children danced for pennies outside Broadway theatres. Young Walker soon started boxing. He was skinny, almost scrawny, but his hands moved like lightning and he was impossibly difficult to hit.

He boxed in the Police Athletic League at the age of 13 for George Gainsford, a huge, corpulent man who ran black amateur boxing in Harlem. On his first AAU outing, Walker wasn't registered and had to borrow the card of another boxer called Ray Robinson. The name stuck. He was a brilliant amateur, winning several Golden Gloves contests and beating future featherweight legend Willie Pep. He lost just a couple of times, including one to future contender Billy Graham, and was called 'sweet as sugar' by sportswriter Jack Case. Ray became 'Sugar' Ray.

Robinson turned pro with a two-round win in Madison Square Garden in October 1940. He was managed by Gainsford with the backing of Curt Horrmann, a white brewing millionaire, though later he effectively managed himself. It was instantly apparent that a star was in the making. He had qualities which set him apart from other young prospects, not least the ability to mix punches in deadly combinations. He outpointed Sammy Angott, the NBA lightweight champ, in his first major main event in July 1941, and by the end of that year he had defeated Marty Servo, another unbeaten newcomer, and Fritzie Zivic, a former welterweight champ. One victory followed another until in 1943, after 40 consecutive wins, he was matched against Bronx caveman Jake LaMotta. Robinson had beaten him a few months earlier but this time the tables were turned. LaMotta knocked him down and, in Robinson's words, 'stomped me for ten rounds'. He wouldn't lose again for eight years.

Robinson fought LaMotta six times in all, winning five. Each was a war. It was a sign of his ability that he could beat one of the most avoided middleweights in America while only a welterweight. His first defeat was avenged three weeks later and by the end of the year he had also beaten the ageing Henry Armstrong, one of the greatest fighters of all time. Witnesses swore Robinson could have knocked him out but held back out of respect. 'I couldn't have handled Robinson on the best night I ever had,' said the gracious ex-champion. Robinson was not averse to 'carrying' opponents — including Charley Fusari in a world title fight — who posed no threat.

At the end of 1943 Private Walker Smith was inducted into the US Army. In his autobiography he described his war record in a chapter headed simply 'Amnesia'. It hides a peculiar mystery. Robinson was part of the 'Joe Louis Troupe', in which Louis, Ray and two other boxers toured camps putting on exhibitions. However, when the troupe sailed for Europe in March 1944, he was not with it. In his book, he said he fell down some stairs and knocked himself out, losing his memory. He came round a week later in hospital. A medical report said he had been brought in by a stranger in 'a confused, disoriented state, complaining of headaches and dizziness'. He was discharged as a sergeant in June 1944. Sports columnists like Dan Parker raised still-unanswered questions about the incident.

It didn't affect him between the ropes. He returned to the ring in October and won 30 bouts on the trot. One opponent, George Costner, also used the nickname 'Sugar'. For his temerity, Robinson flattened him in one round. He had a few close calls, including one against Artie Levine, whom he called the hardest puncher he ever faced. Levine dropped Robinson twice but was knocked out himself with 19 seconds left.

Sugar Ray had now been the best welterweight in the world for five years and in December 1946 won the vacant title on points against Tommy Bell. He made five successful defences of the title. Tragically his first challenger, Jimmy Doyle, died. Doyle had been badly concussed a year earlier by Artie Levine. Despite fears that Doyle could be permanently harmed, his fight with Robinson went ahead. In round eight he was floored by a short left hook and his head cracked off the canvas. He lapsed into a coma and died the next day from a clot on his brain. At the inquest, the coroner asked Robinson if he meant to get Doyle in trouble. 'Mister,' he replied, 'it's my business to get him in trouble.' The coroner also said a great deal of pressure had been put on him to 'divert the investigation'. He didn't reveal by whom.

Many believe Robinson reached his peak as a welterweight. He had his sights on the middleweight title but was kept waiting for years because he wouldn't play ball with the new promotional force in the US, Jim Norris's International Boxing Club. In June 1950 the Pennsylvania commission recognized him as world middleweight champion after his victory over Robert Villemain. He defended this fringe version of the title against Carl 'Bobo' Olson and José Basora, whom he beat in 52 seconds. In the same year he fought Charley Fusari for one dollar, giving the rest of his $30,000 purse to the Damon Runyon Cancer Fund.

Finally, the real champion, LaMotta, consented to fight him in Chicago Stadium on St Valentine's Day, 1951. Robinson still held the welter title and reached an agreement with the NBA that he would relinquish it if he beat LaMotta, but his name would go down in official records as having held both crowns at the same time. He also received an offer to fix the fight from the ubiquitous Frankie Carbo, who told him 'I want you and the "Bull" to have three fights. You'll win the first. He wins the second. The third is on the level.' Robinson said no.

They called it the St Valentine's Day Massacre. For eight rounds, the Bronx 'Bull' forced the action but was caught by deadly accurate crossfire. Going into the ninth it was even. But LaMotta had suffered from drastic dieting and was beginning to tire. Robinson's punches became deadlier. The 11th was one of boxing's classic rounds. LaMotta trapped Robinson on the ropes and unloaded his full artillery in a last-ditch effort. The 'Sugarman' rode the storm and blazed back with a glorious sequence of punches. LaMotta was punched half silly in the 12th, but the man who had never been knocked down refused to buckle. 'You can't do it, you black bastard. You can't put me on the deck,' he growled through bloodied lips. In the 13th he was soaking up blows like a human shock absorber, groggy but still standing, when the referee stopped it.

The Sugar Ray show was now in full swing. His flamboyance was legendary, his flamingo-pink Cadillac — 'I'd had other nice cars but this one had soul' — was almost a Harlem landmark. He bought one of the most elaborate hairdressing salons in New York and had interests in real estate and a bar. His wife Edna Mae, a gorgeous former nightclub dancer, was set up in a lingerie shop. Robinson's personal wage bill was estimated at £1,000 a week.

There was an air of burlesque about Robinson's camp followers.

Reporter Jack Birtley wrote, 'Each member of his "circus" had a special task to do during a fight, while manager George Gainsford talked to him during the rest periods. For example, Bert Neal was delegated with the task of smoothing Robinson's hair down, while Harry Wiley patted the champion's superb stomach muscles with cold water. Then there was Honey Brewer, who held the satin-covered water bottle while Robinson rinsed his mouth, June Clark (a man) was in charge of the spittoon and Roger Simon had the job of adjusting the American's gumshield. There was also an "odd-job man", Harry Johnstone and, finally, Jimmy Konrabi, a midget who could often be seen sitting on the champion's knee outside boxing venues, but during fights pranced gleefully about, wisecracking and wishing his master luck.'

To keep the cash coming in Robinson signed for six fights in Europe in 41 days — in Paris, Zurich, Antwerp, Liège, Berlin, Turin — and British promoter Jack Solomons added a record purse offer of about £30,000 for him to defend against Randolph Turpin in Earl's Court, London. Robinson moved through Europe's best boxers like a buzzsaw. The only blip was a fiasco in Berlin when Gerhardt Hecht fell in round one claiming a kidney punch. The referee counted him out and he was carried to his corner, where his manager and the crowd protested loudly. He was allowed to continue, but in the second round again fell, clutching his back. The ref now disqualified Robinson. The crowd erupted, raining bottles into the ring, and the West Berlin boxing authority later declared it a no-contest. Hecht wasn't the first opponent to accuse Robinson of kidney punching; Chuck Taylor had been treated in hospital for an enlarged kidney after a match in 1947.

Finally, the Robinson circus arrived in London, complete with 53 suitcases, for the title defence against Turpin. Robinson had lost once in 131 bouts, one of the best records in the boxing history. He didn't know much about Turpin, but it didn't matter. How could he lose?

Randolph Turpin was a black boy in a white town. It was a good job he could fight. His father, Lionel, an immigrant from British Guiana (now Guyana) did his battling on the Somme, where he was wounded and gassed in the Great War. His mother, Beatrice, who was white, was the daughter of a bare-knuckle fighter. His brothers were pretty good with their fists too. They lived in a shoddy basement flat in

Leamington, a genteel provincial spa town in the English Midlands. Lionel was the first black man there. Sneers and gossip from neighbours were often silenced by a swift punch from Beatrice. Randolph was the youngest of their five children, born on 7 June 1928. Three months later, his father died from the effects of his war-time injuries. Beatrice worked as a cleaner while her mother and aunt helped look after the children.

The three Turpin boys started boxing as children and Randy was known as 'Licker', because he could lick his schoolmates by the age of 12. 'Grown men didn't seem to want to try their chances with him, even at that age,' said one old friend. He was a natural athlete whose love of swimming caused partial deafness after he was trapped underwater; his seeming indifference to some people stemmed from this; he simply couldn't hear what they were saying.

Dick was the first brother to turn pro, while Randy and Jackie would fight on his undercards as 'Alexander and Moses'; their payment the 'nobbins' thrown into the ring after. 'Jackie used to thrash me, and I'd cry my eyes out,' recalled Randy. He soon developed, however, into one of Britain's finest-ever amateur boxers. He won three national junior titles, two senior ABA titles and international honours. His most famous victory was a punch-perfect 90-second knockout of Harold Anspach, star of the US boxing team, which helped England to win an international meeting five–three.

Turpin joined the Royal Navy in December 1945 and was made an assistant cook. The first sign of his fragile emotional state appeared when he was charged with attempted suicide by overdose following a row with his Leamington girlfriend, Mary Stack. The incident was glossed over. In 1946 he turned professional, joining Dick and Jackie in the stable of George Middleton, a local grocer. In his debut he crushed Gordon Griffiths in two minutes. Peter Wilson said it was 'like a bronze tiger devouring a tethered kid'.

He was unbeaten in 18 bouts before leaving the navy. Only four went the distance, while the well-regarded Mark Hart held him to a draw. At the age of 19 he beat British middleweight champ Vince Hawkins in a non-title fight. But five weeks later, he was out of sorts and lost on points to Albert Finch. Women problems were again to blame; his deteriorating relationship with Mary Stack, now his wife, contributed to his poor frame of mind. Five months later he received a far worse defeat. He was dropped several times by France's Jean

Stock and was stopped in the fifth. This time his excuse was that he
had separated from Mary and their baby son.

At this time the British Boxing Board abolished its colour bar
forbidding black men from fighting for British titles. Dick promptly
dethroned Hawkins. Randolph was a leading contender, but the
brothers vowed never to fight each other. The younger brother won
all eight fights in 1949, seven inside the distance, his victims
including Cyrille Delannoit. In 1950 he beat a series of imported
fighters. Opportunity knocked when Albert Finch took the title off
Dick. In a display of power-hitting, Randolph avenged his brother's
defeat by knocking out Finch in five rounds in London.

Turpin rose to number four in the *Ring* world ratings and in
February 1951 met Luc Van Dam for the vacant European title. Van
Dam, an experienced pro, was ripped apart. Turpin trapped him on
the ropes and cracked in a left and right. Van Dam collapsed and was
on the floor for ten minutes. A month later, Turpin dismembered
Stock in five rounds. Three more impressive inside-the-distance wins
followed. Then came Robinson.

Turpin, who trained at a Welsh castle, was unfazed by his
opponent's reputation. Robinson, tired after his hectic European
adventures, came in very light at 11st ½lb. Still, the 18,000 fans at
Earl's Court held only faint hopes of an English victory. Turpin
started with great confidence, however. His ramrod left and his
peculiar defence, crouching low, legs splayed, confused the
champion. Turpin was also tremendously strong, and tossed
Robinson around in the clinches. The American's eye was cut after a
clash of heads in round seven and Turpin pulled away in the later
rounds to win a clear decision on points. He was proclaimed
champion as the crowd sang 'For He's a Jolly Good Fellow'. Turpin
later praised American sparring partner Mel Brown, who had once
worked with Robinson and had, said Turpin, 'taken the Robinson
machine to pieces for me and showed me exactly how it worked'.

Success was failure for Turpin. A simple, emotionally vulnerable
man, he simply could not handle fame. He was obliged to give
Robinson a return 64 days later in New York and flew over in advance
to train at Grossingers, a well-known holiday resort. Rumours
circulated of late-night parties with dancing girls and friction in the
training camp. Eleven days before the bout, a boxer called George
Flores died in hospital after being kayoed at Madison Square Garden.

Its significance would soon become apparent.

A massive crowd of 61,000 packed the Polo Grounds on 12 September 1951. Turpin was hurt early on, but his strangely effective defence often made Robinson look ordinary. As they came out for the tenth, it looked as if Turpin might spring another upset. Then it happened. A looping Turpin right split Robinson's left brow, and blood trickled down his cheek. Robinson, staring at defeat, exploded. A short right hurt Turpin and he was pursued to the ropes, where a blizzard of blows cut him down. He rose at 'nine' and backed into the ropes near his corner. Gilbert Odd described what happened: 'Then was seen some of the fiercest, fastest and most accurate punching ever thrown. Blows were rained on Randy from every conceivable angle. Hooks, uppercuts, swings, the lot.'

Turpin rolled from side to side, doubled over, trying to sway from his tormentor, weaving, wrote Red Smith, 'like a cobra dancing to a flute'. But Robinson was deadly accurate. The champion seemed unable to raise his gloves to protect his chin and gradually slumped forward. Before he could fall, referee Ruby Goldstein jumped in and grabbed him, stopping the fight. There were just eight seconds left in the round. Much debate followed about whether Goldstein, with the Flores death in his mind, stopped it too quickly. But Turpin looked totally gone.

Robinson was king once more, but chinks were showing in his armour. He needed a strong closing rally to outscore Bobo Olson in March 1952 and a month later he found himself facing Rocky Graziano in Chicago. The 'Rock' was as dangerous as ever and in round three bounced one of his patented right hands off the champion's neck and knocked him down. Sugar Ray rose immediately, waited for Graziano to open up again, and levelled him for the full count with a vintage left hook-right cross combination. 'He must be good,' cracked Rocky, 'because he knocked out *me*.'

In June Robinson tried to make boxing history and become the third man to win titles at three weights when he challenged light-heavyweight champion Joey Maxim. The bout, as A. J. Liebling noted, was 'memorable, but chiefly for meteorological reasons'. It was the hottest 25 June on record in New York, with a ringside temperature of 104 degrees under the arc lights. Referee Ruby Goldstein collapsed at the end of the tenth, to be replaced by Ray Miller. Robinson raced ahead on points, but by the 13th was dehydrated and exhausted. At one stage he swung, missed and fell on his face. He was unable to come out for the 14th round.

While Robinson contemplated his future, Randolph Turpin's form was unimpressive. He won the British and Empire light-heavyweight titles from tubby Don Cockell before 50,000 people at White City, London and also won the Empire middleweight title. But generally his performances were listless and unmotivated. (The one Empire middleweight who could have beaten him, Dave Sands, tragically died in a car crash.)

Plans for Robinson to meet Turpin again in London were scotched when Bob Christenberry, chairman of the New York Boxing Commission, stripped Robinson for failing to defend his title within six months. On 18 December Robinson announced his retirement. The British proposed making a Turpin–Charles Humez Euro-title fight into a world title contest. Instead, it was agreed that the Turpin–Humez winner would meet the victor in a US elimination series involving ten boxers: Norman Hayes, Ernie Durando, Paddy Young, Walter Cartier, Eugene Hairston, Rocky Castellani, Lee Sala, Joey Giardello, Pierre Langlois and Carl Olson.

Humez, aged 26, was an ex-coalminer known as the 'Lion of Flanders'. He had lost just twice in 65 bouts and was impervious to punishment. The bout was a 54,000-ticket sell-out. Turpin had to have a Turkish bath to make the weight at the third attempt. He still had too many guns for Humez, winning on points, but was booed for his inability to finish off his opponent and for his safety-first approach.

Olson beat Paddy Young in a box-off and then agreed to meet Turpin on 21 October at Madison Square Garden. Turpin's behaviour again came under scrutiny. He refused to speak to the British press at his Catskill training camp and gave London reporter George Whiting a letter saying he was going to quit after the contest. He ignored his trainers, rarely sparred, and said if anyone upset him he would pack up and go home. The *New York Post* lampooned him in a cartoon entitled 'Training, British style', showing him in a 'Fast set-to with a tea-bag' and 'Four rounds with the mail'. The odds shortened on Olson.

Yet Turpin came out like his old self and had Olson on the rack for three rounds. Things changed in the fourth, when Olson buckled Turpin's knees with a hard blow and opened a cut under his left eye.

The American took charge, bossing Turpin on the ropes. Olson was one-paced but persistent. In the ninth, he sent Turpin down with a flurry. The bell rang at 'four' but the referee couldn't hear above the din and continued to count until he realized what had happened. A thoroughly demoralized Turpin was pummelled for the rest of the fight. At the final bell he was exhausted, bloody and well-beaten. Olson took the unanimous decision and the undisputed title.

On 2 November, the day before he was due to sail back to England, Turpin was arrested in New York for the rape and assault of a 24-year-old woman. Adele Daniels said they had become lovers after the second Robinson fight, but before the Olson bout he had attacked her. The police charge was subsequently dropped but Miss Daniels and her flamboyant lawyer Roland Sala, known as 'Sala the Magnificent', announced they would sue the boxer for $100,000. Turpin, who denied the charge, had to lodge a $10,000 deposit before he was allowed home. There, he received little respite. He and Mary had divorced and he was pursued by journalists anxious to report his relationship with a Welsh girl, Gwen Price. The pair tried to hide but were chased through several counties by a small army of reporters and photographers. Soon after, they were married.

Turpin had a history of women trouble. He was cited in a divorce case by a policeman who said Turpin had committed adultery with his wife. There was a girl who claimed he raped her on a train. In 1948 Mary Stack had brought a charge of assault against him, saying he had hit her with a broomstick and kicked her in the stomach while she was pregnant. The case was dismissed, though Turpin admitted he had slapped her several times.

Not surprisingly, Turpin was in a poor frame of mind when he defended his European title against Tiberio Mitri in May 1954 in Rome. He fell heavily from a beautiful left hook in the first round and his head banged against the canvas. He staggered up but the referee decided he was too dazed to continue. Mitri was not a big puncher and one Italian paper reported that 'Mitri himself was astonished'. It was a sign of Turpin's decline. He announced he wanted to fight as a light-heavy in future.

The Daniels trial started in 1955. She told an American courtroom that Turpin attacked her the day after he arrived in New York for the Olson fight. Miss Daniels told the hushed court, 'He was a charming English gentleman and he told me I was everything he longed for.'

But back at her flat, she said, he put a pillow over her head and raped her. Afterwards he said, 'It's OK, everybody does this in England.' Sala described him as 'a jungle beast in human form, and a dangerous killer'. He and Turpin's lawyer argued loudly and even the judge called the trial 'a shambles'. One the fifth day, before Turpin could be called to stand, Daniels accepted £1,250 in settlement. Sala was disgusted, claiming the jury would have awarded her 20 times as much. Turpin said he considered the rape story 'a big laugh' and returned to England to revive his boxing career.

He fought erratically for seven more years, winning a Lonsdale Belt outright but losing to Gordon Wallace and Hans Stretz. He was mooted as an opponent for Willie Pastrano, the world light-heavyweight champion, but the British Board forbade it. Though his punch never deserted him, his chin and legs had 'gone'. In September 1958 he faced Yolande Pompey of Trinidad before a big crowd in Birmingham. Near the end of round one, a Turpin right put Pompey on one knee. Instead of moving in for the kill, Turpin touched gloves in a sporting handshake. The brief respite allowed Pompey to recover. He knocked Turpin out in the next round.

Turpin retired and went to work in his manager's scrap yard. Most of his money had gone, the Inland Revenue was after him for back taxes and a hotel venture failed. In 1959 he scraped together enough cash to rent a small transport cafe in Leamington. He also turned to wrestling, which became his main source of income.

The taxman's axe fell in 1962. Turpin, who said he was 'illiterate' with money, was hit with a bill for £17,126 on his boxing earnings. He didn't have it. He said he had never received much of the £100,000 he was reputed to have earned and muttered darkly about those who had 'cheated' him. He was declared bankrupt. According to Jack Birtley, 'From the moment he walked out of the Warwick court-room, Turpin became a changed man.' He fell out with his family and turned inwards, concentrating more on his wife and three daughters. In November 1962 an article bearing his name appeared in the American magazine *Boxing Illustrated* under the headline 'Hate in my Heart'. Prepared just before the conclusion of his bankruptcy hearing, it began, 'Meet the biggest boxing sucker of all time. I'm broke. I'm bitter. And I have been bled to bankruptcy which is just around the corner.' It carried on in the same savagely self-pitying vein.

There was another boxing comeback, as a heavyweight, which lasted just two fights, in England and Malta. One newspaper headline read, 'Leave Us the Memory, NOT THIS.' In 1964 a compulsory purchase order was served on the cafe. The site was needed for a car park. The Inland Revenue also started chasing him for his wrestling earnings. He told Jack Solomons he was at his wit's end and tried to sell his boxing trophies and title belts. The wrestling engagements dried up.

On 14 May 1966 a final tax demand arrived on his doormat. Three days later, Gwen noticed him writing a letter. Then he disappeared into the attic, followed by his youngest daughter, Carmen, not yet two. Just after 2.30 pm Gwen went up to see what they were doing. She found Turpin was slumped against the side of a bed, soaked in blood, a revolver by his side. Carmen was sitting on the same bed, her face covered in blood. Gwen screamed, 'What have you done to her?' There was no reply; Turpin was dead. Pinned to the bedroom door was a suicide note. Gwen picked up the child and ran with her to hospital.

Carmen survived with bullets in her head and chest. Turpin had actually left two notes, one of which referred to threats to his life, a gang of hired killers, and men who had allegedly cheated him. It created an air of mystery around his death. He had two bullet wounds; one in the chest, the other on the left side of the head. At the inquest, one of his notes was read, in which he said, 'Naturally they will say my mind was disturbed, but it is not.' The verdict was suicide. His family doctor later expressed the opinion that he was punch-drunk. His eyesight had deteriorated and he had complained frequently about his health in recent years.

Randolph Turpin last tasted glory six months before his death. He had been invited to Madison Square Garden, all expenses paid, on the night of the Emile Griffith–Manuel Gonzales welterweight title fight. A farewell gala for Sugar Ray Robinson, retiring at the age of 45, was being held in the ring on the same evening. As Turpin stood in the ring next to fighters like Carmen Basilio, Gene Fullmer, Bobo Olson and the great Robinson, he heard for the final time the cheers and applause of more than 12,000 fans. During the last few weeks of his life, he often pulled a newspaper cutting of the evening from his pocket, fingering it, reading it over and over. It was, he said, 'one of the few times I have been treated like a human being'.

★   ★   ★

If bad company makes good boxers, Bobo Olson had a flying start. He began boxing to keep in shape for all the gang brawls he was in. 'I always went around with guys older than myself. We did a lot of fighting on the streets,' he said. His crew was a motley collection of European, Japanese and Korean delinquents who ruled the back alleys of their Honolulu home. 'You couldn't ever call them good boys. They liked to drink and hell it up. Some are dead, some are in jail. Wanting to be a fighter kept me out of the real trouble they used to get into.'

Olson was born on 11 July 1928 to a Swedish–American father and a Hawaiian–Portuguese mother who met when his father, a US Army sergeant, was stationed in Honolulu. Carl got the nickname 'Bobo' from his baby sister's mispronunciation of the word 'brother'. It stuck throughout his boxing career. He remembers hearing the bombing of Pearl Harbor six miles from his home, in December 1941. He never had much of a childhood. His parents split when he was 12 and he was put to work on a dairy farm. He fought with much older boys to join a gang and by the time he was 15 was a bouncer at a cheap dance joint. At the gym pros refused to spar with him because he was so aggressive.

Bootleg bouts at army camps hardened his muscles and he turned pro at 16, lying about his age, using a false ID card, and having two tattoos to make him look older ('Mother' on his left arm and a dragon on his right). He won four bouts inside the distance before the Hawaiian Commission found he was under their age limit and withdrew his licence. So he travelled to San Francisco and won more fights until it was discovered there that he was not 18. He lost his licence again. He returned to Honolulu. In the week following his 18th birthday he resumed his career *and* married Helen, a girl he met at school. They lived with her brother because they didn't have a home.

Good wins over boxers like Flashy Sebastian, Anton Raadik, Tommy Yarosz and Earl Turner brought Olson to the attention of the ratings compilers. His style was reminiscent of old-timers Ben Jeby and Vince Dundee. He wasn't big or powerful, but he was durable, persistent and threw plenty of leather. In March 1950 he travelled to Sydney to fight Dave Sands, the best Australian middleweight since Les Darcy. Sands had too many guns for him and knocked him down for the first time in his career. Olson toughed it out, but lost a close

12-round decision. He came back with three wins, including a verdict over Henry Brimm, and in October took a huge step in class to fight Ray Robinson for the Pennsylvania version of the world title. Olson gave it all he had but was knocked out in round 12.

After a five-round defeat of fading Lloyd Marshall, Olson moved to San Francisco, where he took on the 15-stone Sid Flaherty as manager. He almost stopped Sands in a losing return engagement and generally fought well enough to justify another title shot. Robinson was now undisputed champion, having beaten Jake LaMotta. Few gave Olson a prayer, but he hurled everything he had at the champion and the 15-round decision in Robinson's favour was booed by the San Francisco crowd. The bout gave Olson a lot of self-belief. 'I had the confidence after that . . . when I came so close to the greatest fighter, Robinson.'

Olson won his next nine fights. When the American authorities announced an elimination tournament to find a successor to Robinson (see page 153), Olson had already beaten four of the other seven nominees. He was put in the ring with Paddy Young in June 1953 for the right to meet Randolph Turpin for the vacant title. Young, a former Greenwich Village street-urchin, was a playboy who disliked training. Olson won on points. In the subsequent battle with Turpin, he looked bad for three rounds. His trainer told him to move inside Turpin's reach, and from then on he won easily. Olson was the champion at 25.

He won his next ten fights, including three defences of his title, against Kid Gavilan (points), Rocky Castellani (points) and Pierre Langlois (11 rounds). He also made headlines when he was discovered to have a wife and four children in Hawaii and a wife and four children in San Francisco. He settled with the second wife, Judy. In April 1955 he dropped the rugged ex-light-heavyweight champion Joey Maxim several times on the way to a ten-round points win. Bobo was excited about a possible challenge to heavyweight champion Rocky Marciano. He really thought he could win. First, he fought Archie Moore for the light-heavyweight title. The 'Ol' Mongoose' knew one move too many, however, and lured Olson onto a left hook, then finished him off. Olson was counted out in round three.

It was Olson's bad fortune to compete with two such champions as Moore and Robinson, and there was more bad news when Sugar Ray returned to the ring. They met on 9 December 1955 in Chicago.

Olson said he had to lose a lot of weight and felt weak and Robinson took him out in two rounds. They fought again in May and this time Olson lasted four rounds. He then retired.

He came back a few months later as a light-heavy and boxed on for ten more years, in 35 fights. He won most of them, but was knocked out by Pat McMurty. Doug Jones and José Torres. He left the ring for good after losing to Don Fullmer in 1966. For several years he was recreation director of a training programme for hard-core young criminals in Santa Rosa, California. He has worked in public relations for the Teamsters union and made personal appearances. Today, he is most proud of his five brawny sons; each weighs over 200lb.

11

No Room for Pity

GENE Fullmer was born to fight. His father, Tuff, was a feared streetfighter in the small copper-mining town of West Jordan, Utah, on the outskirts of Salt Lake City. His mother Mary was an avid boxing fan, naming her first son after Gene Tunney, and his brothers Jay and Don became professional boxers. They were raised as Mormons, members of the Church of Jesus Christ of Latter-Day Saints. Clean living and the work ethic held sway. When he was eight Gene took boxing lessons at the local athletic club. The instructor was Marv Jenson, a mink farmer, who would steer Fullmer until the day he retired.

Fullmer was a versatile athlete with the meaty muscularity of a wrestler. In his first bout, he recalled, 'they paired me against a boxer named Keith Nuttle. He beat me badly. If I'd had any sense I would have quit then, but I didn't.' He won more than 80 amateur bouts and lost about five, reaching the semis of the Olympic trials in 1948 and losing to future welter champ Johnny Saxton in National AAU finals in 1949.

His style was dictated by his build. 'He does everything wrong but it's right,' said one frustrated opponent. He was only 5ft 8in, with short arms, and needed to get close to land his punches. On the plus side, he had a 17-inch neck, sturdy legs and great strength. He became a swarming, clubbing boxer, barging in behind a cross-arm defence and hurling overhand rights like grenades. He attributed his stamina to the high altitude of West Jordan and his lifelong work ethic: for much of his career he continued to work in the copper mines.

Fullmer turned pro in 1951 and won 29 in a row, 19 inside the distance (11 in the first round). He also served with the army during the Korean War in 1952–3. In November 1954 Marv Jenson took him to New York, where matchmaker Teddy Brenner was so unimpressed that he offered to pay their fare home. But a lop-sided win over Jackie LaBua made an impact and Fullmer stayed to beat several more opponents, including Paul Pender. In April 1955 he suffered his first loss in 30 fights to Gil Turner. 'He beat the hell out of me,' conceded Fullmer. He dropped two other decisions at the end of the year but came back in 1956 to beat the cream of the division, including Rocky Castellani, Turner, Ralph Jones and Charles Humez. The Humez bout was seen as an eliminator to find the next challenger for Ray Robinson.

Robinson gave Fullmer the runaround for months. When they finally signed to fight on 2 January 1957 at Madison Square Garden, Robinson demanded, and received, a huge share of the purse. Fullmer was bitter but determined. 'The only people who thought I could beat Robinson were me and Marv,' said Fullmer. 'And I'm not so sure about Marv.' It was the classic matador–bull confrontation, but on this occasion the bull won. Fullmer drove the great champion through the ropes in the seventh, whacked and bullied him, and was not too particular where he hit him. He won a clear 15-round decision. A few days later he was back working in the copper mines for $17.65 a day.

On 1 May Fullmer gave Robinson a rematch in Chicago. For four rounds the new champion pressed the action. In the fifth, as he barrelled in, Robinson hit him with a short left hook. Fullmer neither saw nor remembered the punch. It landed with perfect timing and he crumpled to the canvas. Fullmer tried to rise but his legs would not obey him. 'Why'd they stop the fight?' he said, as he finally staggered to his feet. 'Because the referee counted ten,' he was told. Robinson was champion for the fourth time. According to Fullmer, he had a contract for a rubber match but Jim Norris threw it out the window. It would be another six months before Robinson defended his title, against a man cut from the same emery cloth as Fullmer.

Carmen Basilio was a flinty man of bone and gristle. He boxed with a cold heart. 'The ring is so many feet by so many feet,' he said. 'There's him, there's me, and there's the referee. And that leaves no room for pity.' His eyes — like 'frozen oysters' according to Peter Wilson — were distrustful, as if someone would cheap-shot him if he did not stay alert. Trainer Angelo Dundee said he was a self-contained man, meticulous about his training and preparation. Others said he was just plain suspicious. His success was based on ceaseless aggression and disdain for hurt. Though he cut easily, it never curbed his vehement aggression.

He was born in Canastota, central New York state, on 2 April 1927, one of four sons and six daughters to Italian parents. His folk were onion farmers. Basilio senior loved to talk with his friends about the exploits of the giant Italian boxer Primo Carnera, the 'Ambling Alp'. He bought boxing gloves for the boys, and sometimes for the girls, to settle family squabbles.

A life farming onions did not appeal to Carmen. As soon as he was old enough he joined the marines. Stationed in Hawaii, he watched a pro fight with Bobo Olson and decided to give the sport a try. He had three amateur fights, all wins. When discharged, he worked in a factory and turned pro in November 1948 to supplement his income. Co-managed by Ralph DeJohn and Joe Netro, he knocked out Jimmy Evans in three rounds.

His early career was erratic, with losses to ordinary fighters like Johnny Cunningham, Eddie Giosa, Vic Cardell, Ross Virgo and Johnny Cesario. His best win at this stage was over former lightweight champion Lew Jenkins. In September 1951 he had to lay off for five months with bursitis in his shoulder. But he was forced to return when his wife Kay, a waitress he met in his favourite cafe, fell ill. His comeback fight was against Chuck Davey. It was first announced as a split points win for Basilio, then declared a draw by the New York commission after an error was discovered in a scorecard.

Basilio started to roll by beating former lightweight champ Ike Williams, then lost, won and drew against Billy Graham, the last two for the New York welter title. He was high enough in the welterweight rankings to get a shot at the classy champion, Kid Gavilan. Basilio lost on a split despite flooring the 'Cuban Hawk' for the first time in his career.

He took the title two years later in a classic bout with Tony DeMarco, whom he broke up with body punching. Basilio also triumphed in a thrilling return, then lost his hard-won crown to Johnny Saxton on another controversial verdict. 'He ran like a deer,' sneered Basilio. The teak-tough farmer took his revenge in a rematch. Saxton made the fatal error of trying to stand and slug with Basilio and had to be rescued in round nine. In their third fight, Saxton was knocked out by a left hook in the second round.

Seven months later, Basilio entered the ring against Sugar Ray Robinson at Yankee Stadium for the middleweight title. Basilio, like Fullmer, disliked Robinson, claiming he had once snubbed him on a New York street. 'I swore then that one day I'd get him in the ring, and lick him. I was thrilled when they made the match, I trained harder than I'd ever done before. I knew I could beat him.' Their battle was an epic of thrust and counter-thrust. Robinson was four inches taller and vastly more experienced but, as Peter Wilson wrote, 'Basilio fought the kind of fight which a man is born to fight just once.' He stormed through the champion's more orthodox blows, swarming over him like rain. At the end of 15 rounds, Basilio's hand was raised on a split decision.

The return, on 25 March 1958 in Chicago, was even better. The first round was blistering, with both swapping punches — and fouls — and they were still swinging after the bell. The pace never dropped. In the sixth, Robinson closed Basilio's left eye with a right cross. The injury was hideous, a huge purple swelling. Cornerman Angelo Dundee told him, 'You can't see Robinson's right hand. I'm going to stop this fight.' Basilio hissed, 'You stop it, I'll knock you out.' He fought on ferociously for the next nine rounds and lost on the closest of split decisions.

Robinson was now champion for the fifth time, an unprecedented boxing achievement. The fans clamoured for a third, deciding bout with Basilio. Robinson rejected an offer of $500,000, claiming he could get more. He finally agreed to $750,000, but that meant Basilio would only get £225,000, and now *he* refused. Haggling went on for months, with Basilio publicly calling Robinson a pig, but the bout was never made.

On 4 May 1959 the NBA stripped Robinson of his title for 'inactivity' and his failure to agree to a rubber match with Basilio. The title was now split again, with New York and the European Boxing Union (formerly the IBU) continuing to recognize Robinson. The 'Sugarman' accepted far less than he would have received against

Basilio when he took on Paul Pender in January 1960. He lost.

The NBA matched Basilio against Fullmer for its vacant title. The fight, on 28 August 1959 in San Francisco, brought together two of the most determined boxers in the ring. Since his dramatic knockout by Robinson, the Utah fighter had learned to pay more attention to his defence and had won nine more bouts on the trot. Basilio expected Fullmer to attack, as usual, but instead he stood off and produced some surprisingly effective boxing. Red Smith said it 'may have been the most skilful battle by an unskilled pug, and the cleverest battle ever planned by amateurs'. Having messed up his opponent's fight plan, Fullmer then started to grind forward. Basilio took a count after stumbling into the ropes and in the 14th round the referee stopped it to save the lighter man. Even then, Basilio begged the referee to let him go on.

Fullmer made seven defences of his version of the title, beating Spider Webb, Basilio again, Robinson, Florentino Fernandez and Benny Paret, and drawing with Robinson and Joey Giardello. The Giardello draw was a bloodbath. Both butted repeatedly and the referee lost all control. The ringwise challenger always maintained he should have won and later called Fullmer a 'crumb'. Fullmer found Carmen Basilio's cruder rushes easier to handle and steam-rollered him in a defence in June 1960, one of his best performances. Basilio seemed mentally unready. He complained frequently about Fullmer's tactics, kept up a running slanging match with his opponent's corner and raged at everyone around him when it was stopped in the 12th. But he had been well beaten.

Meanwhile, Robinson, having lost his title to Paul Pender, failed to regain it in a return fight. In December 1960 he challenged Fullmer. The 'Sugarman' had one last great show in him. After a slow start, he opened up in the fourth, and over the next two rounds unleashed some of the old combos from memory. He also held a lot. Fullmer came on strong in the ninth and tenth, but in the 11th Robinson produced another glimpse of his past. A beautiful left hook spun the champion into the ropes and he was shellacked before wobbling back to his stool. The last few rounds evened out but most thought Robinson had won. The referee and one judge went either way, while the second judge called it a draw. They fought again three months later. A buzzer was used instead of a bell and, at the end of the third round, Fullmer pretended he hadn't heard it and pounded Robinson for several seconds. The 39-year-old former champion never properly recovered and lost clearly on points.

Fullmer's reign continued. In August 1961 he outpointed Florentino Fernandez, despite taking some crunching hooks, including one in the 13th that broke a bone in his arm. Middleweight legend Mickey Walker told the *New York Daily News*, 'Out of all today's fighters, Fullmer is the only one who could have been a champion or contender in my time.' Four months later, Fullmer hit welterweight Benny Paret with 'the hardest punches I ever threw' and knocked him out in the tenth. When Paret died in his next contest, against Emile Griffith (see page 181) many attributed it to the beating he took from Fullmer. Finally, a title unification bout with Paul Pender was mooted for June 1962 at Bozeman, Montana.

Paul Pender was one of those champions who live in the shadow of others. He took the title from a living legend and lacked the charisma to make his own mark. Ray Robinson had not expected to lose when he travelled to Boston to fight Pender on 22 January 1960. The champion started fast, as if he knew he no longer had the stamina for a 15-rounder. Pender suffered in the sixth and seventh but managed to evade his hardest blows and came on strong in the second half to jab to victory. The split decision was controversial, with many thinking Robinson had won. *Boxing News* called it 'one of the major upsets of the century', which seemed a little extreme.

Pender was a talented but colourless boxer with no love for the sport. In an interview before he challenged Robinson he said, 'Why should boxing, as it is conducted today, be allowed to exist? Recent investigations — I know they are true, because I've kept my eyes open in this business — proved boxing is rotten clear through, infested by gangsters and thieves. The public has lost all confidence. I have too.' He later retracted the remarks when questioned about them by the local commission.

His style, conditioned by his brittle hands, was effective but unpopular. He had a superb straight left which he turned into a slicing hook, a long reach and a tight defence. Pender was a stiffer puncher than he is given credit for. His injured hands often prevented him from using full force. He was born in Brookline, Massachusetts,

on 20 June 1930. After winning a New England amateur title he
turned pro in January 1949 with a one-round win. He was unbeaten
in his first 21 fights, which included wins over Roy Wouters and
Ernie Durando. Then he broke a bone in his right hand in his 14th
bout against Leon Brown and suffered from it ever after.

His first loss was in December 1950 to Norman Hayes. He knocked
out Hayes in seven rounds a month later, lost and drew against Joe
Rindone, and in April 1951 was stopped in three rounds by Gene
Hairston. His hands gave him constant pain, but doctors were unable
to find the cause of the trouble. After another stoppage loss, to Jimmy
Beau, and 'a lot of internal conflicts with my own organization of
supposed advisers', Pender joined the marines in disgust. He kept fit
as a boxing instructor.

After an absence of two-and-a-half years, he returned to the ring in
August 1954 with a points win. A Boston doctor finally located the
source of his hand trouble and operated to remove a piece of bone, but
Pender broke his hand again in a fight with Ted Olla. In 1955 he
knocked out Freddie Mack but dropped a ten-rounds points decision
to Gene Fullmer, and retired for another two years. In his comeback
fight, a points win over Jimmy Skinner in December 1956, he broke
his hand again and retired again.

Pender had fought only six times in seven years. Yet the
demoralizing injuries never defeated him. He worked as a fireman in
Brookline and had another operation to remove a bone spur. It was a
success and though he continued to be troubled by his hands, they
never broke again. In November 1958, at the age of 28, he gave it one
last shot, advised by John Cronin, a Boston lawyer and former FBI
man who had replaced his manager Johnny Buckley. By the end of the
year he had won three fights inside the distance. Punching with new
confidence, he scored three more wins early in 1959, then outpointed
Ralph Jones. A win over Jackson Brown brought the New England
middleweight title and a decision over Gene Hamilton put Pender in
line for a world title shot.

Sam Silverman, the leading Boston promoter, managed to
convince Robinson that Pender wasn't much of a threat. Pender's
view of Robinson differed from most. In Peter Heller's *In This
Corner*, he said, 'Robinson was not a great boxer. I tell people that and
they look at me like I'm positively insane. He was the greatest
puncher that ever lived, with a repertoire of punches that nobody

could throw. Did you ever see a fighter that could throw four left hooks, a left hook uppercut, another left hook, and a right hand? Robinson threw these automatically. But . . . he couldn't shine Willie Pep's shoes as far as pure boxing ability.'

Pender supported his thesis by outboxing Robinson in a return on June 1960. His next opponent, Terry Downes of England, he labelled 'a commonplace tough guy who could take a whack'. Downes had also served with the US Marines while living in the States and both entered the ring with a marine escort. Their styles couldn't have provided a greater contrast: Pender fought with his head, Downes with his heart. Pender knocked Downes over with a good right in the first but the Englishman chased him for the rest of the round. Pender's jab was rarely out of Downes's face and in the third it split his nose, a zigzag cut an inch and a half long. The blood ran freely and after 57 seconds of the seventh the referee called a halt.

Pender's next defence was against Carmen Basilio in April in Boston. He called Basilio 'one of the most inept fighters in the world as far as boxing ability is concerned', a 'guy who fought with nothing but his face'. Basilio found it difficult to keep that face away from Pender's spearing jab. 'He was nothing but a punching bag and you would have to get tired hitting him and he would probably beat you.' Pender won comfortably on points over 15 rounds. He floored Basilio for only the second time in his career and put him into retirement.

It was the end of the line for Basilio, who had decided before the bout to retire. He had already become a pillar of the community in Syracuse, New York state, where he was a scout master. He made a success of retirement, with interests in several businesses, including Carmen Basilio Italian Sausages. He still guides a few fighters, makes after-dinner speeches and personal appearances, and — feisty as ever — wishes he hadn't retired so early.

Memories of Terry Downes are always coloured by blood. He seemed to get cut in every fight. The bravest of men, he couldn't resist a good ruck. 'Unless you've boxed a bit it's hard to explain the satisfaction you can get from a decent punch-up,' he said. Injury never deterred him. Boxing writer Hugh McIlvaney described his attitude as 'a seam of the most fundamental optimism, a spirit that somehow impresses as too positive to be destructible'. It never occurred to Downes that he might lose, even with the claret spilling down his face.

Downes was the son of a soldier, born on 9 May 1936, in Paddington, London. His father, Dick, was one of 16 brothers and there was an army of cousins: 'The Downeses of Paddington were a right notorious mob. We weren't murderers or mobsters, but I can't pretend we were always a bunch of do-gooders.' Though born beyond the sound of Bow Bells, he was the archetypal Cockney: brash, loud, confident, quick-witted. He was also quick with his mitts and joined a boxing club in his early teens.

Downes's family moved to America in 1952 to be with his sister Sylvia, an acrobat with Ringling Brothers' circus, after she lost an arm in a road accident in Baltimore. Terry became a newspaper copy boy and boxed for the Baltimore YMCA. In January 1954 he joined the US Marines, where he had been told boxers received privileged treatment. Instead he was sent to a camp in Paris Island, Carolina, where discipline was so harsh that two other recruits committed suicide. Eventually he was transferred and won a string of armed services boxing titles. He missed a berth for the Melbourne Olympics because he hadn't been a US resident long enough.

Downes decided to turn pro and signed a management deal with the boxer Walter Cartier, a front man for Irving Cohen, Rocky Graziano's former manager. Before his debut he returned to England for a holiday. There he boxed a few more amateur fights before promoter Jack Solomons talked him into ignoring the American contract and turning pro in England. Tycoon Jarvis Astaire became his manager. His first pro outing, in April 1957, lasted 90 seconds, 26 of which opponent Peter Longo spent on the canvas in four separate trips. Downes topped the bill in his next fight, a short win against hard man Jimmy Lynas. His Stateside experience had given him a distinctly American style; though not a big puncher, he threw loads of leather and could switch easily between head and body.

An obscure Nigerian was picked for his third contest. Dick Tiger, who worked in a Liverpool paint factory, had lost five of 11 fights in England and Downes was the 5–1 favourite. Tiger made a mockery of the odds by dropping him twice in the first round and once in the second. Downes piled back in and forced Tiger to hold. They exchanged fire for the next four rounds, with the Nigerian's blows causing most damage. Downes's right eye swelled shut, his left was badly cut, and at the end of the sixth his corner pulled him out. 'Who will you fight next?' he was asked in the dressing room. 'The geezer who made that match,' Downes replied. He received £125, Tiger £60. Within five years they had both won world titles.

Downes lost again on cuts in January 1958, but in June he whipped the British middle champ Pat McAteer into retirement in a non-title fight. In September he won the vacant British title in 13 rounds from an experienced Welshman, Phil Edwards. The *Daily Mail* called it 'the most thorough beating a man can take without going down'. Downes now wanted to challenge the European champion, Gustav Scholz, but Solomons and Harry Levene, Britain's leading promoters, were Jewish and would not book a German boxer.

Instead Downes made a major mistake: he fought Chicago's Ellsworth 'Spider' Webb. The American was rated number three in the world and oozed class. The British papers were aghast. Once again, Downes took a sucker punch in the first round and landed on his back. Dead game, he refused to buckle, and turned a potential walkover into one of the best fights ever seen in a British ring. 'In the next few rounds, we tore each other apart,' wrote Downes. 'The crowd were going raving mad.' They dislodged each other's gumshields and shook each other repeatedly. Again Downes bled heavily. At the end of the seventh, the ref examined gashes over both his eyes, and one round later it was stopped. The press had nothing but praise for Downes and he was made Young Boxer of the Year.

Downes was cut repeatedly in his next few bouts, despite plastic surgery and a specially made headguard that protected his nose during sparring. He also lost his British title in a farcical contest with John 'Cowboy' McCormack. Downes dropped his ungainly challenger ten times, nine from body punches. Incredibly, he was then disqualified in the eighth round for an alleged low blow. He stopped McCormack in a rematch.

To earn a world title bout Downes needed to beat a leading American. Having failed against Spider Webb, he now tried Joey Giardello. It was a bold move. Giardello was 30 and had a record of 108 fights. The British press referred to him as 'Scarface', which did not please him one bit. He was well-versed in the dark arts of boxing and was more than capable of opening Downes's old wounds. So the Londoner chose to box at distance for once. It worked. Downes won the ten-round decision.

His first attempt at the world title ended in honourable defeat against Paul Pender in Boston (see page 167). Downes's nose was cut to the bone and required 12 stitches. 'Pender won by a nose,' rued Downes. The London *Daily Mail* concluded: 'Nobody wins world titles by leading with his face.' The Londoner, however, was guaranteed a return on home territory on 11 July 1961.

There was a sensation when Pender was retired on his stool by trainer Al Lacey with a cut after nine rounds. Downes bled as usual, but dropped the American for a short count in the sixth. Pender was also cut over both eyes and, after a storming effort in the ninth, was pulled out by his corner. The papers were unconvinced; many hinted Pender quit knowing he had a return clause. John Cronin had insisted that a large part of Downes's purse be held in escrow in a US bank to ensure he would give Pender a rematch in Boston. In the early hours of the next morning, Boston promoter Sam Silverman was beaten up in a London night club by Albert Dimes, a notorious villain who was wrongly convinced it had been a betting coup. Pender's faction said their man had been suffering from a virus.

Their rubber match was a rough and tumble affair in Boston on 7 April 1962. Pender started by grabbing Downes, who butted him in return. It turned into a contest between Pender's jab and Downes's close-quarter work. Both boxers staged a grandstand finish. Pender got the nod. Surprisingly, it was the first and only time Downes went a full 15 rounds.

The Paddington boxer scored a few more useful wins at middleweight, beating Gene Fullmer's brother Don, a 41-year-old Sugar Ray Robinson, and Phil Moyer. He moved up to light-heavyweight to challenge Willie Pastrano, the world champion, in Manchester in November 1964. For ten rounds Downes set the pace and ran off with the points. In desperation, trainer Angelo Dundee whacked Pastrano's backside and swore at him at the start of the 11th. The champion let fly with a right-hander and down went Downes. He got up, then went down again on one knee during a follow-up attack. The referee stopped it, despite Downes's protestations.

Downes retired from boxing but had more than enough to keep him busy. His business interests had started with a car showroom in the 1950s. He was sharp enough to move into bookmaking when the 1963 Gaming Act legalized off-course betting. With Sam Burns he became an executive with the Hurst Park Syndicate of betting shops, eventually bought by William Hill in the early 1970s. He dabbled with acting and sent his children to private schools.

One thing Downes never forgot was how to use his fists. On one occasion a blackmailer threatened to petrol-bomb his north London house if he didn't hand over £5,000. Downes agreed to meet him and sent him flying with a single punch before the police moved in. Then there was the motorist who took exception to Downes's driving, jumped from his car and swung several punches. 'I took my glasses off and hit him two or three times,' Christopher Holloway told a court. 'It didn't have any effect on him at all'. Downes's right cross did have an effect, putting Holloway in hospital for five days with a broken jaw. The boxer was cleared of any blame.

In the late 1980s Downes lost an estimated £250,000 in share and property deals. He is still comfortably off and travels the country raising funds to buy Sunshine coaches for handicapped children on behalf of the Variety Club of Great Britain. He is also an unmistakable voice at boxing matches.

After beating Downes, Paul Pender lost interest in boxing, and the various commissions and associations began to withdraw their recognition of him. New York removed his title in November 1962 and recognized Dick Tiger instead, a move adopted by all other major ruling bodies. On 7 May 1963 Pender formally announced his retirement. He became a prison recreation director, a dog-track security officer, later gained a university degree and entered local politics. And he had his broken nose straightened.

Gene Fullmer lost his version of the title to Tiger in October 1962. He was unsuccessful in two attempts to regain it (see page 175) and retired in July 1964. He made some bad business deals but is still comfortably off. Now semi-retired and still in West Jordan, he raises pigs, cows and horses, which he sells, and lives off his real estate holdings. His most arduous duty is babysitting for his nine grandchildren. He maintains an interest in boxing as president of the Rocky Mountain Gloves and looks as though he could still go a few rounds.

The curtain on Sugar Ray Robinson's career came down against Joey Archer, who floored and beat him in November 1965. It was the last of 45 bouts he had boxed since his last world title bout with Fullmer. Robinson had recently fought wherever he could pick up a purse, in France, England, Scotland, Mexico, Italy and Hawaii, losing to men who couldn't have laced his boots in his prime. He announced his retirement on 10 December 1965 at a glittering farewell party at Madison Square Garden. Four of the five opponents he had beaten to win the world middleweight title were there (LaMotta was barred). Johnny Addie announced him as 'the greatest fighter in the history of boxing'.

Robinson became an actor, starring in films and TV shows. He devoted most of his energies to the Sugar Ray Youth Foundation to counter juvenile delinquency. It has helped thousands of deprived youngsters. Sadly, he was stricken with Alzheimer's Disease and towards the end of his life he could not even recognize old friends. He was cared for by his wife Millie (he and Edna Mae had divorced).

An era ended when he died on 12 April 1989. Two thousand mourners, from Mike Tyson to Elizabeth Taylor, attended his funeral. The mood was perhaps best captured in a piece written years earlier, during Robinson's decline, by W. C. Heinz: 'When I am old I shall tell them about Ray Robinson. . . . When the young assault me with their atomic miracles and reject my Crosby records and find comical the movies that once moved me, I shall entice them into talking about fighters. Robinson will be a form of social security for me, because they will have seen nothing like him, and I am convinced that they never will.'

12

The 1960s

TRIBAL scars are a sign of manhood among the Ibo of Nigeria. Richard Ihetu received his when he was ten. They were seared across his chest with a hot sharp knife in a thin, almost invisible line. Born in Amaigbo, Nigeria, on 14 August 1929, he inherited the proud and haughty bearing of the Ibo from his father, Naajuogu ('Knife fears no war'). Once, perhaps, he might have been a great warrior. Instead, under the name Dick Tiger, he became a great boxer.

A. J. Liebling wrote that Tiger 'had a chest like an old-fashioned black office safe, dropping away to a slender waist, big thighs, and slender legs; he boxed classically, his arms tight against his sides at the beginning of a punch, his savagely methodical blows moving in short arcs and straight lines.' Outside the ring he was 'a quiet man, with the temperament of a disciple'. He was serious in thought and speech, a student of politics. Just occasionally, his big cheekbones widened into a dazzling grin.

Tiger worked as a farm labourer while attending a small rural school. He left home for Aba, one of Nigeria's larger towns, and worked as a janitor while training to be a boxer. The sport there was booming with the success of Hogan 'Kid' Bassey, who was to become world featherweight champion. After a brief career as an amateur, Tiger turned professional in 1952. Colourful ring names were an African tradition: he fought men called Easy Dynamite, Mighty Joe, Lion Ring, Koko Kid, Black Power and Super Human Power. He also picked up the Nigerian middleweight title. In the winter of 1955, with just one defeat in 16 contests, he followed Bassey's path and sailed to Liverpool, England.

Tiger lived in a boarding house and manager Tony Vairo found him work in a paint shop. But he was painfully homesick and lost his first four fights in England on points. Gradually, however, he began to show his true form, but his record was still far from impressive when, in May 1957, he met former amateur star Terry Downes. Tiger won after a brutal punch-up (see page 168). After more useful performances against Britain's best middleweights, he knocked out Pat McAteer in nine rounds to become British Empire champion in March 1958.

Three months later, Tiger tangled with one of the best boxers in the world, the American Spider Webb, in London. He was outpointed but not outclassed. After a points win over Yolande Pompey, he lost and won in two bouts against another top American, Randy Sandy. Soon after, he moved to the United States. 'America made me a better fighter,' he said. 'There I got good training and sparring, but best of all I could go to many fights. I watched and I learned.' He was managed in the States by Jersey Jones, a sportswriter and man-about-boxing.

Over the next three years Tiger fought and beat the cream of America's middleweight division. In that time he lost three decisions, to Rory Calhoun, Joey Giardello and Wilf Greaves, who took his Empire title. He beat Giardello, Gene Armstrong, Holly Mims and Henry Hank, and regained his title from Greaves. He also stopped Spider Webb and beat the Cuban bomber Florentino Fernandez in five hectic rounds, leaving him with a broken nose.

Tiger outpunched the punchers and outboxed the boxers. Nobody took a better punch. He was never fast on his feet — he was 'like a man rushing a wheelbarrow uphill', said Jimmy Cannon — but he stalked implacably. He was sparing with his punches, drawing his opponent's leads before slotting in counters. Privately, he was a conservative man with a reputation for thrift. He wore old, patched clothes and lived in a cheap hotel. 'Dick Tiger wouldn't pay a quarter to see an earthquake,' said trainer Charlie Goldman. He sent his earnings to his wife Abigail, a former teacher, and their brood of children in Nigeria, where he owned a nine-room house, seven apartment buildings, a ranch and a couple of shops.

On 23 October 1962 Tiger challenged Gene Fullmer for the WBA middleweight title in San Francisco. It had the makings of a gruelling ruck. Tiger's shorter punching cut inside Fullmer's swings and he was strong enough to resist the champion's rushes. Fullmer was forced to back off, a new experience for him. Sometimes, wrote A. J. Liebling, Fullmer 'drove in with his left forearm across his face, throwing his right fist over it, like a man ducking behind a bar to throw beer bottles'. It had little effect. Tiger won the decision. They fought another dour battle in Las Vegas in February 1963. This time it was a draw, with Fullmer convinced he should have won.

Tiger deeply wanted to perform in front of his own people. On 10 August 1963 he fought Fullmer for a third time in Ibadan, Nigeria. It was the first major sports event ever held there. The promotion was backed by the government and all of Nigeria was exhorted to buy tickets. Tiger was fiercely proud of his country, refusing to pose in tribal robes by a tree-trunk because he said it would make Nigeria look like a jungle. He did kid reporters that he ate white men for breakfast. That was pretty much what he did to Fullmer. Before 25,000 people, Fullmer was pulled out by his corner after seven rounds, thoroughly beaten and with one eye shut tight. *Boxing News* called it 'a frightening display of scientific slaughter'.

Tiger lost the title in his third defence four months later to the hugely experienced Joey Giardello. The decision was hotly debated. The African had a return clause but was kept waiting for almost two years. He refused to wrap his high world ranking in cotton wool and continued to fight the best opponents. He beat Don Fullmer, Gene's brother, dropped a decision to clever Joey Archer, wiped out Rocky Rivero, flooring him for the first time in 54 fights, and outpointed the fearsome Rubin Carter.

On 21 October Tiger regained his title from Giardello on points in New York. It was a battle of veterans: Giardello was 35, Tiger 36. Something apart from age bothered the African; he was starting to suffer pains in his lower back and right side, and occasionally saw blood in his urine. He lost his title six months later, again on a disputed decision, to welterweight champion Emile Griffith in New York on 25 April. Weight problems nudged him up to the light-heavyweight division and on 12 December he became a world champion at two weights by beating José Torres in an all-action encounter.

Tiger should have been contemplating retirement. But bad things were stirring at home. In May 1967 the Ibo of eastern Nigeria seceded from the central government to form the new state of Biafra. It caused a hellish civil war. Thousands were massacred on both sides, but the

Ibo suffered most. Tiger fought on, earning money for his people's cause. He defended the light-heavyweight title against Torres and Roger Rouse and sent more than $100,000-worth of food and medicine on the 5,000-mile journey to Aba in a private plane. As the war wore on, thousands more were threatened with starvation from an economic blockade. The Ibo appealed for arms and aid from the outside world; none came.

In 1968, desperate for cash, Tiger defended against Bob Foster, a lanky American sheriff who hit with concussive force. The champion took a ballistic left hook in round four and was counted out for the only time in his life. In Nigeria, members of his family were imprisoned and his Lagos properties were confiscated. In 1969 he returned the CBE he had been awarded by the Queen as a protest against the lack of British support for the Biafra cause. Finally, Aba fell after a bloody battle. Tiger, in New York, told reporters, 'Nothing matters any more.'

He fought four times after the Foster defeat before retiring in July 1971 at the age of 42. He worked as a guard at the Metropolitan Museum of Art, living in a low-rent room in Brooklyn. In October 1971 he was stricken by a stabbing pain in his back while at work. He was diagnosed as having advanced cancer of the liver. With the civil war over, the Nigerian government allowed him to return home to die in Aba. According to author Sam Toperoff, 'His plane landed in Port Harcourt. For days thereafter thousands of visitors — mourners, really — from miles around walked the hot, dusty roads to Aba. When they found his house they saw a muscular but pain-withered man sitting in the shade of a solitary acacia tree, his best fights behind him.' He died in hospital, his dreams destroyed, on 14 December 1971.

★　　★　　★

Joey Giardello was not a model citizen. 'I loved to fight in the street', he told Peter Heller. 'I wanted to be champion when I was a kid. So I made what I wanted to be. I just loved to fight.' An Italian–American punk with a mean streak, he sometimes carried the tricks of the street into the ring. If you wanted it dirty, Joey would oblige. He rarely trained, getting by on natural ability, savvy and a cool head.

Carmine Tilelli was born in Brooklyn, New York, on 16 July 1930.

He was raised in Flatbush and spent much of his youth fighting with gangs. At 15 he bought a birth certificate from an older cousin and used his name, Joe Giardello, to join the army. He became a paratrooper with the 82nd Airborne Division. Part of their training was done in the boxing ring and 'Joey' took to the sport, though his first love was baseball. His parents eventually found out where he was and told the authorities, and he was discharged.

He stayed in Philadelphia for a spell, digging sewers, and at 18 turned pro to earn extra cash, keeping the name Giardello so his folks wouldn't know it was him. He beat Johnny Noel in two rounds in his debut in October 1948. Giardello's first manager was Jimmy Santore, who later sold his contract to Carmine Graziano and Tony Ferrante. The latter was a relative of Joe Bonnano, otherwise known as 'Joe Bananas', a notorious Mafia boss. Partly for this reason, Giardello was known as a 'Mob fighter'. He always denied this, pointing out that it would not have taken him so long to get a title fight if he had been well-connected. He did not become champion until Frankie Carbo was in jail.

Giardello was a throwback to the 1920s and '30s, when boxers fought at least once a month. He had an up-and-down early career, going unbeaten until 1950, when he lost three fights, two inside the distance. He learned his boxing in the ring rather than the gym, his style based not on boxing theory but on what was needed to survive and win. Writer Sam Toperoff said 'Giardello was what they call a "cutie pie", an excellent defensive fighter who could avoid being hit, counterpunch and minimize the damage to himself with a combination of leaning, holding, spinning and leverage tricks he'd learned and mastered.' He had more tricks than a conjuror, but was often let down by lack of training and a weak punch.

He took a couple of good scalps in 1951, beating Roy Wouters and Ernie Durando, but dropped a few decisions as well. In 1952, having moved back to New York, he broke into the rankings, beating, among others, Pierre Langlois, Billy Graham and Joey Giambra. A return with the veteran Graham in New York ended up in court. Giardello won the split decision, but two members of the New York commission then changed the referee's card, giving the win to Graham. Giardello took the case to the New York Supreme Court, where a judge found in his favour: the original decision stood.

Newspaper coverage of the case put Giardello in the public eye and his fists did the rest. He was to stay in the world rankings for the next 14 years. In 1953 he lost to Graham and Johnny Saxton but beat Harold Green, Gil Turner, Ernie Durando, Walter Cartier and others. (Giardello claimed the Saxton defeat, in Philadelphia, was engineered by mobster Blinky Palermo). He showed hitherto unsuspected punching power in 1954, stopping Garth Panter, Cartier and Willie Troy in quick succession before losing to Johnny Saxton. He lost to Pierre Langlois but was guaranteed a title fight with Bobo Olson on 15 December. By a cruel twist of fate Giardello was injured in a car accident and the title shot went to Langlois.

He recovered from his injuries to win three bouts at the start of 1955. Then, disastrously, the old Carmine Tilelli surfaced. He was with two friends filling-up at a gas station when a fracas broke out. Giardello, who was on crutches with a foot injury, whacked the attendant with one of his sticks. The man was also hit with a pistol butt. Giardello was jailed, serving four-and-a-half months, and his New York boxing licence was later revoked. While in jail, his father died. The boxer was allowed out for his funeral, flanked by guards, and swore he would one day win the world title for his dad.

It was almost a year before he would fight again. He found a new manager, businessman Frank Laurenzi, and his career resumed its meandering course. After dropping a couple of decisions to Charlie Cotton, he put together an unbeaten run of 17 fights, including a knockout of highly rated Bobby Boyd. It seemed he must get a title shot, but Sugar Ray Robinson was conducting his own personal feuds with Gene Fullmer and Carmen Basilio, and Giardello was frozen out. His bubble burst in June 1958. Joey Giambra, another tough Italian–American who never got the breaks, beat him in ten rounds in San Francisco. Giambra said gangsters told him to fall in the second round, but he defied them and made a sharp exit after the bout in a getaway car ready outside the arena. Demoralized, Giardello also lost his next two bouts, to Spider Webb and Ralph Jones.

Once again, he clawed back into contention, beating Holly Mims, Del Flanagan and Chico Vejar and losing and winning in two bouts with Dick Tiger. Finally, after almost 12 years of boxing, he was granted a title shot by NBA champion Gene Fullmer. They fought in Bozeman, Montana, in April 1960. Fullmer started in his usual ruffian style and bored his head into Giardello's face. The challenger responded with blatant butts of his own and the bout turned into a bloodbath. After 15 rounds it was declared a draw. Giardello was incensed and his supporters almost came to blows with Fullmer's.

Giardello took the result badly. He lost three of his next six bouts and appeared to stop training completely. But he never gave up. Two points wins over Jesse Smith restored his confidence and in January 1962 he came back from an early battering to pip Henry Hank in a classic. He won four of his next five bouts and in June 1963 was matched to meet Sugar Ray Robinson. Robinson did not want the bout, but was persuaded to accept by matchmaker Teddy Brenner. He pointed out that Giardello was one of the few white middleweights who had never avoided the top black fighters, men like Spider Webb, Holly Mims, Henry Hank, Randy Sandy, Willie Troy and George Benton. Giardello duly outpointed Robinson.

Machinations were now afoot to match Giardello with Dick Tiger for the title. Lou Duva, who helped handle Giardello, said he had waited so long for a shot because his management would not cut Frankie Carbo into the action. Duva told reporter Dave Anderson, 'I manoeuvred Joey into a title fight because I had the right connections. I sat down with the right people and worked out the right deal. I never sat down with Carbo, but there was other people I sat down with. It wasn't so much giving a piece, it was more or less a friendship thing. . . . I was never involved to the point where I was part of a plot.' Carbo had been jailed for 25 years for extortion in 1961, but his 'people' were still influential.

Giardello trained for nine weeks and was in the best shape of his life when he faced Tiger in Atlantic City on 7 December 1963. He carried with him the experience gained in 123 pro fights and was, in the words of Jimmy Cannon, 'a guy who understood the forgotten practices of a once graceful sport'. It was a fight for the purists, with the champion's harder, more methodical hooking countered by the challenger's longer reach and greater mobility. 'I just moved and moved and nobody could believe I'd go fifteen rounds like that,' said Giardello. At the end of 15 rounds, luck smiled on him for once. He took a tight decision and the title. The celebrations lasted for days.

Giardello didn't change. He was just as ready to fight anyone as he had been as challenger. After two non-title wins over Rocky Rivero, he defended his title against Rubin 'Hurricane' Carter, the division's most feared fighter. Carter, survivor of an appallingly violent youth in a bleak black ghetto in Paterson, New Jersey, had developed into a

malevolent puncher with a shaven head, goatee beard and Sonny
Liston stare. But Giardello had far more experience and knew too
much for his challenger, winning on points. Carter later became a
cause célèbre when he was jailed for triple murder. Many media
figures backed a campaign to establish his innocence and he was
finally exonerated after two decades in prison.

Not every title fight came off. Lou Duva lined up two well-paid
defences against Nino Benvenuti, the darling of Italy. The first would
be in Benvenuti's home country. If the American lost the decision,
the return would be in Jersey, where only the referee scored. As that
would be former heavyweight champion Rocky Marciano, a pal of
Duva's, any decision would be sure to go the 'right' way. The bouts
never happened. But life was good for Giardello, who had changed.
He lived in a smart colonial home in Cherry Hill, New Jersey, with his
blonde wife Rosalie and children. Carmine, his second son, was
retarded from birth. Caring for him altered Joey's outlook on life:
'My kids were the reason I matured, the reason for going to church
and saving my money and taking adult education courses and
becoming a different person.' His New York licence had also been
restored.

On 21 October 1965 Giardello met Dick Tiger in a return match in
New York. Seventeen thousand fans turned out on a Thursday night
to watch two of the best boxers of their day wage war. From the
blackness of the vast arena came the rhythmic beat of an African
drum. Tiger rumbled forward, used his strength to pin Giardello
down and won the decision.

Giardello fought a few more times, but even his appetite for the
ring was waning. He retired at the end of 1967 and became an
insurance salesman in New York. Later he was made a regional
distributor for a chemicals company. Today he is involved in church
and community affairs and raises funds to help disabled children. A
model citizen.

Emile Griffith was the Ol' Man River of the middleweight division.
He just kept rollin' along. He boxed in 22 officially sanctioned world
title bouts and remained at the top of his profession for almost 20
years. A great body-puncher, he could change tactics to suit the

occasion. He could beat anyone on his day, and could just as easily lose to them the next. *Boxing News* in 1967 said, 'He is a complex character who wants to be loved and admired, especially by the fight crowd.' A superstitious and sensitive man, he always carried a jade Buddha charm for luck. He was deeply affected by the death of his opponent Benny Paret early in his career.

Griffith was born in the Virgin Islands on 3 February 1938, the oldest of eight children with a widowed mother. He went to New York at the age of 11 and eventually found work in a West Side hat factory. His boss, Howie Albert, an enthusiastic boxing fan, noticed his impressive physique (he had a 27in waist) and encouraged him to box. Albert sent him to the Park Department Gym where, under the tutelage of Gil Clancy, he won 51 of 53 amateur bouts, taking the New York and Inter-City Golden Gloves welter titles.

He turned professional in June 1958 and won 19 of his first 21 matches, losing only to Randy Sandy and Denny Moyer. Wins over the hazardous Florentino Fernandez and Luis Rodriguez brought him a shot at the world welterweight title in April 1961. It was held by Cuba's Benny Paret, a brave but inconsistent fighter. Griffith was trailing after 12 rounds. In a desperate bid to motivate his boxer, Gil Clancy slapped his face before the 13th. Griffith stormed out and knocked out the champion with a left hook.

After one defence, he lost to Paret in a hard return. Neither man liked the other and when they were matched a third time the bad blood rose to the surface. Paret called Griffith a *maricon* (homosexual) and touched his buttocks at the weigh-in in New York. Griffith was incensed. The bout took place on 24 March 1962, and Griffith was knocked down early on. Paret, however, had taken a terrible beating from Gene Fullmer in a middleweight title fight some months before and had not fully recovered. In the 12th round, Griffith pinned him on the ropes and jerked his head back repeatedly with right hands. Paret took 22 punches without reply before collapsing as referee Ruby Goldstein stepped in. He never regained consciousness. Videotape replay had been used for the first time on television and the barbarous ending was shown across the world. Broadcaster Don Dunphy recalled: 'Apparently people were calling friends and telling them to tune in, that a guy was getting beaten to death on the TV.' Paret died ten days later.

There were immediate calls for the abolition of boxing. Griffith was devastated and still carries the mental scars. 'I've never stopped anybody since then, really,' he told an interviewer in the early 1970s. But boxing was his business, and later that year he successfully retained his title against Ralph Dupas and Jorge Fernandez. In 1963 he lost his welterweight crown to Luis Rodriguez, then won it back three months later. In all, Griffith met the skilful Rodriguez in four excellent fights. Norman Mailer called their bouts a 'dialogue between bodies'.

Gil Clancy believed Griffith had the ability to move up to the more prestigious middleweight division and beat Dick Tiger, the champion. A win over Holly Mims encouraged him further and in December 1963 Griffith tackled Rubin Carter in Pittsburgh. It was a risky piece of management, and proved disastrous. The 'Hurricane' was in one of his lethal moods and blasted Griffith to bits in less than a round.

Griffith concentrated on the 147-pounders for the next two years, defending his title four more times. He did make an excursion into the middleweights again on 20 August 1965, against not Tiger but Gene Fullmer's brother Don. The contest, in Salt Lake City, was recognized by the World Boxing Association (formerly the NBA) as a world title fight and Griffith lost a 12-round decision.

Everyone knew Tiger was the real champion, however, and he gave Griffith a shot in New York on 25 April 1966. It was a very close fight and many thought Tiger unlucky to lose the 15-round decision. No less an authority than Nat Fleischer called it 'one of the worst decisions rendered in New York for many years'. Under boxing rules Griffith had to relinquish his welterweight title to take the middleweight one. He protested and took the matter to a Supreme Court judge, but lost. Bronx Irishman Joey Archer gave Griffith a tough time in two title defences, taking him to a split decision in New York. The champion boxed better when they met for a second time six months later and again won the decision.

His next opponent, Italy's Nino Benvenuti, had lost just once in 72 contests. They fought in New York on 17 April 1967. The champion was on the floor in the second but came back to put Benvenuti down in the fourth. The challenger prevailed, however, his precise punching and longer reach taking him to a 15-round win. In their return bout, on 29 September, Griffith was at his best, boxing brilliantly to regain his title on points. He said he had really felt like fighting for the first time since Paret's death. Their third contest took place at the new Madison Square Garden on 4 March 1968. Benvenuti won, again on points. They were so evenly matched that there would never have been more than a couple of points between them.

Griffith could still make welterweight and decided to chase the 147-pound title. He met José Napoles, a truly exceptional champion, on October 1969 and was well beaten. Several writers called for his retirement. He proved them wrong by winning ten in a row and securing a challenge against Carlos Monzon of Argentina, who had taken the middleweight mantle from Benvenuti. The Argentinian was too strong for him and won in 14 rounds.

In 1973, in a rematch with Monzon, the 35-year-old Griffith gave one of his greatest performances, pushing a superb champion to the limit. He frequently beat Monzon to the punch and drove him to the ropes, but could not keep the attacks going. Monzon countered strongly in the final third to win a fiercely disputed decision. Griffith suffered several more defeats and there were calls for his retirement. Then, in 1974, he scored a big upset over Bennie Briscoe. He became an international journeyman and, and at the age of 39, came within an ace of winning his sixth world championship, at light-middleweight, against Eckhard Dagge in Berlin. The split decision in Dagge's favour was jeered.

Griffith retired after losing in his 112th fight to Alan Minter. He became a trainer and cornerman, working at the Times Square Gym with stars like Wilfred Benitez, Bonecrusher Smith and Simon Brown. But his money all went and he was reduced to working as a nightclub bouncer. In September 1992 he was hospitalized with a serious kidney ailment. One report said he had been beaten up by a gang of men after a fracas at the nightclub.

Giovanni 'Nino' Benvenuti was the son of a fish peddler from the Adriatic seaport of Trieste. He was born on 26 April 1938. A sporty youth, he was inspired by the success of his hometown hero, Duilio Loi, who was to win the world junior welterweight title. Benvenuti followed him into boxing and became the finest amateur Italy had ever produced. He lost only one of 120 contests, took the national and

European titles and in 1960 won an Olympic gold medal at
welterweight before an ecstatic crowd in Rome. He also received the
award for best stylist, ahead of a flashy young American called
Cassius Clay. Benvenuti would always say that winning the gold
medal was his biggest career thrill.

Tall and dark, with film-star looks, Benvenuti was the idol of Italy.
With the nation behind him, he had little choice but to turn pro,
beating Ben Ali Allala on his debut in January 1961. He boxed all over
Italy, fighting often and taking the vacant Italian middleweight title
against Tomasso Truppi in his 30th straight victory. His opponents
were not very good, but his supporters did not seem to mind.
Benvenuti was also active outside the ring. An avid admirer of Benito
Mussolini, he was elected in 1963 to the Trieste City Council as a
member of the neo-Fascist Italian Social Movement.

He defended his Italian title three times, but generally his
management kept him in cotton wool. Only gradually was he allowed
to meet decent foreign boxers like Gaspar Ortega, Denny Moyer,
Mick Leahy and Rip Randall. In June 1965 he was the obvious choice
for a bout with fellow Italian Sandro Mazzinghi, holder of the junior-
middleweight title, which had been created by the NBA three years
earlier. Mazzinghi was very strong and had lost just once, but he was
caught by one of Benvenuti's right uppercuts and was knocked out in
round six.

Now a champion and still unbeaten, Benvenuti marched on. He
took the vacant European middleweight crown against Luis Folledo,
beat Mazzinghi again in a world title fight, outpointed Don Fullmer
and defended his Euro title against Jupp Elze in Berlin. Then his
handlers made their first error. They accepted a world title defence
against Ki-Soo Kim in Korea in June 1966. Benvenuti had been the
only man to beat Kim as an amateur, in the Olympics, but now the
Korean turned the tables. He took the Italian's title on points and
handed him his first loss in 66 pro fights.

Benvenuti got back on the winning track with six wins and made
his second venture out of Europe to challenge Emile Griffith for the
middleweight title in New York on 17 April 1967. This time he was
more successful. Roared on by a huge contingent of New York
Italians, he won by a wide margin after a hard tussle which saw both
men on the floor. He lost the title back to Griffith in his first defence,
but regained it in March 1968, clinching the decision with a

A classic fight: Randolph Turpin taking the title from the great Sugar Ray
Robinson...

...Turpin out-pointed Robinson on a fabulous night for British boxing at Earl's Court, London. (*Press Association*)

Turpin beats Charles Humez to win European recognition as champion after Robinson's retirement.

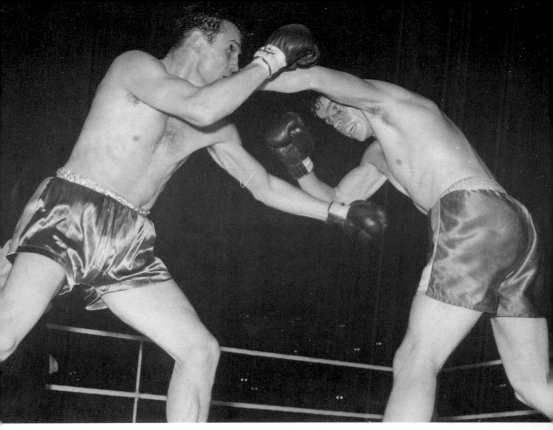

Paul Pender and Terry Downes fight it out for the championship in July 1961. Pender was forced to retire with a bad cut to his left eye after the ninth round. (*Press Association*)

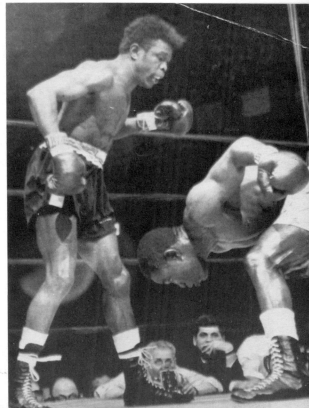

Two of the most under-rated champions, Dick Tiger and Emile Griffith, clash for the title.

Carlos Monzon's huge reach is apparent as he picks apart welterweight champion Jose Napoles.

Britain's Alan Minter chops up Vito Antuofermo, the man from whom he took the title. (*Press Association*)

Marvin Hagler and Tommy 'Hit Man' Hearns go to war in their classic slugfest at Caesars Palace in 1985. (*Allsport/David Cannon*)

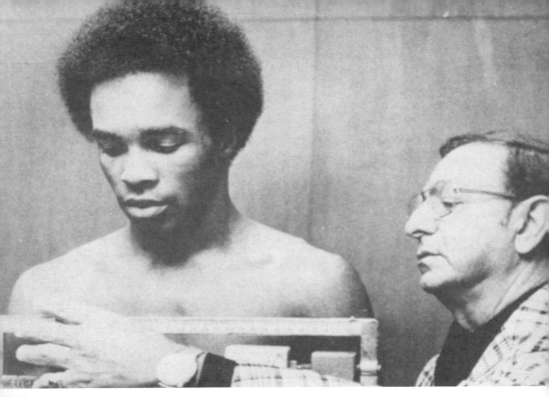

Mr Perfect: Sugar Ray Leonard at a weigh-in with Angelo Dundee.

Roberto Duran, the first man to beat Leonard and one of the most ferocious fighters of all.

Nigel Benn ducks defensively to avoid an attack from Chris Eubank during their championship contest at Birmingham Exhibition Centre in November 1990. (*Press Association*)

Chris Eubank lands a punch to Michael Watson's head during their super middleweight title fight in September 1991. The fight ended in near tragedy when Watson fell into a coma. (*Press Association*)

knockdown in round nine.

The Italian was never convincing as a world champion. He had been managed too carefully and had not faced the variety of styles needed to hone a great boxer. He won several non-title bouts and in December 1968 defended successfully against Don Fullmer in San Remo, but not before he had been on the floor. His limitations were exposed by Dick Tiger, who outpointed him in a non-title contest. The once-unspoilt features were also looking marked. Fraser Scott, who faced him in a title fight in Naples in October 1969, wrote, 'The nose resembled putty that had been bent and twisted around, and then straightened out again. It wasn't wrong for a fighter to look like that. It was his badge.' Scott professed bemusement when he was disqualified in the seventh.

In November Benvenuti was losing to Luis Rodriguez, but found a left hook in the 11th round to knock him senseless and save his crown. Disaster struck in his next bout. Tom Bethea, an American who had lost his last five bouts, three inside the distance, forced him to retire in eight rounds in a non-title bout. In a quick return, Benvenuti was in better shape. A left hook–right cross combination took care of Bethea in round 11 in the first-ever title bout in Yugoslavia. Then the champion drew with Doyle Baird in another non-title affair.

An unknown Argentinian was selected for his next defence, in Rome on 7 November 1970. Carlos Monzon was in fact the hardest puncher Benvenuti had ever faced and matched the champion in height and reach. He jolted the Italian as early as the first and gave him a lesson in controlled, effective ferocity. Benvenuti rallied several times but was heavily punished in the 11th, and in the 12th he was caught by a succession of pinpoint blows. He was trapped in his own corner, and a left hook set him up for a straight right to the jaw. He slumped to his knees, then toppled onto his face. By the time he struggled up he had been counted out.

Benvenuti was granted the now-customary rematch (rematches had been the bane of the division in the 1960s, denying many good challengers a chance at the title). His tune-up bout turned to farce when he was drubbed by José Chirino and lost on points. He still went ahead with his challenge to Monzon in the first-ever title bout held in Monte Carlo. The Italian was walloped and knocked down twice before his manager Bruno Amaduzzi threw in the towel in round three.

Benvenuti has since made a successful career out of the ring, travelling widely for a publishing company and appearing in films and as a television and radio pundit.

13

King Carlos

VIOLENCE surrounds Carlos Monzon. It has been the constant theme in his life. In the boxing ring he mastered it; no middleweight has been more dominant. But outside the ropes, violence was his master. From his youth as a street fighter and pimp to the shootings and arrests of his adulthood, he has never escaped it. A brother died in a gunfight; another faced murder charges. And today Monzon, one of the greatest of all boxing champions, himself languishes in an Argentine prison cell for killing his ex-wife.

How different it is from his days as King Carlos, the arrogant, imperious monarch. 'He doesn't look like a tough guy, he *is* a tough guy,' said one awed interviewer. Nearly six feet tall, with thick black hair, high cheekbones hinting at his Indian ancestry and limbs like steel cables, he seemed indestructible. 'Monzon's method is related to profound confidence,' wrote Hugh McIlvaney, 'the conviction that he has the animal authority to dominate almost any man they put in front of him.' His manager, Amilcar Brusa, put it another way: 'He's a cold man with extraordinary strength of will.'

Monzon was born on 7 August 1942, one of 12 children, in the village of San Javier in Argentina. Later, the family moved to the filthy slums of Santa Fe. To eat, Monzon shined shoes and peddled papers. He was aggressive and difficult, but found some outlet for his energies in a boxing gym. He had his first amateur bout as a 16-year-old lightweight and reportedly won 73 of 87 unpaid contests over five years.

He turned professional in 1963 under Brusa, winning his first contest in less than six minutes. Low purses and high inflation forced Argentinian boxers to fight often and Monzon entered the ring 11

times before the end of the year, losing just once. That wasn't enough
violence for him. He also landed in jail for starting a riot at a soccer
game. In his next legitimate fight, against Roberto Carabajal in
January 1964, he re-aggravated an old hand injury. It put him out of
boxing for six months. Again he was in trouble with the law, this time
for brawling on a bus, and was also involved in pimping girls.

He returned to boxing with a win in June, then travelled to Rio de
Janeiro to meet Brazilian Felipe Cambeiro. His swagger briefly
disappeared when he was dropped three times and beaten on points.
In October he lost for the third time, to Alberto Massi. None could
have forecast it then, but Monzon would never lose again. The slum
kid avenged two of his defeats in 1965, beating Cambeiro and Antonio
Aguilar. A year later, he won the Argentinian middleweight title from
Jorge Fernandez and reversed his defeat by Massi. Now no man
could say he was his better.

Monzon boxed on average once a month against hungry,
determined men. He learned subtle, unshowy defensive skills. He
threw punches sparingly but to great effect and his stamina never
failed him. He tended to start contests slowly; of 61 fights won inside
the distance in his career, not one was in the first round. Monzon
liked to appraise his opponents before chopping them down with
straight, accurate blows. Sometimes he looked awkward and stiff, but
he was cruelly efficient.

In May 1967 he faced a huge step-up in class before a big crowd in
Buenos Aires. Bennie Briscoe, a shaven-skulled product of the
Philadelphia bearpits they called gyms, was one of the most
dangerous middleweights in the world. It was the kind of war the fans
love and at the end of 12 rounds a draw seemed fair. It should have
brought Monzon to a wider audience, but Argentina was something
of a boxing backwater then. It took three and a half years more for him
to get a sniff of the world title.

In the meantime he won the South American middleweight title,
defended it twice, and beat a few more Americans imported by the
leading Argentinian promoter, Tito Lectoure. It may have been that
Monzon's lack of international stature helped his cause, for when
champion Nino Benvenuti was looking for a payday, the man from
Santa Fe didn't seem to present too many risks. After all, he had never
even been outside Latin America. A title fight was set for November
1970.

'Who is Carlos Monzon?' asked one Italian paper when the challenger arrived in Rome. They soon found out. He gave an icy display, his face an Inca mask, as he broke the champion's resistance and dispatched him with clinical finality in round 12. A return six months later gave even more compelling evidence of Monzon's superiority. He mopped the floor with Benvenuti in three rounds. The Italian later said, 'The Argentinian is the expression of instinctive, uncontrolled strength, with those whirling, irregular barrages. And he has that natural gift of punching power, meaning that he can emerge from the most critical situations at any time.'

Monzon was to defend his title a record 14 times. The champion who smoked a pack of cigarettes a day (though not when training) fought every kind of challenger: boxers, punchers, cagey veterans, sluggers. All were grist to his mill. In his second defence, in September 1971, Monzon stopped 33-year-old Emile Griffith with a whirlwind barrage in the 14th round in Buenos Aires. Another canny veteran was next in March 1972 in Rome. Denny Moyer, 32, had won the inaugural junior middleweight title 10 years before. Short and stocky, he was not expected to give Monzon trouble. But there was controversy when the bout was stopped in the fifth. Moyer had more than held his own for the first four rounds, and though he had been down in the fifth, did not appear unduly troubled when the Argentinian referee, Lorenzo Fortunato, stepped in. Moyer looked bewildered and the crowd of 20,000 chanted, 'Fix, fix, fix.' They pelted the ring with fruit and bottles and police had to escort Monzon away.

'Monzon the Unstoppable' was one headline after his next defence, when he vanquished European champion Jean-Claude Bouttier in Paris in June. The Frenchman had lost only three of 60 bouts and was a relentless fighter. Before an estimated crowd of 35,000, setting a gate receipt record for Paris, he was floored in the sixth but rallied repeatedly. His best shots had no effect on the champ. Bouttier failed to come out for the 13th round, saying he had been thumbed in the left eye in the tenth and could no longer see properly.

Tom Bogs was dismissed in five rounds in Copenhagen in August and two months later Monzon took on former foe Bennie Briscoe. Even the champion's iron jaw was vulnerable to Briscoe's thunderous hooks and in the ninth round the American hit home. Monzon was badly hurt but called on his years of experience to get through. He won a close decision and always had great respect for Briscoe. 'My God! He had a head of stone — and a big heart,' said Monzon years later.

The champion's strength was as much mental as physical. Amilcar Brusa told a disturbing story of his calm. On the morning he was due to box Roy Dale in a non-title bout in Rome, Brusa had to break the news that one of Monzon's brothers had been killed in Argentina. The champion just grunted. He won his fight in five rounds, then said: 'Now we catch an earlier plane to the funeral.'

In June 1973, in Monte Carlo, the ageless Emile Griffith came closer than anyone to separating Monzon from his crown. The old master beat Monzon to the punch and gave him a lesson in human geometry. But the champion gritted his teeth and raised his work-rate to wobble Griffith in the 14th. He clinched a win with a big last round, though the unanimous decision was greeted with catcalls. Gil Clancy, in Griffith's corner, claimed the scorecards were changed before the decision was announced. Monzon was also given a hard bout in a return with Bouttier, who had won six in a row since their previous contest. He made a good start, but in close Monzon was actually laughing at him. The champion cut loose briefly in the fifth and sixth, then went back into his shell. Finally he changed gear to drop Bouttier in each of the last three rounds and win the decision.

These two bouts raised doubts about Monzon. He did only enough to win, critics said, and a skilful boxer would catch him out. He had a good excuse for his performances, however. In February 1973 he had been shot by his wife Beatriz in the right arm and shoulder. The bullet in his arm was later removed but the other remains lodged in his body to this day. He and Beatriz subsequently divorced.

José Napoles, they said, was the man to expose Monzon's failings. Napoles, from Cuba, was one of the best welterweight champions there has ever been. His style was so smooth he was known as 'Mantequilla', the Spanish word for butter. Many good judges thought he would beat Monzon when they met in Paris in February 1974. The Argentinian turned it into a massacre. His jabs set up Napoles again and again for full-blooded right smashes. The challenger was torn apart and was a befuddled, blinking wreck when he quit on his stool after six rounds. 'It was a target against a marksman,' said Frank McGhee in the London *Daily Mirror*.

In April 1974 the World Boxing Council did what no opponent

could: it took away Monzon's title. The champion had been hinting at retirement and his failure to fight leading contender Rodrigo Valdes was deemed reason enough to strip him. Valdes beat Bennie Briscoe for the WBC crown in Monte Carlo in May, while Monzon remained WBA champion.

A powerfully built Australian, Tony Mundine, was his next challenger, in Buenos Aires. Mundine, who had 41 inside-the-distance wins to his credit, forced the fight until Monzon warmed up. Then the champion unleashed a stream of combinations and Mundine was counted out in round seven. Soon after, a Right-wing death squad threatened to kill the champion. It was unclear why, though possibly it was over his relationship with Suzanna Gimenez, a gorgeous Argentinian actress known as the 'Bardot of South America'. He shrugged off the threats to beat Tony Licata, a Chinese–Italian, in his first fight in the United States. Licata was knocked out in the tenth round and later complained that he could see 'two Monzons' because his vision had been blurred by a thumb in the eye. 'One Monzon would be enough for anybody,' commented Henry Miller in the London *Daily Telegraph*.

One Monzon was certainly enough for his next challenger. Gratien Tonna, a strong but erratic Frenchman, was counted out on his hands and knees claiming he had been hit on the back of the head in the fifth round. It was the Santa Fe slum boy's fourth bout in Paris, where he thoroughly enjoyed his fame. He became a well-known figure on the French Riviera, living life to the full, the glamorous Miss Gimenez often by his side. He was even offered the lead part in a film called, fittingly, *El Macho*. There was only one man left to challenge the king.

Rodrigo Valdes, too, was born to poverty. He saw the light of day on 22 December 1946, the fourth of nine children to Perfecta Hernandez, who was left to raise her tribe alone when her husband died in a fishing accident. They lived in Cartagena, the Heroic City, in Colombia. Rodrigo never went to school. He left home when he was very young, sleeping rough and living on scraps. Like the other street boys, he learned to fish with a loose line or to swim into the bay, braving the sharks to pick up fish when the men threw in dynamite. Sometimes the dynamite killed the boys.

He loved to fight and was training in a gym by the age of 15. But he
was clearly underfed and was rejected at local tournaments. Then, at
one show, a boxer didn't turn up. Valdes stood in for him and won.
He turned professional as a 16-year-old lightweight, beating Orlando
Pineda in October 1963. A local restaurant manager gave him food to
beef him up and he won eight bouts before Rudy Escobar knocked
him out in 1965. It was to be the only kayo loss in an 18-year career.

A Cartagena sports journalist, Melanio Porto Ariza, offered to
become his manager and over the next three years guided Valdes to 14
wins and two draws, all in Colombia. The last of these was in the
capital, Bogotá, where the young fighter was fascinated by the
escalators at the airport. 'Look Melanio, they carry you up all by
themselves,' he said to his manager. Despite this, Valdes never liked
leaving home, even for a few days. He lost his next contest, in Quito,
Ecuador.

It took all Ariza's powers of persuasion to get Valdes to travel to
America to improve his skills under Gil Clancy. Valdes fought nine
times in nine months, winning seven, before homesickness got the
better of him and he fled back to Cartagena. He returned to New York
in June 1971. In August he stopped Benny Cassidy in seven, but
caught hepatitis from him. The symptoms developed several months
later and Valdes was too ill to fight for four months.

He returned to the ring in 1972, winning four times in six months,
then travelled to Paris to beat Carlos Marks of Trinidad. The boxing
world was beginning to pay attention, and in September 1973 Valdes
became the number one contender by beating Bennie Briscoe in New
Caledonia. It was a great fight. Briscoe punched harder and left the
Colombian badly bruised, but Valdes took the verdict with better
boxing and flashy counters. He had developed into a class boxer, with
rhythm, movement and a choice selection of hooks. He also had the
deep-down toughness of the truly hungry competitor. His nickname
was 'Rocky'.

Valdes had won 20 straight when the WBC ordered Monzon to
fight him in 1974. Tito Lectoure, Monzon's promoter, claimed
Valdes rejected his purse offer for the fight. In any event, Monzon
was stripped and the Colombian was matched with Briscoe for the
vacant WBC title in Monte Carlo on 25 May. The shaven-headed
Philadelphian, who had given Monzon all the trouble he could handle
in two fights, was one of the best middleweights never to win the

world title. His record was studded with knockouts, the most recent a masterful demolition of Australia's Tony Mundine.

It was one of those fights that comes along once in a generation. Briscoe knew only one way to fight. He marched forward and threw bombs. Valdes matched him with blazing hooks and they slugged away in the middle of the ring. A right blasted Briscoe back on his heels in the first round and he was forced to cover up against the ropes, but he was soon ploughing forward again, hunting the body. Both put their all into every punch. Briscoe was pulled up by an uppercut in the fourth and he was belted repeatedly in the fifth. But the man the French called the 'Robot' kept going and by the sixth blood dripped from a gash over Valdes's left eye.

Briscoe stood at the end of the round, eyeing Valdes, and came out for the seventh as if he meant to settle it. He landed a heavy right but, just as the danger signals were flashing, the Colombian responded with a stunning set of hooks, all bang on the jaw. *Boxing News* reported, 'Valdes spread his feet and swivelled his body to hit Briscoe with everything he had. Briscoe's legs buckled, his arms came down, and Valdes drove in a final, crunching right-hander to the jaw.' The toughest man in boxing went over on his back and was counted out. In his dressing room Valdes complained of a burning pain in his left eye. He collapsed and was taken to hospital. After two days of tests, doctors said he had suffered an attack of 'suppressed anxiety'.

The Colombian defended his version of the title four times. France's Gratien Tonna fell in 11, counted out on one knee while claiming a rabbit punch. Ramón Mendez went in eight and Rudy Robles was outpointed before the champion's people in Cartagena. In September 1975 Valdes badly hurt his right hand in a car crash. He was out for six months but the hand looked good as new in ending the challenge of Max Cohen in four rounds in Paris.

The bout all boxing wanted to see was Valdes versus Monzon. It was set for Monte Carlo on 26 June 1976.

Five days before the fight Valdes's younger brother, Raymondo, was stabbed to death in a brawl at a party in Colombia. He got no sympathy from Monzon. The Argentinian called him *chico* (little boy). He added, 'Valdes is a paper tiger. I intend to send him home

looking like he has been run over by a train. I'm going to let him last
the full 15 rounds. That way I can watch him bleed slowly until the
end.'

Valdes took several trips to the scales to make the weight. It boded
ill for his chances; Monzon already had a $5\frac{1}{2}$-in reach advantage and a
2in height advantage, and knew how to use them. Valdes got off to a
poor start and allowed the Argentinian to dictate for too long. By the
middle rounds he was trailing badly. He pulled back the deficit with
characteristically flashy hooking, then ran into a Monzon right in the
14th and was floored. He was up quickly, but the damage was done.
Monzon took the decision and unified the world title once more. Gil
Clancy moaned that the ropes had been loose, allowing Monzon to
lean back out of range of the shorter-armed Valdes.

Monzon took time out to make films and have fun with his
glamour-puss girlfriend. Thirteen months later he was tempted back
into the ring in Monte Carlo to renew his rivalry with Valdes for
$500,000. Monzon said before the fight that it would be his last. He
nearly went out a loser when Valdes caught him with a cracking right
and sent him to the floor. More blows opened a cut across the bridge
of his nose. But Monzon was never more dangerous than when stung.
He blasted back in with measured, chopping punches. In the tenth
Valdes was on the verge of being stopped as Monzon belted him
around the ring. The challenger's left brow was badly cut and he had
swellings around both eyes. Valdes took more wicked blows in the
12th but again surged back and seemed to hurt Monzon in the 13th. It
was desperately close, but at the end of 15 tense, thrilling rounds,
Monzon was again the winner. Recovering afterwards, he looked in
the mirror and said to himself, 'Monzon was never floored and never
cut. Monzon is a great champion. He must be remembered as a great
champion.' Then he quit. He had lost just three of 101 fights.

The turbulent champion did not have an easy retirement. At one
time he had a Santa Fe ranch, two apartment buildings and a sports
equipment company, but he lost money with bad investments,
including a scheme to import Korean televisions. He dabbled in
boxing management. In 1981 he was jailed for a month for possessing
a firearm. There had been other offences during his career, including
two convictions for hitting photographers, and in 1975 he had been
convicted, though later pardoned, for hitting his estranged wife in
public.

He had found a new girlfriend, a beautiful Uruguayan dancer called Alicia Muniz, who bore him a son. Theirs was a stormy relationship, a saga of rows and reconciliations. On 14 February 1988 Monzon finally snapped. He had a blazing argument with Alicia in a first-floor apartment in the Argentinian resort of Mar del Plata. Their fight spread to the balcony. There was a violent scuffle. Muniz, who was semi-naked, and Monzon both fell. The boxer broke two ribs and a hip; Alicia was dead. Monzon was arrested and charged with her murder.

His trial attracted huge publicity. Monzon took the stand and testified that he and Alicia started arguing when she asked him for money. He told the court, 'I don't remember very well, but I suppose I took her by the neck with my hand. She was very near the balcony . . . and I can't remember what happened. It was just as if we were in a fog. I can only remember trying to catch her with my left arm. I can't say what happened. I woke up on the ground, with Alicia near me. I started to shout, asking for help.'

Pathology reports indicated that Muniz was strangled by hand before she fell from the balcony. Argentina's hero was convicted and sentenced to 11 years in jail, where he remains to this day. The shadow of violence lingered. In 1992, his brother Reinaldo was accused of murdering a 72-year-old man whose body was found outside Santa Fe.

Rodrigo Valdes was matched with Bennie Briscoe for the vacant title on 5 November 1977 at Campione, Italy. It was the third time they had fought; both were showing their years. They competed as hard as ever, but some of the old fury had gone. Valdes won in 15 rounds. He always admired Bad Bennie. In 1992 he told writer James Dusgate, 'Bennie had the hardest punch of anyone I ever fought, twice as hard as Monzon, who was much more of a technical boxer.'

Valdes was to lose his title at the first defence, to Hugo Corro (see page 198). He eventually retired in 1978. Unlike Monzon, his attitude to life is essentially happy-go-lucky. After four wives and (at the last count) ten children, he lives a contented life in his beloved Cartagena, where he owns properties, houses and some buses. Plumper than in his boxing days, he hangs out in the Park of Martyrs, instantly recognizable in his brightly floral shirts. Sometimes he goes to the cinema. His favourite film is *Rocky*.

14

The Bleeders

HUGO Corro looked like a young Carlos Monzon. There the similarity ended. He had none of his fellow countryman's steel, nor his power. A counter-puncher with fast hands, Corro moved well and hit straight and accurately. He was sometimes a little cocky, and once or twice paid the price. Corro always seemed something of a stop-gap champion until the next big gun arrived. He beat only two top-quality opponents in his career and disappeared into obscurity once he had lost the title.

Outside the ring, Corro was a quiet lad, born in San Carlos, Mendoza, Argentina, on 5 November 1953. Monzon's success inspired a generation of South American youngsters to punch their way out of poverty and Corro won a national amateur title in 1973. He turned professional in the same year, beating Gaston Diet inside six rounds. His manager was Diego Corrientos, who had trained him as an amateur.

Corro was unbeaten in his first 13 contests. Over-confidence surfaced in his 14th bout, against Hugo Saavedra in November 1974. Corro started showboating and dropped his hands. He was knocked out by a right cross in the eighth round. After a six-month break and a lot of work on his technique, he came back to reel off a string of victories. He was also punching harder. He outpointed Saavedra in September 1953 in his first contest in Buenos Aires. Ten days later, he comfortably outpointed another leading middleweight, Norberto Cabrera, taking great care not to mix it.

He was now top contender for the Argentine middleweight title, but champion Rodolfo Rosales dodged him. After two more wins, he agreed to fight Cabrera again. His opponent was an intimidating, irascible man who had been sent home from his country's Munich Olympics squad for beating up his flyweight team mate. Again, Corro started showing off and was caught. He was knocked down early on, took several rounds to recover and lost on points.

His lesson learned, he won eight bouts on the trot, seven inside the distance. In December 1976 the Argentine Boxing Federation stripped Rosales of his title and awarded it to Corro. To prove his superiority, Corro then fought Rosales twice, winning both easily on points. He was nominated to challenge Peruvian Marcelo Quinones for the South American title in May 1977, and survived a difficult patch in the middle to win on points after 12 rounds. In June he successfully defended his Argentinian title against Cesar Duarte.

Despite his titles Corro was virtually unknown to the wider boxing fraternity when, on 22 April 1978, he challenged world champion Rodrigo Valdes in San Remo, Italy. Experts gave the Argentinian little chance; many predicted he would last only a few rounds. Valdes was a warrior with 15 years' experience. But once the bell rang, it was the 31-year-old champion who struggled. Valdes looked frayed from all those tough battles and his normally accurate hooks missed. Corro, 24, boxed intelligently, sticking and moving, throwing the odd quick burst of hooks. The champion could not penetrate Corro's defence nor dodge his rapid-fire one-twos. He grew wilder with desperation and was thoroughly beaten at the end. In the upset of the year, Corro won a unanimous points decision. It was his 17th win in a row.

The new champion's first defence was in Buenos Aires on 5 August. His opponent was Ronnie Harris, an unbeaten American southpaw and former Olympic gold medallist. Harris was quick and slick. But Corro fought out of his skin to pip him with a grandstand finish. On 11 November, again in Buenos Aires, he gave Valdes another chance. Corro adopted the same stick-and-move plan. He was booed by the crowd, who wanted more action, but he still won easily. The bout was not recognized by the WBC because the referee was South African. Valdes, who had little left, said he would defer a retirement decision until he had finished work on a motion picture in Buenos Aires.

Even as he reached his peak Corro's status was under threat. The looming presence of a ferocious American middleweight, Marvin Hagler, cast a pall over his future. On 30 June 1979, in Monte Carlo, Corro put his crown on the line against Italian-born Vito

Antuofermo. On the undercard, Hagler met Norberto Cabrera, the caveman who had once beaten Corro. Hagler fought first. He gave an awesome performance, wrecking Cabrera 'like a contractor demolishing a building' according to *Boxing News*. In the title fight that followed, Corro was strangely lacklustre, allowing the crude Antuofermo to scuffle and butt his way to the decision. Corro blamed weight-making problems for his sluggish showing. Leading promoter Bob Arum said Corro had been so cowed by Hagler that he was actually relieved to lose his title.

The Argentinian announced his retirement in February 1980, saying he no longer had the incentive to make the weight. Eight years later he returned to the ring, weighing 12st 4lb and unimpressively knocking out Juan Ledesma in four in Tunuyan. His comeback came to nothing.

'No one can knock me out', Vito Antuofermo used to boast. His face bore battered testimony to those who had tried. Rims of scar tissue jutted like ramparts from his brow. It was once estimated that Antuofermo took around 400 stitches in his ten-year career. At only 5ft 8in, with short arms, he was always going to take punishment as he moved into range. He could not break an egg with his own punches and his boxing was woeful. But his jaw was solid granite. 'I've sparred with 200-pound heavyweights,' he liked to say, 'and when they hit you, you know you've been hit.' It was his dauntless determination that made him a success; that, and the services of his venerable cut-man, Freddie Brown. 'If Freddie had told me to go through a concrete wall I woulda done it.'

Antuofermo was born in the small Italian hill town of Palo dell Colle, near Bari, on 9 February 1952. His father farmed grapes and olives. Vito first showed an interest in boxing after watching the Benvenuti–Griffith title fight on television when he was about 14. Two years later a series of poor harvests drove the family to Brooklyn, New York. They lived in two poky rooms, sharing beds. Antuofermo worked on building sites, cut meat and loaded trucks to bring in a few bucks. He also joined a gang. During one fight he was too slow to run away before the police arrived and was taken to the local precinct, then home where 'my old man beat the hell out of me'. The next day the cop who arrested him took him to see the owner of a boxing gym. Vito started to work out and in 1970 won the New York Golden Gloves sub-novice title in 1970. His hero was Jake LaMotta.

He met Tony Carione, who ran a sanitation service, and turned pro. He won 17 and drew one of his first 18 fights until Harold Weston beat him on cuts. 'I don't worry about blood but the referee thought I was bleeding too much,' said Antuofermo. He continued to box fairly ordinary opposition until stepping up in class to beat veterans Denny Moyer and Emile Griffith in 1974. He won all seven fights in 1975, then returned to Europe to take the continental light-middleweight title from Germany's Eckhard Dagge. (Dagge later won the world title.)

Antuofermo defended his European title once before losing a non-title decision to the German southpaw Frank Wissenbach. He claimed the referee would not let him fight at close quarters, a common whinge from the Italian. Good pay days enabled him to buy a house on Long Island, but he spent more time in Brooklyn because 'there's nothing to do'. In October 1976 he lost his title to England's Maurice Hope in Rome. His manager blamed weight reduction. Antuofermo was stopped with just ten seconds left in the final round, as Hope drilled in punches without reply. The Italian had received two standing counts and was covered in blood but refused to buckle.

Moving up to middleweight, he beat his next eight opponents, including Philadelphia badmen Eugene Hart and Bennie Briscoe. He beat Hagler to a world title bout with Corro and lifted the crown after 15 rounds in Monte Carlo (see page 199). He was America's first middleweight champ since the 1960s. 'It's like a dream come true,' he said. 'One minute I'm a tough streetfighter from Brooklyn, the next I'm the champion of the whole world.' John Schulian of the *Chicago Sun-Times* wrote, 'The story belongs to another time in this country, a time when immigrant kids got off the boat and punched their way out of poverty.'

A daunting prospect awaited the new champion. He was ordered to face Hagler in a mandatory defence in November 1979. To make things harder, Hagler was a southpaw, and left-handers always gave Antuofermo difficulty. He approached the bout in his usual fearless way, however. By the fifth round he was cut around both eyes, but he fought back strongly. After 15 hard rounds, most of the Las Vegas crowd thought Hagler had won a close decision. But the judges declared it a draw. Antuofermo later needed 45 stitches.

The champion returned to the unreality of Vegas for his second defence, against Alan Minter, on 16 March 1980. He was plainly outboxed by the Britisher, who took the decision after 15 rounds. For some reason a myth grew up that Antuofermo was robbed, partly because of British judge Roland Dakin's lop-sided scorecard of 149–137 in Minter's favour. Antuofermo, who complained that the referee had broken clinches too early and stopped him working on the inside, was supported by ten out of 15 American writers at ringside. A clearer perspective seemed to come from the editor of the British *Boxing News*, who said of Antuofermo that 'his battle plan, in so far as he had one, seemed to be to burrow his head onto Minter's chest as if he was trying to knock him out with his ears'.

All arguments were settled in a London rematch three and a half months later. Antuofermo's corner pulled him out at the end of eight rounds with both his eyebrows ripped (see page 204). He had plastic surgery in November 1980, paying $4,000 to have his brows filed down, but was cut up again in his next fight, against Mauricio Aldana. In June 1981 he challenged Hagler, who had won the title from Minter. The shaven-headed champion was determined to make amends for his previous draw with Antuofermo. Two sickening head clashes left the Italian looking like 'a candidate for a Red Cross blood donor's poster', according to one observer. He was dropped in the third and stopped, with six cuts on his head, in the next.

Antuofermo never fought again and announced his retirement in January 1982, turning down a $75,000 offer to meet the promising Bobby Chyz. Brooklyn honoured him with a Vito Antuofermo Retirement Day. He was never a great boxer but he did have his supporters. Sportswriter Mike Katz said, 'I think Vito Antuofermo was a hell of a lot better boxer than he was given credit for. He knew how to make a guy miss, how to roll with punches, he knew how to bob and weave.' He landed a public relations job with Coca-Cola and remains a popular figure. During a recent senate investigation into boxing, a *mafioso* called Mike Franzese claimed the Mob had owned some of Antuofermo's contract and were sometimes told what the results of his fights would be in advance. There appears to be no independent corroboration for such claims.

★　★　★

Opinion about Alan Minter is divided by the Atlantic. One US magazine rated him the worst middleweight champion of all time. English fans regard him as one of their best modern boxers. The anomaly seems to date from his title-winning bout with Antuofermo, when some Americans thought he was lucky. In reality, Minter was a highly competent southpaw who could box, move and punch and was as tough as they come. He had the qualities to be champion for a long time but couldn't overcome two major drawbacks. One was his tendency to cut. The other was Marvin Hagler.

Minter liked nothing better than a good scrap and his rashness sometimes led to defeat. He admitted, 'When I got banged I used to go berserk, charging in like a lunatic and trying to take the geezer's head off.' Sometimes he would, indeed, take the geezer's head off. Other times he would suffer disastrous cuts and lose. The stoppage losses on his record before he won the title were all due to injury.

He was born on 17 August 1951, in Bromley, Kent, to an English father and German mother. His dad Sid liked a scrap and had his own ideas why his son was a good boxer: 'Alan's the product of an English bulldog and a German alsatian. Breeding obviously has a lot to do with the creation of a boxing champion. Don't forget — poofs don't breed fighters.'

Alan was raised in Crawley, a new town south of London. In his autobiography, he wrote, 'One word sums up my youth: trouble. I was never out of it. At my junior school . . . even if I wasn't the playground bully, I certainly managed to get other boys to give me a piggy-back ride all the way . . . to my home.' His first wife Lorraine told a Sunday newspaper, 'Alan was a bit of a tearaway at school. He didn't like it and he wasn't very good at anything. But when he started boxing and had won a fight, the whole school would stand up in assembly and clap him.'

Minter followed in his father's footsteps as a plasterer when he left school. Under the tutelage of Doug Bidwell, who ran Crawley Amateur Boxing Club, he became one of Britain's leading amateurs. He was ABA middleweight champion in 1971 and an Olympic light-middleweight bronze medallist a year later, losing a highly controversial decision to a German opponent in the semi-final in Munich. He was known as 'Boom Boom' for his habit of snorting loudly as he threw punches.

Bidwell, who was also Minter's father-in-law, carried on guiding him when he turned professional at the end of 1972. He won his first five bouts inside the limit to serve notice to Britain's middleweight. More wins improved his rating, but from June 1973 it all went wrong. Minter's tendency to become recklessly aggressive in the heat of battle was partly to blame. He lost on a cut to Don McMillan, won two bouts, then lost four of his next five. The very awkward Jan Magdziarz stopped him on cuts in two bad-tempered meetings and he was similarly beaten by American Ricky Ortiz. Next, a British title final eliminator against Magdziarz was declared no-contest in the fourth round after neither man showed any inclination to attack.

Minter had grounds for believing that none of these losses had been on merit. He ended 1974 with an excellent win over the dangerous Shako Mamba in Germany. Bobby Neill, an ex-British champion, was brought in to train him. He calmed Minter down and taught him to pick his shots and work for openings. More confidence-boosting successes followed, and Minter was nominated by the boxing board to meet former champion Kevin Finnegan for the British middleweight title vacated by Bunny Sterling.

It was the first of three extraordinary battles between two talented ringmen. Each reached deep inside himself to compete at a level of chilling intensity. They were so well-matched that it was almost impossible to separate them. Minter was the harder puncher, Finnegan the better boxer. Neither flinched from punches. Minter won the first on points after 15 rounds. He followed it with stoppages of Billy Knight, who never lived up to his promise, and Germany's Frank Reiche.

In his second fight with Finnegan for the title, Minter's jabbing took the first three rounds, but then Finnegan began to find the range and landed a greater variety of blows. In the ninth Minter was stunned by two quick rights and fell against the ropes. Finnegan swarmed all over him as the champion fired wildly back. Both fell over, Minter lost his gumshield, then Finnegan's left eyebrow began to bleed. It was riotous stuff. If anything, the frenzy increased over the final rounds, with defence scorned in a toe-to-toe contest of wills. The rounds were almost impossible to score. In the 15th, Finnegan threw everything he had, and it seemed certain that Minter would crumble. He fought back on instinct alone, and it was enough to get referee Roland Dakin's decision.

Minter completed 1976 with wins over name imports Tony Licata and Sugar Ray Seales (the latter, an Olympic gold medallist, is now blind as a result of injuries). He picked up the European title with an easy knockout of Italy's Germano Valsecchi in Milan in February 1977. But an elusive fellow southpaw, Ronnie Harris, badly gashed Minter's mouth and eyes to force an eighth round stoppage in London.

Minter ended Emile Griffith's career in his next fight. Then cuts struck again as he fell into a punch-up and lost his European title to the heavy-fisted Frenchman Gratien Tonna. The referee stopped it because of a laceration on Minter's forehead. The injuries were now becoming a serious hindrance and Minter underwent hypnotherapy to overcome his fear of being cut.

It must have worked: Minter now won ten in a row. They included a third thriller with Finnegan and a tragic 12-round knockout of Angelo Jacopucci. The Italian had faced charges that he lacked fibre and seemed determined to prove he was brave, if nothing else. He took some awful punches in their European title bout before he was counted out. He collapsed and was dead by the time Minter had flown back to England. The Crawley man put the tragedy behind him and showed discipline in the rematch with Tonna in September, ignoring a cut caused by a butt to pick his punches beautifully. He demoralized the Frenchman and stopped him in six rounds.

Restraint was again Minter's strongest suit when he beat Antuofermo to win the world title. His best friend Ron Patterson had died just four days before of a brain haemorrhage, but Minter went out and gave a thoroughly professional performance. He endeared himself to a national TV audience in Britain by tearfully declaring, 'I did it for England, my country and all my fans. And when I get back to Crawley we're all going to get pissed.'

Minter settled all arguments in a return at Wembley in June. He heard Antoufermo had been nicked in training and let the punches flow, busting up the rock-hard Italian and forcing him to retire, covered in blood, at the end of the eighth. He never really had much time to enjoy being champion, however. On 27 September 1980 he made a mandatory defence against Marvin Hagler, the brooding Boston southpaw.

The build-up to the bout was charged with xenophobia. Minter was a patriotic man. He had a Union Jack in the garden of his Sussex home and the doorbell chimed Land of Hope and Glory. He was obviously affected by the fervour before the bout and told reporters he would 'never lose the title to a black man'. The comment was widely reported. Minter recollected, 'I could kick myself over the remark. As soon as I said it I could see journalists rushing for phones and I suddenly realized exactly what I'd done.' He subsequently claimed that he hadn't meant black people in general, just Hagler in particular, but the damage was done.

Minter didn't help by wearing Union Jack underpants at the weigh-in. The Wembley atmosphere was electric as they walked to the ring. Beer-swilling yobs booed and jeered at the challenger. Both men eyeballed each other in the ring. But whereas Hagler remained cool, Minter stupidly let it get to him. He started too aggressively. Both landed hard blows but Hagler was more controlled and busted the champion up, forcing a stoppage in round three. The ending was followed by disgraceful scenes, with police having to usher the new champion to safety (see page 209).

Minter comforted himself with a new Rolls-Royce with personalized plates (AM 69). He tried to force a rematch and travelled to the US to fight the rough, tough Mustapha Hamsho. Minter lost a hotly disputed decision. He then received a hammering from left-hooking Tony Sibson, the European champion, in another emotionally charged encounter on 15 September 1981. Minter was counted out in the third round for the first time in his career.

Like most former champions, he had his ups and downs adjusting to life out of the limelight. Minter attracted lurid headlines such as 'Sex and Pain With My Wildman Minter' after a messy break up from his second wife Liz. She claimed he sometimes hit her, as did his first wife, Lorraine. In May 1992 he was hired by a private detective agency in Surrey to train bodyguards. 'The ability to protect yourself when the going gets tough is one of the cornerstones of my life,' he said.

15

Marvelous Marvin and Sugar Ray

MINUTES after being led to safety through one of the worst riots seen at a British boxing match, Marvin Hagler was asked for his response. He shrugged his powerful shoulders. 'The violence doesn't really bother me,' he said. After all, violence was his profession, and Marvelous Marvin was the ultimate professional, a driven, almost fanatical fighter who wouldn't even shake an opponent's hand before a bout. Fighting was *personal* with him. His bitterness came from years of being ignored when he knew he was the best in the world. Joe Frazier once told him, 'You've got three strikes against you: you're black, you're a southpaw, and you're good.' It was true.

Hagler made no compromises. He stayed loyal to his managers, the Petronelli brothers, throughout his career when a deal with Bob Arum or Don King would have brought a title bout much more quickly. As it was, he became one of the richest of all boxers, with gross earnings of well over $40 million.

Hagler's youth was the familiar tale of deprivation and decay. He was born on 23 May 1954 in Newark, New Jersey, the first of six children to Robert Sims and Ida Mae Hagler. Sims left when he was a small boy. In 1968 Newark, a bleak industrial town, was swept by race riots. Twenty-six people died as blacks fought running battles with police. For three days the Haglers moved about their house on all fours, too terrified to show their faces. Their mother then moved them to Brockton, Massachusetts, determined to give them a better life.

Brockton was the home of legendary heavyweight Rocky Marciano. Goody and Pat Petronelli, brothers of Italian descent, ran a boxing gym there. They were puzzled by the moody kid who came in and just hung around, too shy to speak. Eventually they asked him if he wanted to box. He nodded. Hagler took to the game straight away. He won 48 of 50 amateur bouts, taking a national AAU title in 1973. He also started shaving his head 'for luck'.

He turned pro a week before his 21st birthday, beating Terry Ryan in two in Brockton. A run of knockouts brought his first big fight. Sugar Ray Seales, the 1972 Olympic gold medallist, was rated an even better prospect than Hagler. They clashed in August 1974 and it was Hagler who emerged with the ten-round decision. They drew in a return two months later.

Hagler's 26-bout unbeaten streak was ended in Philadelphia in January 1976, by lanky Bobby 'Boogaloo' Watts. Many called it a hometown decision; Hagler seemed to have won clearly. He ventured back to Philly two months later. This time there were no arguments when he was outpointed by Willie 'the Worm' Monroe. In retrospect, his two defeats can be seen as a turning point. From then on, the Hagler legend was born. He became the baddest of all the bad-ass middleweights, Public Enemy Number One, busting up the division's most feared fighters in their own backyards.

The legend was forged in Philadelphia, renowned as the world's toughest fight city. It had a particularly mean and nasty bunch of middleweights: Bennie Briscoe, Eugene Hart, Willie Monroe and Bobby Watts. Hagler locked his sights on them. In September 1976 he beat Hart into surrender in eight rounds. Monroe was stopped in 12 for the North American Boxing Federation title early in 1977. In a return in August, he was crunched in two.

Highly rated Mike Colbert showed that a clever mover could give Hagler trouble, but the shaven-headed warrior with the 75-inch reach finally broke through his guard in the 11th round, floored him twice and broke his jaw to force a 12th round stoppage. In 1978 Hagler had two very tough fights against Britain's gutsy Kevin Finnegan, who refused to be intimidated and gave as good as he got. Hagler won both on injuries (Finnegan needed more than 60 stitches) and also stopped Doug Demmings in eight. Then it was back to Philly to meet the toughest of them all, Bennie Briscoe. Not even Hagler traded punches with 'Bad Bennie'; the Brockton man sensibly used his right jab to win on points. A victory over sawn-off Willie Warren rounded off 1978.

Hagler was now the most avoided man in boxing. He was bitter at his inability to get a title fight, but turned the hate to his advantage: 'People may have thought they were cutting out my heart, but they were only making me meaner.' Sugar Ray Seales, who had failed to live up to his early promise, took the brunt of his ire and was broken up in less than a round. After two more quick wins, Hagler was invited to showcase his talents on the Corro–Valdes title bill in Monte Carlo. His opponent, Norberto Cabrera, was the kind of man sensible contenders dodged. Hagler showed him a glimpse of hell and stopped him in eight rounds.

The case for giving Hagler a title fight was now unanswerable. He had won 20 in a row, 18 in short time, against the very best in the world. He even recruited influential politician Tip O'Neill to lobby on his behalf. Yet when his chance arrived, against Vito Antuofermo in November 1979, he was strangely unimpressive. Perhaps it was the knowledge that, in what should have been his finest hour, he was overshadowed by superstar Sugar Ray Leonard, who challenged Wilfred Benitez for the welterweight title on the same Las Vegas bill. As Ralph Wiley wrote in his book *Serenity*, 'Leonard had charisma. Marvin, on the other hand, didn't have a pulse as far as the world was concerned at that time.'

The fight was disappointing. Hagler's clinical approach too often seemed like hesitancy and he did not change gear fast enough when needed. He allowed Antuofermo to bull and scuff his way to a draw, though many thought Hagler won. 'This will just put bitterness in me and make me a better fighter,' he said. But he was not guaranteed an early return. Effective lobbying by British promoter Mickey Duff secured the next title fight for Alan Minter, not Hagler.

Marvelous Marvin (he incorporated the 'Marvelous' by deed poll) went back to work. Training with monastic zeal on a windswept spit in Cape Cod, he shattered a good prospect, Loucif Hamani, gained emphatic revenge over Bobby Watts in two rounds and outpointed Marcos Geraldo. Meanwhile, Minter had beaten Antuofermo. He agreed to defend his title against Hagler in London.

The racial overtones to the bout have been dealt with earlier (see page 205). Suffice to say that the American and his wife, Bertha, who was at ringside, faced appalling abuse. But Hagler remained the calmest man in the building. Minter shared the first round and shook Hagler with a left in the second, but his aggressive tactics were foolishly misconceived. Hagler, a precise and incisive hitter, hooked, crossed and slashed him to pieces; Goody Petronelli said it was like a guy walking into a buzzsaw.

The racist minority in the audience bayed as the black referee, Carlos Berrocal, stopped it in the third. As Hagler knelt in his corner in a prayer of thanks, plastic beer bottles and cans began to rain into the ring. The new champion's seconds threw themselves around him to protect him, and police escorted him to the dressing room without waiting for the verdict to be announced. Even in his moment of glory, he was denied the pleasure of being crowned champion in the ring. *Boxing News* called it 'the ugly and unacceptable face of British sport'. Minter needed 15 stitches in four cuts above and below both eyes.

Some had doubted Hagler's ability as a contender. He proved to be an outstanding champion. He was to make 12 successful defences of his title, remaining unbeaten for 11 years, a record to compare with any in the past. His first seven defences ended inside the distance: Fulgencio Obelmejias (eight rounds), Vito Antuofermo (five), Mustafa Hamsho (11), Caveman Lee (67 seconds), Obelmejias again (five), Tony Sibson (five) and Wilford Scypion (four). There was variety in those opponents, a wide mixture of styles and qualities. Hagler bested them all.

Obelmejias was a tall boxer–puncher from Venezuela. Hamsho, a New York–Arab, was impossibly strong but was clinically chopped up by the champion before his cornerman jumped into the ring to stop it. Reg Gutteridge wrote: 'Hamsho had begun with contempt for the champion . . . sneering at him, challenging his manhood. He ended by almost paying homage, extending handshakes, looking as forlorn as a boy who has had his bike stolen.'

Caveman Lee came with a puncher's chance but barely had time to swing a fist. Britisher Sibson, a noted left-hooker with a good chin, was stopped in a punch-perfect display, after which Hugh McIlvaney of the *Observer* wrote: 'There are two middleweight divisions. Hagler and the rest.'

And yet. Doubts were raised in his eighth defence against Roberto Duran. The Panamanian, an all-time great at three weights, was 32 and past his prime. Hagler had all the physical advantages. But Duran performed with proud defiance and Hagler failed to dominate him. The bigger man was even shaken at one point and there was booing at the decision in Hagler's favour, though it was fair.

In his next two bouts he did what he did best — chop up strong men who came to fight. Juan Domingo Roldan knocked him down for the first time ever, but paid the price in round ten, and Hamsho went again in three. Any lingering doubts were dispelled in his next contest, perhaps the most exciting title fight of all. Tommy 'Hit Man' Hearns was the WBC light-middleweight champion, an elongated puncher of spectacular power. He was matched to challenge Hagler for $8 million apiece on 16 April 1985. Fittingly for such gladiatorial combat, it was at Caesar's Palace, Las Vegas. The two boxers genuinely disliked each other and were almost in a frenzy by fight time. Hagler punched his own head in his corner as he waited for the bell to ring.

Few had witnessed anything like the apocalyptic conflict that followed. The first round contained enough excitement for an entire fight. *Boxing News* editor Harry Mullan wrote: 'It was three minutes of mayhem, of controlled, educated violence sustained at an almost unendurable level of intensity . . . they smashed terrifying hooks at each other, full-blooded blows which were designed to intimidate and destroy.' There was no attempt at defence. This was a blood brawl conducted on an elemental level. With 30 seconds left in the first round, Hagler suffered a vertical cut on his forehead. Blood gushed down but he was hurling himself at Hearns at the bell.

In the second round he came out knowing he would never last the distance. A Hearns right split his cheek. Still he blazed away. Hearns took huge punches on the ropes, all the while blasting back. In the third, referee Richard Steele took Hagler to a corner to wipe away the blood. 'Can you see?' he asked. 'I'm hitting him, aren't I?' replied Hagler. He was allowed to fight on and charged back into the maelstrom. It was Hearns who cracked. A right hook to the chin took away his control of his legs and three more rights sent him onto his back. Incredibly, he got up — but he was gone. Steele wrapped him in his arms and stopped it.

Hagler rested for nearly a year. Typically, the opponent he chose for his next fight was as dangerous as Hearns. John 'the Beast' Mugabi, a light-middleweight from Kampala, Uganda, had won 25 fights in a row, all inside the distance. Victims seemed to dissolve in fright when he hit them. Again, the high-rollers of Las Vegas were treated to a blood-and-guts drama. Hagler soaked up Mugabi's best shots without flinching and gradually increased the pace. Both took punches that would have flattened ordinary men. Hagler prevailed on willpower and conditioning, battering Mugabi defenceless and finally out for the count in round 11.

Hagler thought of retiring. But there was an offer too tempting to resist. Sugar Ray Leonard, a boxer who had often overshadowed Hagler, was returning to the ring after a long lay-off. He challenged the middleweight king. Pride and the promise of an unprecedented purse persuaded Marvelous Marvin to get it on one last time.

The nickname 'Sugar' is spoken with reverence in boxing circles. Pretenders adopt it at their peril. But it fitted Ray Leonard like a glove. He was as talented and versatile as any boxer who ever climbed into a ring. Speed, rhythm, punch, movement, an acute brain, awareness, balance and control: he had it all. Charisma, that intangible quality, allowed him to succeed Muhammad Ali as boxing's superstar. Trainer Angelo Dundee even claimed he would have beaten the original Sugar Ray. Who knows?

Many people find it difficult to like Ray Leonard. He shared with a contemporary athlete, Carl Lewis, an overweening self-belief that made them brilliant achievers but also deprived them of the human vulnerability that people seek in their favourite performers. Ray Charles Leonard (he was named after the singer Ray Charles) was born on 17 May 1956 in the port of Wilmington, North Carolina, one of six brothers and sisters. He hated his first experience of boxing, at a boys' club when he was seven, but returned to the sport when his family moved to Palmer Park, Maryland.

Leonard's parents were not rich, but his was not the classic story of urban delinquency. He started boxing seriously at 14 and found he excelled at it. He was so talented that he almost made the 1972 Olympic team when aged just 16. His glittering amateur career culminated in a gold medal in the 1976 Olympics in Montreal. Amateur boxing is not a big spectator sport but Leonard's lightning hand speed and machine gun bursts of punches, coupled with an Ali-like showmanship, reached a wide TV audience. Olympic team manager Rollie Schwartz said, 'Ray Leonard is the greatest amateur I've ever seen in my 38 years of amateur boxing. He has the fastest reflexes and the greatest balance.'

Ironically, given the multi-millions he was to earn, it was financial hardship that forced Leonard to turn pro. He had intended accepting a college scholarship to study for a business degree, but his parents were taken ill and his girlfriend, Juanita Wilkinson, had to apply for welfare to support their three-year-old son. He made a deal with a Maryland lawyer, Mike Trainer, to handle his financial affairs. Trainer put together a consortium of business men to back Leonard; he later paid them all off. Angelo Dundee, the most famous trainer in boxing, was brought in to oversee his career with the help of Janks Morton and to select his opponents, something he did brilliantly. Dundee matched Leonard with a succession of good, experienced boxers with a variety of styles, giving his charge a good grounding in all aspects of the game.

Given the hype, Leonard disappointed in his debut, a six-round decision over journeyman Luis Vega in May 1977. His pay was $40,000. He reeled off five more wins before the end of the year, and by 1978 had convincingly made the transition from amateur to pro, winning 11 more times. Good welters like Randy Shields and Armando Muniz were easily beaten. Leonard moved up in class carefully; the ever-improving standard of his opponents could be charted on a graph almost as a perfect diagonal line. In 1979 he stopped Johnny Gant and Fernand Marcotte, then knocked out Daniel Gonzales in one round. He outpointed tricky Adolfo Viruet and a tough middleweight, Marcos Geraldo, and stopped Tony Chiaverini. Dundee did veto one match, with a young prospect called Tommy Hearns. 'I did not feel that it was a good match at the time,' he said. They would later make a fortune together.

In August 1970 Leonard beat Pete Ranzany for the North American Boxing Federation welterweight title. Ranzany, who had an excellent if slightly inflated record, was well beaten in four. Six weeks later, Leonard defended against Andy 'the Hawk' Price, a fine boxer who at one time held wins over both the WBC and the WBA welterweight champions. Leonard stunned the Las Vegas crowd by taking him out with a single shot in round one.

The welterweight division at this time had the greatest depth of talent boxing had seen in any weight class for years. Wilfred Benitez, a Puerto Rican whose natural ability rivalled Leonard's, was WBC champ. Pipino Cuevas, who frequently left opponents with broken bones, was WBA champ. Tommy Hearns and the legendary lightweight Roberto Duran were waiting in the wings. Leonard secured a bout with Benitez. It was a battle of prodigies and Leonard won on a stoppage in the 15th round.

Leonard's welterweight career is the stuff of legend. There were two sensational bouts with Duran, the first of which he lost in a magnificent battle, the second which he won with a masterpiece of boxing skill. There was the unification bout with Hearns, another classic between two all-time greats. Leonard pulled out a dazzling finish to stop Hearns in the 14th round. He also won the WBA light-middleweight title from the superb Ayub Kalule.

In 1982 Leonard was training for a bout with Roger Stafford when a sparring partner thumbed him in the left eye. His retina was detached. He had surgery and was told the eye was as good as new, but instead chose to retire while at his peak. The news shocked boxing.

More than two years later, Leonard caused another shock by returning to the ring. He chose Kevin Howard as his opponent. Leonard's timing was off, his rhythm gone, and in round four Howard knocked him down with a right hand. Leonard got up to eventually stop his foe in the ninth, but said later, 'I knew even before the knockdown it was over for me. I kept trying to get my hands to work but they never did.'

But fame was Leonard's drug. He couldn't resist the lure of the stage, the worship of his followers. As British writer Ken Jones put it: 'Intelligent, articulate, astute, commercially successful, heavily invested, rich beyond anything he could have imagined when growing to manhood in Palmer Park, Maryland, he still found the mysterious thrill irresistible.' Leonard had closely followed the career of Marvin Hagler and believed he had detected chinks in the champion's armour. He announced he was returning to the ring, and the Marvelous one consented to meet him with his title on the line.

It was a fatal misjudgment. Hagler agreed to Leonard's demand that their bout, on 6 April 1987, should be cut from 15 rounds to 12. The sop was extra money. From a promotion that grossed $70 million, Hagler eventually received upwards of $18 million, Leonard a 'mere' $11 million. The huge purse also made up for the fact that Hagler had been stripped of his title by the WBA and the IBF for meeting

Leonard instead of the leading contender, Britisher Herol Graham. Anyway, everyone knew who the real champion was.

'Destruct and destroy' became Hagler's mantra before the bout, adorning tee-shirts and baseball caps and repeated endlessly by his camp. Few experts gave Leonard much of a chance. He had been out of the ring for too long, his skills were too far gone. But, said *KO* magazine, 'It was Hagler who didn't realize what he was facing: a brilliant tactician who had trained for over a year, and who, for more than three years, had been watching Marvelous more closely than the IRS.' Others agreed. As one of Leonard's trainers put it, 'Marvin is like a computer. Ray is versatile.'

Hagler entered the arena at Caesar's Palace, Las Vegas, to the sound of Edwin Starr's *War*. He banged his chest and yelled 'Let's go,' at Leonard during the pre-fight instructions. But once the bell rang, he came out cautiously in an orthodox stance. Although he stalked, he scarcely threw a punch, while Leonard, bulky and muscular at middleweight, flurried flashily to steal the points.

And that was the pattern of the bout. Leonard went through his wind-ups, sticking his chin out, show-boating, but also nicking rounds with eye-catching combinations, displaying a still-remarkable hand speed. In the fifth, Hagler suddenly went for it, hurting Leoard with a right and catching him with more punches than in the whole of the previous four rounds. Leonard survived.

There were already traces of tiredness from the challenger, but he boxed a brilliant tactical bluff, keeping Hagler wary by threatening more than he delivered and relying on speed to score points. The ninth was a thriller, with both trading blows. Leonard fought off his weariness to counter spectacularly in the tenth. At the end of 12 unbearably tense rounds, it was Sugar Ray who took the narrowest of split decisions. The Hagler camp were disgusted, muttering darkly about 'Vegas' and 'boxing politics'.

'I had fun tonight,' Leonard said afterwards. Hagler, however, proved to be one of the sorest losers in history. 'He couldn't deal with it,' said Pat Petronelli. He started drinking heavily and his wife of 17 years, Bertha, left him and said she would consider reconciliation only if he underwent drug rehabilitation, something his half-brother Robbie Sims had already undergone for cocaine addiction. Hagler denied taking drugs. Bertha, the mother of five of Hagler's six children (he had his first child to a Newark woman in 1973), met with top American divorce layer, Marvin Mitchelson. She said she was in fear of her husband and he was barred by court order from visiting their home in Hanover, Massachusetts. She claimed he threw her out of the house and heaved a rock at one of their cars. Hagler had often been seen in the company of other women.

Hagler announced his retirement in June 1988, accusing Leonard of 'playing games' over a possible rematch. He wore his bitterness on his sleeve. 'I still feel in my heart that I won my last fight,' he said. 'I set out to mess up his life and that's what I did,' was Leonard's unrepentant riposte.

In March 1990 it was reported that Hagler and Leonard had agreed terms to fight again that autumn, but that the formal announcement would be delayed until after Hagler's divorce from Bertha had been finalized. However, the deal fell through. Recently Hagler appears to have come to terms with losing a contest that many believe he won. He has made several films in Italy and does inter-round boxing analysis on TV.

Leonard subsequently relinquished the middleweight title without bothering to defend it. He did fight again, but without his great trainer, Angelo Dundee. Many credited Dundee as the architect of the Hagler defeat. Press agent Irving Rudd said, 'If Hagler had had Angelo in his corner, Hagler would have knocked Leonard out.' But they argued over the trainer's payment. He said he received only $175,000. Ten per cent would have netted him about $1.2 million. They went their separate ways. 'There is no sense in being bitter,' said Dundee. 'Life is too short for that.'

Leonard was in the enviable position of being able to pick and choose his opponents. The governing bodies just fell in line behind him. He picked up a version of the light-heavyweight title, and something called the super-middleweight title, by beating Donny Lalonde, outscored old foe Duran in a dreary bore, and was finally well beaten by hard-hitting Terry Norris. He retired, this time for keeps.

Sugar Ray Leonard was the last man to stand alone as undisputed middleweight champion of the world. There may never be another single champion.

16

No Time To Bleed

BOXING fractured at the end of the 1980s. The damage may be permanent. The proliferation and greed of governing bodies, hungry for sanctioning fees, and the voracious appetite of television companies for so-called 'world' title fights between second-rate contestants, made a mockery of the sport. Powerful promoters rode roughshod over the rule books. Hype ran amok. As the number of weight divisions multiplied like lice, fans lost interest. Few casual supporters could today name all four current middleweight champions; only a serious boxing nut could identify every claimant in every extant weight category.

Instead of the WBC and WBA moving closer together (something once mooted but never achieved), their duopoly was challenged by two new monoliths, the International Boxing Federation (IBF) and the World Boxing Organization (WBO). Neither has yet achieved the status of the older bodies, indeed the WBO is something of a joke, though some boxers, notably Britain's Chris Eubank, have earned plenty of money defending its titles. Yet they survive and prosper.

Having stripped Marvin Hagler of his title, the IBF was first to produce a rival champion, matching two unbeaten contenders. Frank Tate was American, a former Olympic light-middleweight gold medallist and the USBA middleweight king. Michael 'The Silk' Olajide, was a Liverpool-born former Canadian and Continental Americas titleist. Both were 23, promising but raw; neither would have been deemed ready for a title fight in saner times. Tate won a

15-round points decision over his more flamboyant opponent on 10 October 1987, in Las Vegas.

Tate, born in Houston, Texas, on 27 September 1964, was a well-disciplined box-fighter, his perfect record compiled against solid journeymen like Curtis Parker, Ricky Stackhouse and Britain's Winston Burnett. He had picked up the vacant USBA title against Troy Darrell in 1987 in his nineteenth contest, and two bouts later beat Olajide. He seemed a promising, well-tutored champion but was far from the finished article. He showed class in his first defence, travelling to England to knock out dangerous Tony Sibson in ten rounds, and followed it with a non-title decision over Sanderline Williams.

On 28 July 1988, Tate met another unbeaten prospect, Michael Nunn, in Las Vegas. They were old amateur rivals, Tate having won two of their three unpaid clashes. Nunn, 6ft 2in tall, had developed into a tactile boxer with great variety and speed. He taunted Tate in the early rounds and built a big lead against the supposedly harder-punching champion. In the eighth, Tate took a gut-busting left and went down on all fours. The bell saved him. Nunn stormed out for the ninth and his two-fisted attack compelled the referee to step in.

'Second To' Nunn looked like a superstar in the making. Born on 14 April 1963, in Davenport, Iowa, he was another former top amateur, an alternate in the 1984 US Olympic team which included Tate. He turned pro that December and bowled over a series of inferior opponents before Charles Campbell took him the distance for the first time. In 1987 he lifted the NABF crown in four rounds against Darnell Knox, retaining it against Kevin Watts and Curtis Parker. The victory over Tate was his 31st in a row. Nunn carried some of Ray Leonard's arrogance and seemed to have all the tools: great southpaw skills and a deceptively conclusive punch.

In November 1988, Nunn knocked out Argentina's Juan Roldan in eight. Four months later, he met the durable Sumbu Kalambay, the WBA titleholder (see page 219). The match offered an opportunity to unify two titles, but in a typical piece of boxing politics, the WBA stripped Kalambay before the fight, in Las Vegas. His bad fortune carried over into the contest. After sparring for the first minute, Nunn flattened him with a single punch, a perfect left hook over the top of his guard. The African staggered up just as the ref completed his count, then collapsed again. Nunn followed this spectacular conquest by outpointing the rugged Iran Barkley, then took a safety-first decision over a good welterweight champion, Marlon Starling, and crushed former two-time kingpin Donald Curry in ten.

With a 36–0 record, Nunn was lauded as one the best boxers pound-for-pound in the world. It came as a shocking upset then, when he was demolished in his hometown of Davenport by the undefeated but inexperienced James 'Lights Out' Toney on 10 May 1991. Nunn had needled his young challenger before the contest, picking imaginary fleas from his head at the weigh-in and sparking 'the obligatory shoving match and shouting that keeps the sport from being confused with golf or chess', according to *Boxing Illustrated*. Toney, from the college town of Ann Arbor, Michigan, fell behind on points but rallied in the second half of the bout. In the 11th, he floored Nunn with a spectacular left hook. The champion hauled himself up but was bent over the ropes by a series of blows. After a further volley, Nunn's cornermen jumped into the ring and the contest was stopped. 'I got lazy and he caught me with a shot,' said the battered Nunn.

The new champion had 26 wins and a draw in 27 outings. He was 22, born on 24 August 1968. A capricious time-bomb of a man, he talks openly of an inner rage fuelled by hatred of his violent father, who shot his mother in the leg before abandoning Toney when he was three. He told *Sports Illustrated*, 'Everything is about that. I look at my opponent and I see my dad, so I have to take him out. I have to kill him. I'll do anything I have to do to get him out of there.' He is also unusual for having a female manager, the blonde Jackie Kallen, a former publicist for Tommy Hearns. 'He's got that side of him that likes violence,' she said. 'If you don't keep him in the gym, who knows what would happen in the street? When he's mad, he'll put his fist through a glass window, throw a chair, knock over a table. There's a valve in James.'

In action he scorns defence, relying on crunching hooks. He almost came unstuck in his first defence when floored in the second by Reggie Johnson, but came back to eke out a decision. Against Francesco dell'Aquila he weighed half a pound over the limit; the challenger agreed to waive any forfeit and was cut down. A disputed draw with the excellent Mike McCallum followed and Toney took *Ring* magazine's Fighter of the Year award for 1991. His 1992 form was uninspiring. A split-decision over Dave Tiberi was deemed so controversial that it sparked a political investigation into alleged corruption in boxing (see page 229). Toney also failed to impress in beating Glenn Wolfe and a rather jaded McCallum in a return. Troubled by weight-making, he stepped up to 12st to beat Doug DeWitt and, in February 1993, was back to his best, taking the IBF super-middleweight title from Iran Barkley. At the time of writing, the future of his middleweight crown is uncertain; Toney still holds it in name, but is almost certain to abandon the division.

The WBA was only 13 days behind the IBF in getting its championship off the mark. It matched a 31-year-old Italian-based African, Patrizio Sumbu Kalambay, with brutish New Yorker Iran Barkley for its vacant title. Kalambay handed out a boxing lesson to win on points in 15 rounds in Livorno, Italy, on 23 October 1987. The new champion was born in Zaïre on 10 April, 1956, but didn't box professionally until he was 24. After an early career loss he won 32 straight, boxing mainly in Italy, before defeat by Duane Thomas in April 1985, and subsequently by Ayub Kalule in his first stab at the European title that December. He eventually won the European title by outpunching and almost stopping the fancied Britisher Herol Graham in May 1987.

The Graham win earned Kalambay his title fight with Barkley. Kalambay showed his ability and easily outpointed the excellent Mike McCallum, then unbeaten WBA light-middleweight champion, in his first defence in March 1988. He outscored Robbie Sims, Marvin Hagler's half-brother, in his second, and crushed durable American Doug DeWitt with a left hook in the seventh round for his third. The lure of a large purse and greater fame then led Kalambay into a showdown with IBF champ Michael Nunn (see page 217). The WBA promptly dethroned him for not fighting Herol Graham. Kalambay lost anyway.

Mike McCallum and Graham met for the freshly vacant WBA championship on 10 May 1989 at the Royal Albert Hall, London. Graham was a defensive genius who dominated British boxing, but in McCallum he was facing a complete pro who had been unquestionably the best light-middleweight in the world for four years. Graham waged a baffling, tactically confused fight, taking far more punches than usual, and McCallum won by split decision after 12 rounds.

The new champion, who hailed from Jamaica, was known as the 'Body Snatcher' for his rib-bending hooks. Born on 7 December 1956, he had been a standout amateur, winning a Commonwealth Games Gold medal, competing in the Olympics and losing only 10 of around 250 amateur bouts. Like Kalambay, he started late as a pro but became one of the game's best practitioners. He won 14 straight in a short time before Kevin Perry took him the distance in 1982. McCallum stopped Ayub Kalule in his next bout. McCallum won the vacant WBA light-middleweight title in October 1984 against Sean Mannion and defended it six times against class opposition. He knocked out lethal Julian Jackson in a 1986 thriller, beat Milton McCrory and flattened Don Curry in five rounds with a memorable left hook in 1987. In 1988, with 32 straight wins, 29 inside the distance, he moved up to challenge and, surprisingly, lose to Kalambay.

After beating Graham, McCallum fractionally outpointed Steve Collins, a US-based Dubliner, knocked out Britain's ill-fated Michael Watson, and outpointed Kalambay. Patient, watchful and ring wise, he was a formidable gladiator, at his most dangerous when stung. He struggled, however, for the recognition accorded more flashy but less talented boxers. In December 1991 he was stripped of his title for failing to sign for a return with Collins. The decision was announced just before McCallum was due to meet James Toney, the IBF champ, in a unification bout. Once more the WBA had acted to prevent two titles being brought together. *Boxing News* editor Harry Mullan wrote, 'There has never been a starker illustration of the way the game is being wrecked by maladministration.' At the time, McCallum had won 42 of his 43 contests. The result was a draw.

Collins was matched with Reggie Johnson for the vacant title. Johnson, an unspectacular southpaw, won on points in a bout marred by fouls before a two-thirds empty venue in New Jersey. The new title-holder was born 28 August 1966, in Cincinnati, Ohio. He turned pro at 17 and won the USBA title by stopping Ismael Negron in February 1990. He lost a split verdict to James Toney in his first title shot (see page 218). After winning the WBA crown, he defended twice in 1992, beating Melvin Wynn and the fancied left-hooker Lamar Parks. He has shown a workmanlike efficiency but is still an unknown quantity.

The WBC title has perhaps the most legitimacy. After Ray Leonard discarded it, perennial assassin Tommy 'Hit Man' Hearns filled the vacancy by kayoing Juan Roldan on 29 October 1987. A lanky puncher from Detroit, Michigan, Hearns has been one of the most feared fighters of the last 25 years. Born on 18 October 1958, he started boxing at the age of ten and was a skilful but not especially dangerous amateur. Success followed his move to the Motor City's Kronk Centre in 1974, under the tutelage of trainer Emanuel Steward. Hearns won 155 of 163 unpaid bouts, taking a clutch of titles, and was voted US amateur of the year in 1977.

He turned pro with a second round win and then compiled a fabulous record, drawing comparisons with the young Ray Robinson. He was well-managed and enjoyed great physical advantages over most of his opponents, but also showed a lashing jab, natural punch leverage and a hunter's instinct. His deadpan mien and laser stare chilled even seasoned pros. Menace was very much part of the Hearns make-up. It was described by New York fight writer Mike Marley, who boxed an exhibition with him as, 'as if you've killed his parents and now he's coming to get *you*'.

By the time he challenged Pipino Cuevas for the WBA welterweight title, Hearns had won 28 straight, 26 inside the distance, 19 inside three rounds. Only Alfonso Hayman, who took a pasting, and Mike Colbert, who suffered a broken jaw, had lasted the distance. But it was his crushing defeat of the highly dangerous Cuevas in two one-sided rounds that truly established his credentials. There was a static charge every time Hearns entered a boxing ring.

The Motor City Cobra went on to feature in a series of memorable contests against great champions like Sugar Ray Leonard, Wilfred Benitez, Marvin Hagler and Roberto Duran. The violence, courage and skill of these contests bear comparison with any ever fought. Leonard stopped him in a famous encounter, but he beat Benitez and crushed Duran, becoming the only man ever to knock out the legendary Panamanian. The Hagler duel, described in chapter 15, was his first attempt at the middleweight title. Despite the finality of his loss, Hearns campaigned vigorously for a rematch even after Haglar had retired. He often accused the ferocious champion of ducking him.

Beating Roldan made Hearns the first man to win versions of world titles at four weights. For his first defence, he chose Iran Barkley.

Barkley, with his wide-open defence, seemed made for Hearns. When Barkley's close friend Davey Moore was killed in a tragic auto accident three days before the fight, the 'Hit Man' was made a 4-1 favourite. He took the first two rounds, cutting Barkley badly. The challenger, noted for his kamikaze courage, launched an assault in the third but ran into more Hearns counters. Bleeding from gashes above both eyes, bruised and swollen, Barkley seemed doomed. In a last desperate assault, he ducked under a Hearns headshot and launched a monster right. It landed. Hearns, separated from his senses, toppled over, helped on his way by another right. He struggled up, but was in deep trouble. A scrambled follow-up by Barkley sent him to the ropes and, as the referee waved it over, he tumbled through them and was left sitting, glassy-eyed, on the ring apron. The new champion was jubilant. 'I don't care about the cuts because I didn't have time to bleed,' he said.

Barkley came out of the Patterson Projects, a high-rise warscape in the terminal zone of New York's South Bronx. Born on 9 May 1960, he had an X-rated youth, running with the Black Spades gang and acquiring the nickname 'Blade'. He had to fight bigger boys to avoid paying extortion money to get in and out of his apartment building. 'I have this crazy madness inside me,' he told *Ring* magazine. 'Those days were periods of great anger for me. I'd sit around and watch the drug dealers do their thing. And when I got bored, we'd go around beating people up, stabbing people and hitting them with lead pipes.'

Barkley was urged into the gym by his sister Yvonne, a woman boxer. He never learned much technique and his style was full of faults, but nobody doubted his guts and firepower. Barkley was *bad* and you swapped punches with him at your peril. He was noted for dramatic late rallies to win fights and for coming back from heavy defeats. He lost his first title challenge, to Sumbu Kalambay, but upset victories over WBC top contender James Kinchen and Michael Olajide secured him a shot at Hearns. Barkley took too many punches and sometimes went over but, as his manager Vinnie Ferguson noted, 'He gets up like a wounded gorilla.'

The 'Blade' lost his title to Roberto Duran on 24 February 1989, in Atlantic City. Duran, 37, turned back the clock in his last great performance. He held the centre of the ring, ducking and swaying and scoring heavily with counters. Barkley nearly dropped him in the eighth with a left hook but was hammered himself in the ninth, and was dominated and taunted in the tenth. In the 11th, the years fell away as Duran unleashed a textbook four-punch combination, culminating in a precisely timed right, to floor the champion. Barkley, as ever, attacked until the end but Duran had done enough for a split decision, the knockdown proving decisive. It was hailed by the press as the fight of the year.

Duran was one of the all-time greats, an indestructible lightweight champion and winner of titles at welterweight and light-middleweight. It would take a whole book to describe his life in detail. Born poor on 16 May 1951, in Guarare, Panama, he was raised in the filthy slums of Colón. Fighting came as naturally as walking; they called him 'Manos de Piedra' — 'Hands of Stone'. The rock-fisted urchin was spotted by millionaire Carlos Eleta and turned pro under his guidance at the age of 16. He plundered the WBA lightweight title from Scotland's Ken Buchanan in 1972, defended it a record 12 times and brutalized the WBC champion, Esteban deJesus.

Moving up to welterweight, he scored a string of brilliant victories and peaked with a magnificent defeat of Sugar Ray Leonard for the WBC 147lbs title in Montreal in 1980. He had lost just once in 73 contests. But in a return with Leonard, Duran amazingly quit in round eight in the notorious *no mas* incident. Further defeats to Wilfred Benitez and Kirkland Laing seemed to signal the end of his career. But Duran was not done. A glorious win over Pipino Cuevas put him back in the frame and on an emotion-charged night at Madison Square Garden, he massacred Davey Moore in eight rounds to win the WBA light-middleweight title.

Duran's next bout, a brave but unsuccessful effort against Marvin Hagler, is described in chapter 15. He was subsequently knocked out for the first time by Tommy Hearns in two rounds. Duran kept going and the pulling power of his name helped him earn the title match with Barkley. As a champion again, he was well past his best. He chose to take on Ray Leonard at super-middleweight rather than defend his honours and was stripped by the WBC in January 1990 for refusing to sign an undertaking to box. He lost to Leonard and later to Irishman Pat Lawlor. As of March 1993 he was in throes of another implausible comeback at the age of 41, heading towards the figure of 100 pro bouts.

Julian Jackson and Herol Graham fought for Duran's vacant title on the Spanish Costa del Sol on 24 November 1990. Graham gave a

boxing masterclass for three rounds, closing Jackson's left eye and
sending him floundering. At the end of the third the ringside doctor
examined Jackson's eye. He looked on the verge of defeat. But in the
fourth, as Graham backed him against the ropes in a corner, Jackson
loosed a perfect right hook to the jaw. 'It was enough to flatten six
middleweights, let alone one,' commented *Boxing Monthly*. Graham
went down as if shot and was counted out.

Jackson, born in St Thomas in the Virgin Islands on 12 September
1960, was used to seeing rivals flat on the floor. He is currently the
hardest one-punch hitter in boxing, and has compiled one of the best
kayo percentages in ring history. His record shows an inordinate
number of clean count-outs. Known as 'The Hawk', he is broad-
shouldered and long armed, with the smooth muscles of a natural
puncher and dynamite in both fists. Surprisingly, his first pro bout,
in 1981, went the distance. He then won 29 straight, 27 inside the
distance, before challenging for Mike McCallum's WBA light-
middleweight title in 1986. Jackson walloped the 'Body Snatcher' in
the first round and was on the edge of victory, but the champion
clubbed his way back and won in the next round. Jackson was later
quoted as saying, 'I was headed in the wrong direction. I had a girl
here, a girl there. I was hanging around with the wrong people. I was
living in the fast lane. I was getting involved in sinful things. God
spoke to me and I listened. I am now a born-again Christian.'

God's warrior took the vacant WBA title in three rounds from
In-Chul Baek the following year and defended it three times,
flattening the likes of Terry Norris and Buster Drayton. The Norris
result looks particularly good in retrospect, as he is currently rated
one of the best fighters in the world. He was dropped and badly hurt
by a single short right, and though he got up was saved by the referee.
Drayton was hit so hard with a left hook in the third round that the
ringside doctor was through the ropes while the referee was still
counting.

Jackson was sidelined for detached retina surgery in late 1989, but
recovered to beat Graham. He won his first four defences inside the
distance, including a don't-blink dismissal of Ismael Negron inside a
minute. In 1992 Thomas Tate took him the distance for the first time
in more than ten years. At the time of writing, Jackson had lost just
once, to Mike McCallum, in his pro career. Yet he had still not
received wide acclaim. According to *Boxing News*, 'Jackson's

problems . . . may not lie inside the ring: his greatest enemy is the anonymity that comes from being a non-heavyweight Don King fighter.' King's strategy is hard to understand — marketed properly, Jackson could surely earn big money. Yet only King's heavyweights seem to get the high profiles they deserve. King's aides bleated that no one wanted to fight Jackson. The fighter himself mused, 'I feel in my earlier years I could have been much more advertised. A lot of other fighters got more attention than me.'

★ ★ ★

The World Boxing Organization, a newly formed fringe body, sanctioned its inaugural middleweight title contest on 18 April 1989, between Doug DeWitt and 'Rockin' Robbie Sims, Marvin Hagler's half-brother. They were hard contestants but neither deserved the honour; both had lost to Sumbu Kalambay in their previous outings. DeWitt won on points in 12 rounds. He came from Youngstown, Ohio, and was a rock-jawed individual with little finesse. Born in 1961, he turned pro at 18 and lost just once in his first 29 fights. His crowd-pleasing aggression brought regular appearances on Atlantic City cards but his limitations were exposed when he dropped decisions to Sims and Milt McCrory. DeWitt still managed to secure a challenge against Tommy Hearns for the NABF title. The 'Hit Man' gave him a merciless hiding, landing bombs almost at will. DeWitt was still on his feet at the end but was arguably never as good again.

He was stopped again in his next bout, toughed his way back to take the vacant USBA title from Tony Thornton, then lost in seven rounds in a challenge to Kalambay. His next bout was for the WBO crown against Sims. DeWitt made one successful defence, forcing Matthew Hilton to retire in 11, then lost to England's Nigel Benn, who climbed off the deck to smash him in eight rounds. The British Board, not affiliated to the WBO, initially refused to recognize the organization, but the WBO title was to become almost a British preserve.

Benn, from Ilford, Essex, did a lot to attract interest in the title with his tearaway style. Born on 22 January 1964, the second of seven brothers, he was a volcanic youngster. He said, 'There was always loads of love in my family but for a time I went off the rails. I did

typical hooligan things like fighting and shoplifting. I was always a
street fighter. You have a good straight-up with your hands and you
get a bit of a reputation and everyone wants to challenge you. I just
grew up having fights, protecting myself. I believe it was my God-
given talent.'

Benn learned discipline and boxing during five years in the British
Army, including a long stint in Northern Ireland. He became a top
amateur, taking the ABA middleweight title in 1986 by beating
Johnny Melfah. He turned pro with promoter Frank Warren, and a
run of 22 straight stoppage victories, 19 within two rounds, made the
'Dark Destroyer' the hottest property in domestic boxing. One
opponent, Ian Chantler, lasted just 16 seconds. Benn won the
Commonwealth title and successfully defended it three times.

Benn's first loss came at the hands of Michael Watson, another
talented British middleweight who took his Commonwealth title on a
sixth-round count-out after a hard contest in 1989 in a tent in
Finsbury Park, London. Benn came back with advisor Ambrose
Mendy, and three wins in the US earned him the bout with DeWitt.
Never intimidated by the Americans, he defended in Las Vegas
against dangerous Iran Barkley. Benn knocked him down three times
to win on a first-round stoppage, though the Americans complained
he should have been disqualified for hitting their man while he was
down.

The British Board gradually came round to recognizing WBO
fights and opened the door for one of the most exciting contests ever
seen in an English ring. Benn's opponent was the unbeaten Chris
Eubank, a Brighton-based boxer with a perplexing style and odd
manner. Eubank was a trade fighter, not widely known among
armchair fans. He could be irritatingly arrogant and a bit eccentric.
'What we have here,' he said, 'is a competent, intellectual boxer
against the shallow-minded puncher. I may just decide to stand back
and play with him before I maul him.' Benn responded, 'I want to
humiliate him, because I detest him.'

They fought at Birmingham's National Exhibition Centre on 18
November 1990. *Boxing Monthly* said, 'Those who bore witness to
this titanic struggle for supremacy will never again refer to boxing as a
"game".' Both men were hurt repeatedly in a trial of almost
unendurable excitement. Benn started fast but Eubank countered
hard. Each was stung in the second. Their antipathy spilled out in the

third, when tremendous blows were exchanged and the ref had to part them at the bell. It was already apparent that Eubank's chin could withstand Benn's bombs.

The challenger seemed tired by the fourth, however, and showed anguish when Benn landed to the body. Benn's left eye was swollen to a slit. Eubank frustrated Benn by drawing his leads and in round six the champion hit low. Eubank was given time to recover but the merciless Benn then launched an attack and hurt him with a body blow. The seventh was furious, with Eubank picking off the body-hunting champion. Benn's left eye was now shut. In the ninth he shook from a one-two and was trapped on the ropes, taking leather without reply, when referee Richard Steele stepped in. Benn had been ahead on the judges' cards. Afterwards, an aching and emotional Eubank said, 'I'll never fight Nigel Benn again. He nearly killed me. I came close to dying.' He also proposed to his girlfriend (now his wife) from the ring.

Eubank was born in Dulwich, south London, on 8 August 1966, the youngest of four brothers, two of whom also became boxers. His parents moved around when he was a child. At 12 he was briefly taken into care and from 14 he lived rough for a year and a half. At 16 his father took him to join his mother in New York to keep him out of trouble. He learned to box at the Jerome Club in the blighted South Bronx. It seemed a strange place to take a wayward son but, as Eubank said, 'If you keep bad company you get killed over there, it's as simple as that.'

He turned pro in 1985 and won five bouts in the States, then returned to England. He continued to win, but his manager, Ronnie Davies, gave him his contract back after his 12th fight and he signed with snooker entrepreneur Barry Hearn. Eubank expressed little love for boxing or boxers, only money. 'Boxing is barbaric,' he said. 'I don't have friends. I'm a natural psychologist. If a psychologist has friends he can't be very good.' He called managers 'slags' and ridiculed his rivals. But he showed a flair for self-promotion, entering arenas to a recording of Tina Turner's *Simply the Best* and leaping over the top rope strand. He was also adjudged one of Britain's best-dressed men.

Eubank defended his title successfully when Dan Sherry retired in the tenth round. However, the champion was fined £10,000 for a blatant back-headed butt. He then beat British rivals Gary Stretch and Michael Watson. The latter bout was an extremely close points decision; Hugh McIlvaney, one of many who thought Watson won, called it 'the triumph of honest orthodoxy over imaginative bombast'. Watson campaigned hard for a rematch and, with both boxers struggling to get down to middleweight, they were matched for the WBO super-middleweight championship (first introduced by the IBF in 1984) on 21 September 1991, at Tottenham Hotspur's football stadium at White Hart Lane, north London.

Again, hype overflowed. The bout was built up as a blood feud. It was another contest of scorching heat, with Watson marching through Eubank's counters to whack his way in front. In the 11th round, with both boxers almost exhausted, Eubank fell from two rights. It looked all over. Time seemed to stand still as Eubank rose and steadied himself, waiting for Watson to come to him. As he did so, Eubank dredged up a single right uppercut that caught Watson flush and knocked him over. He clambered up at 'eight', when the bell rang. Watson came out for the last round but was all in and after taking punches without reply was saved by the referee. Tragically, he collapsed in the ring. Suffering from an acute haematoma, he was rushed to hospital and underwent emergency surgery to reduce pressure on his bleeding brain. He survived after being in a prolonged coma, and is bravely but slowly struggling back to recovery. He receives daily physio and speech therapy and has restored lost weight.

For Eubank, the curse of the middleweights continued. Shortly after, he lost control of his Range Rover while driving to Gatwick Airport and killed Kevin Lawlor, a hod-carrier. His image as a hate-figure continues, though lately he has tried to mitigate it with boxing exhibitions in deprived areas of the country. He continues, unabashed, to defend against second-rate challengers and to denigrate the sport from which he earns his living. He rightly says, 'I'm not seen today as a boxer, I'm seen as a personality.' A return with Nigel Benn is on the cards and may happen in 1993.

Gerald McClellan won the vacant 160lbs title vacated by Eubank by knocking out the once-deadly John Mugabi in one round on 20 November 1991, at the Royal Albert Hall, London. Born on 23 October 1967, in Philadelphia, McClellan has scored 15 first-round wins in 27 contests (two losses). A tall, strong boxer from the Kronk gym, to date he is largely unknown and unproven.

★   ★   ★

At the time of writing, the four 'world' middleweight champions were Julian Jackson (WBC), James Toney (IBF), Reggie Johnson (WBA) and Gerald McClellan (WBO). Despite the confusion, there is some cause for optimism, with plans for a Jackson–McClellan match that could amalgamate two of the championships. But it seems unlikely that there will ever be a single champion again. The sport is now so fissured that nobody could pull it back together. Though some boxers may have benefited from bigger purses on offer for bouts which have the words 'world title' attached, the overall effect has been to cheapen the titles, damage the game and disillusion its followers.

In August 1992, the US Senate's Permanent Subcommittee on Investigations conducted an inconclusive two-day hearing into boxing corruption, partly as a result of argument over the verdict in the James Toney–Dave Tiberi bout (see page 219). The hearings were held in conjunction with a bill, sponsored by senator William Roth, calling for the creation of a Professional Boxing Corporation. The bill, due to reach the Senate floor some time in 1993, would help US state commissioners to administer the sport in a more systematic way. It has promise. However, *Ring* magazine pointed out, 'Boxing is an international game, and a federal body won't have the power to run the sport throughout the world. Whether the PBC is created or not, the WBA, WBC and IBF aren't about to disappear. Damn.'

The middleweight class remains exciting, but lacks the dominant characters that made it so compelling in the past. Its fragmentation means the best boxers don't need to fight each other; they can make easy cash defending their titles against nobodies. There are even indications that the fledgling super-middleweight division is poaching the top men, who feel more comfortable at the slightly heavier weight.

The future of the class will lie, as always, in the quality of its young prospects. They seem thin on the ground. America's Roy Jones, for one, has shown signs of deep talent, but the horizon is otherwise empty. Charisma, defined as television appeal, will be the guiding light in the 1990s. Boxing fans can only hope. Certainly the game will survive; the vast wealth on offer at the top of pyramid will ensure that. And it is not inconceivable that another Monzon, Robinson, Greb or Ketchel, a true inheritor of the legacy of the Men of Steel, will emerge from the shadows to rule as a champion should, alone.

Index